M
11.95

DATE DUE

DEC 1 4 2006

card games
david parlett

For over 60 years, more than
50 million people have learnt over
750 subjects the **teach yourself**
way, with impressive results.

be where you want to be
with **teach yourself**

For UK order enquiries: please contact Bookpoint Ltd, 130 Milton Park, Abingdon, Oxon, OX14 4SB. Telephone: +44 (0) 1235 827720. Fax: +44 (0) 1235 400454. Lines are open 09.00–17.00, Monday to Saturday, with a 24-hour message answering service. Details about our titles and how to order are available at www.teachyourself.co.uk

For USA order enquiries: please contact McGraw-Hill Customer Services, PO Box 545, Blacklick, OH 43004-0545, USA. Telephone: 1-800-722-4726. Fax: 1-614-755-5645.

For Canada order enquiries: please contact McGraw-Hill Ryerson Ltd, 300 Water St, Whitby, Ontario, L1N 9B6, Canada. Telephone: 905 430 5000. Fax: 905 430 5020.

Long renowned as the authoritative source for self-guided learning – with more than 50 million copies sold worldwide – the **teach yourself** series includes over 500 titles in the fields of languages, crafts, hobbies, business, computing and education.

British Library Cataloguing in Publication Data: a catalogue record for this title is available from the British Library.

Library of Congress Catalog Card Number: on file.

First published in UK 1994 by Hodder Education, 338 Euston Road, London, NW1 3BH.

First published in US 1994 by The McGraw-Hill Companies, Inc.

This edition published 2006.

The **teach yourself** name is a registered trade mark of Hodder Headline.

Copyright © 1994, 1999, 2003, 2006 David Parlett

Typeset by Transet Limited, Coventry, England.
Printed in Great Britain for Hodder Education, a division of Hodder Headline, 338 Euston Road, London, NW1 3BH, by Cox & Wyman Ltd, Reading, Berkshire.

The publisher has used its best endeavours to ensure that the URLs for external websites referred to in this book are correct and active at the time of going to press. However, the publisher and the author have no responsibility for the websites and can make no guarantee that a site will remain live or that the content will remain relevant, decent or appropriate.

Hodder Headline's policy is to use papers that are natural, renewable and recyclable products and made from wood grown in sustainable forests. The logging and manufacturing processes are expected to conform to the environmental regulations of the country of origin.

Impression number   10 9 8 7 6 5 4 3 2 1
Year   2010 2009 2008 2007 2006

contents

introduction

Game plan

This is the third edition of *Teach Yourself Card Games* and replaces the 1999 version. The aims of this book are:

- to introduce you to the delights of card play if you haven't yet discovered them
- to remind you of details in case of dispute or forgetfulness
- to introduce some games you may not have played before.

It also includes, for the first time, a section on how to use the Internet to get more information about card games, download software and play online, where possible; and to each game is appended a list of URLs (addresses) of sites specifically devoted to it.

From the many hundreds of card games worth describing, I have selected those which are: (1) easy to learn, (2) most widely played, (3) venerable classics, or (4) any combination thereof. I have substantially rewritten most of the previous material, added some new games, and rearranged the contents by types of game rather than by number of players.

Where a given game is played in different ways in different countries, or in different social contexts, I have opted for the British and the domestic versions because these are what will be encountered by most readers. For example, I have described the British rather than the American form (and spelling) of Kalookie, and Pontoon rather than the American Blackjack. (Blackjack is, in any case, a casino game, and therefore is more appropriately covered by Belinda Belez in *Teach Yourself How to Win at Card Games,* which describes casino games to the exclusion of domestic ones.)

If you have any queries or disputes, or spot any errors, please contact me via my website, *http://www.davidparlett.co.uk*

Have fun!

David Parlett
London, June 2002

Why play cards?

No well-educated person should be unable to play at least half a dozen card games. You may decline to endorse Dr Johnson's possibly tongue-in-cheek comment that card-playing 'is very useful in life: it generates kindness and consolidates society', but there is no doubt that among the 'socially intelligent' it does in fact promote sociability, that it can be used to develop social behaviour and logical thinking in children, and that (as a matter of simple observation) people who have played cards for most of their lives retain their mental faculties for as long as they continue to breathe. I played Crib with my great-aunt Ada a year before she died at 99, and some of my Bridge-playing companions today are well over 90.

Cards have been a popular source of enjoyment for over 600 years, and remain so largely because they are cheap and sociable. For less than the cost of a foaming pint you can buy a pack of these pretty pasteboard objects and assure yourself of hours of entertainment. Unlike telly, it's an entertainment that puts you in the active role and credits you with a modicum of intelligence. (The idea that card games are all luck and no skill is as contemptible as it is ignorant, except in so far as stupid people can always find something stupid to play.) And there's as much variety in the programmes as you want: the games described here just scratch the surface of the wealth available.

You may wonder how come there are so many different games to choose from. There are several answers to this. One is that the gaming material is so ingenious and versatile that you can do almost anything with it – unlike, say, a Chess set, with which you can only play Chess. (Or Chess variants, but they are still varieties of Chess, not significantly different games.) Given this inherent versatility, another is that different nations and communities have developed their own particular favourites, and there has been plenty of time (historically speaking) for them to have diversified and evolved. Another is that people of

ames is based on the fact that
ble only from the front and not
e cards are first randomized by
n to players, who then pick them
ay that you can only identify the
elf and have no idea of who else
n, card games are technically
fect information'. Intelligent card
to simple betting games, hinge on
rmation by a variety of methods,
erence and deduction. (Yes, by
cates the issue.) They are therefore
'developing information', for this
bout.

card games involve playing cards to
card played by each player in turn
fore consists of as many cards as
r – the first to play – is normally
like. The others are then normally
of the same suit as the one led, if
mplete. Whoever played the highest
e trick, turns it face down in a
and then leads the first card to the

t suit from that led cannot take the
s permit one suit to be designated
ch games, a player unable to follow
mp) lead can beat the suit led by
f trick-winning therefore becomes:
ghest card of the suit led, or by the
ed.'

s rule, though slight variations will

ormal trick-play. Of four players,
abs, and that two players have no

different temperaments develop different types of game: there are games of pure fun, for children; games of pure chance, for gamblers; and games of great intellectual skill, for people who like games to be the mental equivalent of strenuous physical exercise.

Another wellspring of variety is that there are games designed for specific numbers of players, which is another advantage of playing-cards over board games like Chess, Backgammon, Scrabble™, and the like. There are games for just one player, generically known as Patience or Solitaire (covered in *Teach Yourself Card Games for One.*) There are some excellent card games for two, such as Cribbage, Piquet, Gin and Bezique. Card games for three are less well known in Britain than elsewhere, but the German game of Skat is outstanding in this respect, and, if you find it too mathematical, you might instead try Five Hundred, Ninety-Nine, or some form of Rummy. Four players are well served by partnership games such as Whist, Bridge and Canasta; but if you prefer to play on your own account you can hardly do better than Solo Whist. Then there are games designed for an indefinite number of players from three to about seven, such as Knockout, Crazy Eights, Newmarket and Poker. There are also casino games played with cards, more of which will be found in *Teach Yourself How to Win at Card Games*.

Poker, unlike most casino games, is a game of skill, contrary to the vague misapprehension of those who have never played it; and perhaps this is the point to address an equally common and related misapprehension – namely, that cards are 'just' a form of gambling, and offer little scope for intelligent play because they are randomly distributed to start with.

First, gambling. This has two meanings, one of which is 'playing for money'. Any game can be played for money, even Chess and Scrabble™, so it is nonsense to single this out as being a defining characteristic of card games. The other is 'wagering money on the outcome of an event over which you have no control', such as Bingo, Lotto (the British National Lottery), or racetrack betting. Here it is necessary to point out that some card games are indeed gambling games by this strict definition of the term: they are the ones played in casinos, and in which most serious card-players have little interest. Others, however, do not fall into this category. Generally speaking, the more skilled and less chancy a card game is, the more interest is derived from the actual play of the game rather than from basing monetary transactions on the outcome. Poker is a game of skill because money itself (or chips or counters representing it) are the actual instruments of play, and players have complete control over how they manage their investments. Hence it is a gambling game in the technical rather than the popular sense of the word.

Other games involve different types and degrees of skill. The fact that you get a random distribution to start with, and don't know which cards are in other players' hands, is not of itself antithetical to the application of skill. On the contrary, one of the skills of a game like Whist or Bridge is that of deducing or inferring other players' holdings from the cards they play and the order they play them in, or from spoken information conveyed in an 'auction' that precedes the play.

Other types of skill may be involved as well, but what they are must be left to emerge from the individual games themselves. Some, like Rummy, involve memory; others, like Cribbage, don't. Skat and Piquet involve a lot of counting; Newmarket and Crazy Eights practically none at all.

One other misapprehension must be dealt with before you set off on your exploration, and that is the myth of 'official rules'. The vast majority of card games are folk games: they do not have official rules of universal applicability, but are played in slightly different ways from town to town, from club to club, from home to home, sometimes even from day to day by the same group of players. The relatively few games that are equipped with universal rules, such as Bridge and Skat, are played at national or international level in clubs and tournaments, where it is necessary for participants to know in advance exactly which rules they will be following, and for which there are well-organized clubs and federations that co-operate in formulating and promoting such rules. Other games, such as Cribbage and Piquet, have rules because they are 'book' games that have been played for centuries by generally literate players and the actual play of the games has been influenced by their descriptions recorded in books.

The skill and fun of c
individual cards are ide
from the back. Invariab
shuffling, then dealt face
up and hold them in suc
cards you are holding y
holds what. For this r
described as games of 'ir
games, however, as oppo
the process of acquiring
including observation,
cheating too; but this co
better thought of as gam
is precisely what they are

Trick-taking games

The vast majority of weste
tricks. A trick consists of
face up to the table. It th
there are players. The le
allowed to play any card t
required to furnish a car
possible, until the trick is
card of the suit led win
squared-up pile before the
next trick.

Normally, a card of a diffe
trick. However, many gar
trump (from 'triumph'). In
suit to a plain-suit (non-
playing a trump. The rule
'The trick is taken by the
highest trump if any are p

Most trick games follow t
be encountered.

Figure 1 is an example of
assume that North leads
clubs to play:

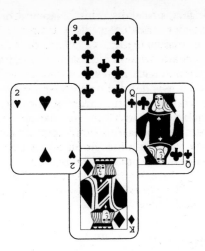

figure 1

North leads the ♣9, East follows with ♣Q, while South and West, having no clubs, play ♦K and ♥2 respectively. If the game is played at no trump, East's Queen wins because it is the highest card of the suit led. South's King, though ranking higher, is of the wrong suit.

If hearts are trumps, West's Two takes the trick, as it is the highest (because the only) trump played. If diamonds are trumps, South's King is the winning card. And if clubs are trumps, East wins again, because a trump suit cannot itself be trumped.

Of many ways of selecting a suit for trump, the commonest are these. In older and simpler games the last card of the pack is turned face up and its suit becomes trump automatically. In more highly developed games a trump suit (or 'no trump') is nominated by the player who contracts to win the greatest number of tricks in return for so doing. Such games are usually preceded by an 'auction' in which players 'bid' to nominate trumps by increasing the number of tricks they offer to win. For greater interest the suits may be graded in a specified order of superiority, so that a bid can be overcalled not necessarily by raising the number of tricks but by bidding the same number of tricks in a higher-ranking suit, or at no trump, which beats every suit. This is the distinguishing feature of Contract Bridge.

Trick-taking games fall into several categories. The most clear cut are:

1 Plain-trick games, such as Whist, Nap and Bridge, in which the aim is to win tricks regardless of their content, all won tricks being equal in value.

2 Point-trick games, such as Skat and Klaberjass, in which the aim is to win point-scoring cards by capturing them in tricks, so that the game is decided not by the number of tricks won but by the total value of the cards they contain.

3 Penalty-trick games, in which the aim is to avoid winning tricks containing penalty cards, as in Hearts, or to avoid winning any tricks at all, as in the so-called 'misère' bids of Solo Whist, Nap and other such games.

Plain- and point-trick games may also involve scoring for making card combinations, as in Piquet, Bezique and Klaberjass.

Many trick-taking games involve an auction, in which the highest bidder or bidders declare a 'contract' to win a minimum number of tricks in return for nominating the trump suit.

Non trick-taking card games

Card games that don't involve trick-play can be divided into other categories, some of them clear cut but others rather miscellaneous.

Rummy games. Of oriental origin, these games of the 'draw and match' variety reached the west in the mid-19th century and throughout the 20th expanded into scores of ingenious derivatives, notably Gin Rummy and Canasta. The basic idea is that at each turn you draw a new card and throw out an unwanted card, add it to your hand or discard one to a discard pile, with the ultimate aim of ridding your hand of cards by laying them out in sets of three or more matching cards called 'melds'. In some such games, notably Canasta, the aim is to score for melds according to the value of cards they contain rather than to be the first to get rid of your cards.

Going-out games. There are other games in which the object is to be the first to get rid of all your cards. A popular western example is Crazy Eights.

Adding and matching games. Some games are based on aiming to make or avoid making certain totals by adding together the face value of cards drawn or played. The greatest of these is Cribbage, which also involves making and scoring for combinations of matched cards.

Gambling games. While all games are potentially gambling games to the extent that they *can* be played for money (even Chess), I use this term in its technical sense of a game that cannot be scored in writing but can *only* conveniently be played with cash or counters. Such games are of two sorts, or at least fall somewhere on a line between two extremes. One extreme is occupied by the completely mindless and trivial, such as Baccarat, the other by those requiring (or at least rewarding) a high degree of skill, such as Poker.

There are other notable types of card game that I have not included in this book for one reason or another. One-player games, known as Patience or Solitaire, are covered in *Teach Yourself Card Games for One*. Many casino games are more appropriately covered in *Teach Yourself How to Win at Card Games*. Tarot games have never become naturalized in the English-speaking world, and in any case have the drawback of being rather complicated and space-consuming. Nor do I cover games played with non-standard cards, such as Rook cards, domino cards, Killekort, Kvitlak, or specially designed commercial games.

Customs and practices

Players. Most games work best for a specific number of players. If played by the wrong number, the balance of a game will be upset, and its enjoyment spoilt. Patience is played by one, and many good games by two or three. Four may play alone or in two partnerships of two, in which case partners sit opposite each other across the table. Games for five or more tend to be more chancy and less skill rewarding.

Cards. Some games are played with what we regard in Britain as the 'standard' pack of 52, with or without Jokers. Some, especially Rummy games, are played with two or more such packs shuffled together. Others are played with packs containing fewer than 52, especially the 32-card pack common to many European games. You can make a short pack by stripping out lower numerals from a 52-card pack, but it is better to buy the appropriate short packs from specialist games shops if you can find them. It is definitely advisable to keep separately packs of different lengths for different games. If you strip 20 from a 52-card pack to play Skat or Piquet, you won't want to put them back again to play Bridge, as the clean cards will give themselves away as being low in value.

Seating and partners. It is usual for players to each draw a card at random from a pack spread face down on the table, the highest rank drawn conferring first choice of seat, and so on downwards. Two or more tied cards will draw again to break the tie. The same draw may be used to establish partnerships. In Bridge, for instance, those drawing the two highest cards play as partners against those drawing the lowest. In games for four or fewer, it is usual to refer to the players by their compass positions at the table – North, East, South, West.

Rotation. In Britain, the turn to deal and play usually passes to the left around the table. However, this varies from country to country, and serious players prefer to play a game the right way round according to its country of origin. All those described in this book are played to the left unless otherwise specified.

Game structure. Depending on the game, the play of a single hand or deal may last anything from less than one minute to ten or more. To make the play worthwhile, and to balance out the receipt of 'good' and 'bad' hands, a game therefore consists of several deals. It may be played (a) for an agreed length of time, (b) up to a statutory or agreed target score, or (c) for a statutory or agreed number of deals.

Shuffle and deal. Whoever drew the highest card usually deals first, and the turn to deal passes to the left. Before dealing, the dealer shuffles the cards in order to randomize the pack. You can't learn shuffling by words, only by observation and practice. In most card games (other than Bridge, which has a lot of rules peculiar to itself), anyone has the right to shuffle on demand, but the dealer has the right to shuffle last. The dealer then offers the pack to his right-hand neighbour, who initiates a 'cut' by lifting the top half and placing it on the table. The dealer then completes the cut by placing the bottom half on the top. The purpose of this rigmarole is to ensure that no one can have seen the bottom card of the pack and so identify a card held by another player. It will of course be frustrated if the dealer is careless enough to hold the pack at an upright, outward angle when dealing.

The deal. This is made by distributing cards face down one at a time around the table, the first card of each round going to the player at Dealer's left (variously called 'eldest hand', 'forehand', etc.) and the last to himself. Some games specify that cards be dealt not singly but in batches of two or three at a time. Such a rule makes a significant difference and should not be ignored. In some games, the whole pack is dealt out. In some, for various purposes, a few neutral cards may be dealt face down to the table as a spare hand or 'widow' or 'talon'. In some, a batch or stock of cards will be left face down, from which players draw additional cards in the course of play so that all are eventually used. In others, the undealt cards are left untouched and play no part at all, except to increase the chance factor by making the acquisition of 'perfect information' impossible until it is too late to do anything with it.

Scores and payoffs. Card games mostly produce more interesting results than the simple 'win, lose or draw' of Chess. They fall into two types as to the way in which scores are made or recorded, which may be designated 'hard-score' and 'soft-score' games.

Hard-score games are played directly for cash, or for objects representing it, like chips or counters. Settlements are made at the end of each deal, so that each deal is a complete game in itself. A session of play has no overall game structure, and can end at any point.

Soft-score games are played for notional points recorded in writing on suitable scoresheets. In this case a game consists either of a specified number of deals, or of as many deals as it takes for a player or partnership to reach a specified target score. This gives the game an overall structure, to which additional scoring interest may be attached, for example, bonuses for reaching the target score soonest, or penalties for failing to reach a minimum level. Additionally, scoring considerations may influence one's strategy ('playing to the score').

All gambling games are played for hard score, and games of chance usually for cash, but it doesn't follow that all games played for hard score are 'gambling games' in the popular sense of depending more on chance than skill. Solo Whist, for example, is almost invariably played for hard score, and for cash at that, but it can be a game of great skill and only an accident of social history has deprived Solo of the sort of highly developed scoring system that has contributed so greatly to the success of Bridge.

Most games of skill are played for the 'soft score' of points recorded in writing. At end of play, these may or may not be converted into the 'hard score' of cash settlements between the players. The more skill-demanding the game, the greater the tendency for interest to attach to the play itself rather than to its capacity for determining cash settlements. Many play such games 'for small stakes' as a matter of temperament or tradition.

Others will not play for money at all. Whatever one's attitude to playing for money, it must be admitted that it is the gambling origin of card games that has led to their fascinating scoring systems and, consequently, to the unique feature of card games where one's strategy is often governed by the various scoring possibilities of a given hand.

Choosing your game

First, decide how many of you there are. In the following table, games are arranged primarily according to the number of players for which they are suitable. Those noted in brackets can be played by the number in question, but are not ideally suited to it.

If there are four of you, decide whether you prefer to play in fixed partnerships, or as individuals ('solo'), as these two groups are listed separately.

Next, decide whether or not you want to play a trick-taking game. On the whole, trick games include some of the deepest and most skill-demanding, while those designed for fun and sociability tend to be of the non-trick variety. Games that are particularly easy to pick up are printed in italics.

Finally, remember that different games appeal to different temperaments, for example, players generally divide into those who favour fixed partnership games like Bridge, and those who prefer solo games like, well, Solo. Some prefer matching games to trick games; some like playing for coins or counters and others for a written score, and so on.

Choosing a game by number of players available

(Games in parentheses are not ideal for the number stated)

Games in italics are particularly easy to learn

	trick games	non-trick games
2 players	Bezique *German Whist* Klaberjass Piquet Sixty-Six	*Crazy Eights* Cribbage *Gin Rummy* *Scopa*

3 players	*Bismarck*	*Adding-up games*
	Five Hundred	Contract Rummy
	(Knockout)	*Crazy Eights*
	Nap	(Cribbage)
	Ninety-Nine	(Kalookie)
	Skat	*Pontoon*
		Rummy
4 players (solo)	*Hearts*	*Adding-up games*
	Knockout	Brag
	Nap	Bum Game
	(Ninety-Nine)	Contract Rummy
	Oh Hell!	*Crazy Eights*
	Skat*	Kalookie
	Solo Whist	*Newmarket*
	Spades	Poker
	Twenty-Five	*Pontoon*
		Rummy
4 players (partnership)	Bridge	Canasta
	Euchre	*Cribbage*
	Five Hundred	*Scopone*
	Spades	
	Whist	
5 players (or more)	*Knockout*	*Adding-up games*
	Nap	Brag
	(Ninety-Nine)	Bum Game
	Oh Hell!	Contract Rummy
	Twenty-Five	*Crazy Eights*
		Kalookie
		Newmarket
		Poker
		Pontoon
		Rummy

*Three active players but usually four at a table, with each in turn sitting out

Card games and computers

Computers in general and the Internet in particular provide a wide variety of useful and entertaining resources for card-players. Such resources fall into two groups: those that give you information about the rules and practices of card games, and those that actually enable you to play, and these can be further split into four as follows:

- websites that give you information about card games, such as rules of play and news of clubs and associations devoted to particular games
- news and mailing groups devoted to specific card games or card games in general
- computer software enabling you to play or practise alone against imaginary opponents, either on your computer or on other electronic devices
- Internet cardrooms and on-line casinos enabling you to play against live but unseen players at their own terminals.

Information on-line

For an authoritative account of any particular card game, whether for learning how to play it or for checking disputed points, your first and probably only port of call will be John McLeod's award-winning website:

http://www.pagat.com

hereinafter referred to as the Pagat website. (Pagat is the name of the lowest trump in Tarock games.) McLeod established this site in 1994, drawing on the twin advantages of being both a computer expert and a card-game expert – one of the few to have played dozens of exotic games in their countries of origin. He is also a founder member of the International Playing-Card Society and was instrumental in setting up the card-games newsgroup.

Rules of games on Pagat are not lifted from books, but are based on first-hand information gleaned either by McLeod himself or from a whole army of field correspondents who recognize the style and standards adopted by it. McLeod is careful to state the 'provenance' of each game – that is, where it is played, by whom, by whom recorded and on what authority. Each game includes further links to other web pages devoted to it.

My own website covers material not included in McLeod's, especially historic card games and card games of my invention. These may be found, respectively, at

http://www.davidparlett.co.uk/histocs
http://www.davidparlett.co.uk/orics

News and discussion groups

Newsgroups are on-line correspondence columns, in which people interested in a particular subject can ask and answer one another's queries, and share and exchange information and ideas. Of general interest is

rec.games.playing-cards

The topics discussed here range from 'How do you score this Cribbage hand?' (which often produces conflicting results) to thought-provoking articles on the origins of particular card games.

Other aspects of the subject, including where to find playing-card bitmaps, fonts and programming tools, makers and sellers of playing-cards and associated equipment, tournaments and meetings, casinos and gambling, books, newsgroups and mailing lists are listed and linked to on the Pagat website. But one that is worth mentioning here is

http://www.playingcardsales.com

from which you can obtain packs of cards appropriate to particular games and associated card-playing equipment.

Playing against the computer

For the computer, any number of card-game simulations are available on CD-ROMs, and the more popular the game, the more versions there are available of it – especially, therefore, of Bridge, Hearts, Euchre, Cribbage, Gin Rummy, and collections of solitaires. Apart from the solitaire collections, individual card games are usually bundled together with equally popular board games such as Draughts and Othello. The only useful way of finding out what is available is to browse through your local software store, note what you fancy, and make sure that it runs on your particular hardware. Older versions of card games, for example designed for Windows 98, are often sold at bargain prices. It is advisable, however, to steer clear of anything that runs only on Windows 3.11, as it may not run under later versions unless you know how to use the backwards-compatible options, and even then it may not work properly.

But CD-ROMs are now virtually antiques. By logging on to the Internet directly you can not only download increasingly sophisticated versions of games for playing alone but also join cyber-cardrooms and play against other players.

You might ask why anyone should want to play alone, and there are two good answers to this. The first is the obvious fact that patiences or card solitaires are by definition one-player games and therefore eminently suitable for singleton computer play, and the second is that it's a good way of getting in some practice for games you play in real life – in order, perhaps, to experiment with lines of play that in real life might prove to be embarrassingly flawed.

An interesting sociological effect of making a game such as Hearts available over the entire computer-using world (since it comes free as part of the Microsoft™ package) is that it tends to establish a particular set of rules as the standard form of a game that previously would have been played in many different versions, sometimes with local house rules and variations. Fortunately, the computer version is based on a highly evolved and well balanced set of rules, rendering older varieties of the game obsolete and probably not worth reviving.

All the most popular card games – Bridge, Cribbage, Euchre, Gin Rummy, Spades, etc. – are available for downloading as either freeware or shareware. In the previous edition of this book I noted the URLs of sites from which you can get them at time of writing. Unfortunately, the nature of the Internet is such that several had dropped out of availability between the time I checked them and the date of publication. Still, you can always find out what is currently available by typing the name of the incomparable search engine Google:

http://www.google.co.uk

Naturally, you will need to think carefully about what you enter. For example, a search for 'Canasta' is hardly likely to bring up anything but references to the card game, whereas a search for 'Bridge' will bring up millions of references ranging from dentistry to civil engineering to British composers of the early 20th century. You will therefore enter something like 'Contract + Bridge', or 'Bridge card game', whatever the format may be.

Other electronic devices

Electronic devices other than the computer are a mixed and as yet still experimental bunch, though they go back to Nintendo's 'Game & Watch' series of the early 1980s. Quite sophisticated Bridge and Poker hand-held machines with LCD or colour screens are obtainable, but they are not easy to find even if you deliberately set out to track them down. You will mostly find them on offer in specialist magazines such as *The Bridge World* and in those mail-order catalogues that come free with newspaper and magazines, or just appear out of thin air as part of your everyday junk mail.

We can expect in the future to see more card games playable on television, further Internet developments, as well as gaming on the Blackberry or other PDAs (Personal Digital Assistant), Nintendo's DS console, Sony's PSP (PlayStation Portable™) or other handheld devices, and even the latest generation of mobile phone. No doubt it will soon be possible to play a lot more card games on our mobile phones, but as yet the industry looks mostly towards games that service providers can charge money for playing – that is, gambling card games such as Poker and Twenty-One. There are of course also solitaire games on some modern mobiles, and you may find websites offering you downloads of various games, including solitaires, to your mobile.

Playing on-line against live opponents

There are a number of cyber-cardrooms which you can join in order to play on-line with real opponents. Typically, you enter the site and fill out a form with basic personal details, including the nickname or pseudonym you prefer to be identified by. You will then get a screen showing which 'rooms' are devoted to which games, and can either join in a game immediately if there is a vacant cyber-seat, or else wait until one becomes available.

This is not an experience that appeals to me, partly because I prefer playing with real people and, even more importantly, with real cards. (I am an inveterate shuffler, by which I mean I tend to shuffle cards at every available opportunity as a sort of nervous habit, the way some people smoke. Indeed, I probably shuffle cards more than I used to before I gave up smoking.) Worse still, you lay yourself open to spam (junk email), so it is as well to have more than one email address and for card-playing purposes to use the one reserved for junk. On the other hand, this is the only option open to you if you wish to learn or practise something outlandish, such as French Tarot, and do not have access to enough friends and acquaintances willing to embark on anything so experimental.

Needless to say, there are also many (too many, in my view) casino game websites that offer some form of indulgence in Blackjack, Poker and other such games. But at this point we leave the world of domestic play and enter realms beyond the scope of this book. It would be well to bear in mind that card-playing and gambling are not completely synonymous – they denote, rather, two circles of activity with a common area of overlap.

part one

plain-trick games

01

German whist

- two players
- easy to learn, quick to play
- practise basic trick-taking

The name of the game

There's nothing particularly German about this game. But when Whist was the western world's most fashionable card game (as Bridge is today) almost any game involving the same rules of trick-play was dubbed Whist with an ethnic epithet – hence Scotch Whist, French Whist, Chinese Whist, and many others.

This excellent game for two players makes a good introduction to the basic principles of trick-play involved in all varieties of Whist including its most advanced descendant, Bridge.

The game

Cards. From a 52-card pack deal 13 each, in ones, and stack the rest face down. Turn the top card of the stock face up. The suit of the turn-up becomes and remains trump for the rest of the round.

Object. To win most of the last 13 of the 26 tricks played.

Play. There are two phases to the game. The first continues as long as any cards remain in stock, and the second begins when the stock is empty.

Non-dealer leads to the first trick. In the first phase you can play any card, whether leading or following. The winner of each trick, before leading to the next:

- draws the top (faced) card of stock and adds it to their hand
- waits for the loser to draw the next (which need not be shown)
- turns the next stock card face up so that both can see which card the next trick-winner will get
- leads to the next trick.

When no cards remain in stock, the last 13 tricks are played to normal Whist rules. This means that, when playing second to a trick, you must follow suit to the card led if you can, otherwise you can play anything.

Score. Whoever wins more of the last 13 tricks scores 1 point for each trick taken above six.

The play

German Whist is a good test of memory and judgement.

In the first half of the game you should only win a trick if you think the top card of the stock is probably better than the one underneath, for example, a trump or a high card in a plain suit. At the same time, you may not want to buy it with a card which itself is higher still, since you need high cards and trumps for the second half.

Figure 1.1 is a nice example of the sort of thing that might happen. Suppose you are to lead from:

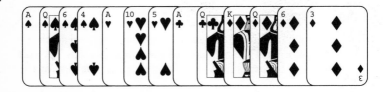

figure 1.1 German Whist

with spades trump and the turned card ♥K. This is a good one and you could probably win it by leading ♥A. A better lead, in fact, is ♦K. Why? Because if ♥K wins the Ace you will only have exchanged one probable winner for another, and if it doesn't you will have lost two probable winners. If you lead ♦K and win you will still have made no difference to the strength of your hand, but if it is beaten by ♦A then your ♦Q will be the highest card in its suit.

The basic principles of trick-play taught by this game are:

- never play a card without a specific reason for it
- remember that any given card is *promoted* (= increases in trick-winning power) when a higher card of the same suit is no longer in play.

02

bismarck

- three players
- easy to learn
- practise basic trick-taking

Bismarck is the simple ancestor of a more elaborated game called Sergeant Major (also known as '8–5–3'), which has long been popular in the British armed forces. It's what I call a 'compendium' game, meaning that it consists of a number of different games strung together in a particular order. The exact components and the exact order are somewhat variable. This one is typical.

The game

Cards. Use a standard 52-card pack, with cards ranking in their usual order A K Q J 10 9 8 7 6 5 4 3 2.

Game. A game consists of 12 deals. Each player in turn deals four times in succession. The deal then passes to the previous dealer's left-hand neighbour.

Deal. The dealer distributes 16 cards to each player, takes the last four themselves, and discards any four unwanted cards face down before the opening lead is made by the player at their left.

Each of the four deals is a different game, as follows:

First deal. The aim is to win tricks, playing at no trump. The dealer scores 1 point for each trick they win above eight, and each opponent scores 1 point for each trick they take above four.

Second deal. The aim is to win tricks, with a trump suit selected at random (such as by turning the last card, or cutting another pack). Score as above.

Third deal. The aim is to win tricks, with a trump suit declared by the dealer after examining his hand but before the first card is led. Score as above.

Fourth deal. The aim is to lose tricks, playing at no trump. The dealer scores 4 points less the number of tricks they took, and each opponent scores 6 points less the number taken by themselves.

The winner is the player with the highest score at the end of the game.

Variations

1 Everyone including the dealer receives 16 cards, and four are dealt face down to the table as a 'kitty'. The dealer must make four discards before replacing them with the cards of the kitty.
2 The target number of tricks for the dealer's left-hand neighbour is not four but five, and that of the third player not four but three. This is the basis of the more elaborate game known as Sergeant Major or '8–5–3'.

See also

http://www.pagat.com/whist/sergeant.html

03
knockout whist

- for three to seven players
- easy to learn, quick to play
- practise basic trick-taking

The name of the game.

So called because players get knocked out one by one, but the game is often called just 'Whist' (confusingly) or 'Trumps'.

A children's or gambling game, however you prefer to regard it, Knockout is a British game played widely in schools and pubs. Much to my surprise, I can't find any reference to it earlier than the 1970s. Perhaps it derives in some way from Oh Hell!, a game of comparable structure some 40 years older.

There are many variations, but the underlying theme is as follows.

Everybody places a single stake in the pot. On the first deal each player receives seven cards, on the second six, the third five, and so on, reducing by one card on each occasion. Dealer turns the next card for trump and leads to the first trick.

Anyone who fails to win a trick is knocked out of the game and has no further part to play. Those who remain contribute another stake to the pot. Whoever wins most tricks (or, if equal, the tied player who cuts the higher card from the pack) gathers the cards up and deals to the next round.

This continues until one player wins the pot by winning every trick played – usually on the last deal of one card, though it can happen earlier.

In another version, the turn to deal passes regularly to the left and no card is turned for trump: instead, the player who won most tricks in the previous deal (or, if tied, the tied player cutting the higher card from the undealt pack) nominates a trump suit after looking at their hand.

See also

http://www.pagat.com/whist/kowhist.html

04

partnership whist

- partnership game for four
- easy to learn
- your first step towards bridge

The name of the game

Dr Johnson described Whist as 'a game requiring close attention and silence', hinting at the popular notion of 'Whist!' as the Scottish for 'Hush!' without actually endorsing it. In fact it was formerly called Whisk, which was short for Whisk and Swabbers, which in turn may have been a disparaging reference to the game of Ruff and Honours.

Many games are called Whist for short, their full names being Solo Whist or Knockout Whist or whatever it may be, but this is the only one to which the single word can properly refer. More long-windedly, it can be described as the classic partnership game.

The game originated in Britain and is nowadays mostly encountered in fund-raising events called Whist drives, in which capacity it remains (with Brag and Cribbage) the basic English folk game that it has been for most of its 400-year history. Before the advent of its natural descendant Bridge, Whist passed through a phase of being the foremost intellectual and social card game of its day. What makes it a great game is the fact that it has extremely simple rules of play, yet can give rise to considerable depth of skill.

If you're planning to learn Bridge, you can hardly do better than to start with partnership Whist.

The game

Whist is played in two forms: the home game and the tournament or 'drive' game. (There was also a third form called Duplicate, but this has been superseded by Duplicate Bridge.) The following description is of the home game. The drive game differs only in minor details given at the end of this description.

Players. Four play in two fixed partnerships. Partners may be determined by drawing cards from a shuffled pack. Whoever draws the highest card has first choice of seats and is partnered by the person drawing the second highest, who sits opposite.

Cards. Fifty-two. It's best to alternate between two packs, one being shuffled while the other is dealt. This ensures thorough shuffling without wasting time.

Object. A rubber is won by the first side to win two games. A game is won by the first side to score 5 points over as many deals as it takes. (But you may find it more logical to follow American practice and play up to 7 points.)

Deal. Whoever draws the highest card deals first, and the turn to deal and play passes to the left. Deal 13 each in ones. The last card goes face up to the table to establish trumps.

Play. The player at Dealer's left leads to the first trick, and the dealer adds the trump turn-up to their hand as soon as it is their own turn to play. Suit must be followed if possible, otherwise any card may be played. A trick is taken by the highest card of the suit led, or by the highest trump if any are played. The winner of each trick leads to the next. All tricks won by a partnership are stored in front of the member who wins the first one.

Revoke. A player who fails to follow suit, though able to do so, may correct their play without penalty before the next card is played. If a revoke is discovered later, 3 points are deducted from the current score of the revoking side, or, if this makes less than zero, are added to the other side's score.

Score. Whichever side took a majority of tricks, seven or more, scores 1 point per 'odd trick' – that is, for each trick won in excess of six. Winning all 13 tricks would therefore score 7 points.

After scoring for tricks, it is possible to score for honours. Honours are the highest trumps (A–K–Q–J). If one partnership held all four trump honours, either in one hand or divided between them, they add 4 for honours. If they held any three, they add 2 for honours. Honours are not scored, however, if the side concerned is 1 point short of game, i.e. standing at 4 points under English rules. (The Americans dispensed with honours entirely, and modern players may wish to do the same, as they depend entirely on chance and obviously form too large a proportion of the total.)

Game and rubber. On winning a second game, a partnership adds 2 points for the rubber. Their margin of victory is the difference between both sides' scores.

Progressive (Drive) Whist. In tournament play, the last card is not turned for trump. Instead, the first hand is played with hearts trump, the second with clubs, the third with diamonds, the fourth with spades, and the cycle is repeated thereafter. Sometimes the cycle is five deals, the fifth being played at no trump. It is not unheard of to play a six-deal cycle, the sixth being misère. This is

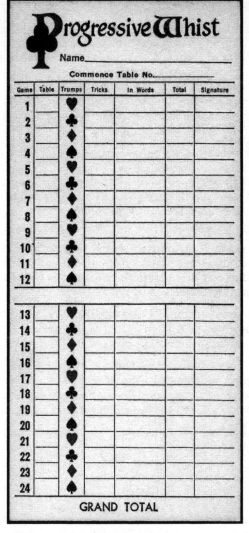

figure 4.1 Progressive Whist score-card

played at no trump, and the side winning fewer tricks scores 1 point for each trick taken less than seven. A leg or rubber is 24 deals, or any other fixed number, after which the partnerships move round to the next table. You can buy printed score-cards for this purpose (see Figure 4.1).

The play

Unless you are exceptionally strong in trumps, your normal strategy as a partnership is to establish and bring home your longest plain suit or suits. To establish a suit means to force out the high cards which your opponents hold in it (preferably by winning them in tricks, though not necessarily) so that those remaining in your hand are the highest left in play. Bringing it home means subsequently leading and winning tricks with those cards without having them trumped.

Consider the underlying principle first. Since there are 13 cards in each suit, each player will be dealt an average of 3¼ of them. Any suit in which you hold four or more is therefore 'long' as far as you are concerned, since you have more than the average number. Those cards of it which are certain to win tricks (disregarding the possibility of trumping for the moment) are described as 'long cards'.

Suppose you have been dealt ♠A K Q 2, spades not being trumps, and the other players have an even three each. How many of these are long cards? At first sight only the top three. But on closer inspection:

Ace draws   3, 4, 5
then King draws   6, 7, 8
then Queen draws   9, 10, J

and now no one has any of the suit left, so your Two is bound to win if led (and not trumped). You have thus established the suit, and if you can reach a position from which you can lead the Two without having it trumped, you will have brought the suit home.

Since few holdings are so clear cut, you and your partner will generally need each other's assistance in bringing home your respective best suits. Your best suit will, normally, be your longest; but if you have two long suits it will be the one with the most likely trick-winners. Clearly, a holding of A K Q 2 in one suit is better than one of 6 5 4 3 2 in another, even though it is normally better to play a five-card than a four-card suit.

The best opportunity you have for declaring your suit is at your first lead to a trick, especially when sitting immediately left of the dealer and so leading to the first trick of the hand. Lead from your best suit, so that your partner will know which one to return to you when he or she gets the lead. Of that suit, lead a card which will indicate to them what sort of holding you have in it, so that by deducting their own holding in the suit they will be able to start building up a picture of where the key cards lie.

In the days when Whist was regarded as a 'scientific' game, the club experts and analysts devised all sorts of ingenious and elaborate leading conventions. Nowadays that sort of brainpower goes instead into devising bidding systems at Bridge, and the tradition of elaborate Whist leads has been lost. In fact, most players tend to follow principles similar to those used at Bridge, which can be summed up as follows:

- lead the Ace if you have it, otherwise
- top card of a high sequence (such as K Q J, Q J 10, etc.)
- top card from an interior sequence (J from K J 10, 10 from Q 10 9)
- fourth highest from a suit with one or two honours (e.g. 5 from K J 6 5 2)
- highest from any other long suit ('top of nothing').

Sample deal

West deals and turns the following hands, turning ♥K for trump:

N	♥ Q 10	♠ Q	♦ A Q J 9 8 5	♣ Q 10 4 2
E	♥ J 9 7 6 3 2	♠ J 10 9 8	♦ K 2	♣ J
S	♥ A	♠ K 7 5 4 3 2	♦ 10 4 3	♣ 9 5 3
W	♥ K 8 5 4	♠ A 6	♦ 7 6	♣ A K 8 7 6

	North	East	South	West
1.	♦A	♦2	♦4	♦7
2.	♦J	♦K	♦3	♦6
3.	♥10	♥6	♥A	♥5
4.	♦5	♣J	♦10	♥4
5.	♥Q	♥2	♠2	♥K
6.	♣2	♠8	♣3	♣A
7.	♣4	♠9	♣5	♣K
8.	♣10	♥3	♣9	♣6
9.	♠Q	♠J	♠3	♠A
10.	♣Q	♥9	♠4	♣8
11.	♦8	♥7	♠5	♥8
12.	♦9	♠10	♠7	♣7
13.	♦Q	♥J	♠K	♠6

North makes the opening lead.

Winning cards are underlined.

East-West win 11 tricks and the game (5 points), thanks to East's trumping with ♥9 instead of ♥7 at the tenth. This enables West to lead the last club, to which East can discard a losing spade, followed by West's own losing spade, which East can trump to yield the extra trick necessary for game (5 points). Had East ruffed with ♥7 at trick ten, South would eventually have made their King, thus denying East-West their game-winning trick. This was not a matter of luck or guesswork. East knew that West held the last remaining trump, from the previous play of trumps; that they held a losing spade (because they played ♠A instead of ♠K at trick nine); and that their other card was the last club because there was nothing else for it to be.

See also

http://www.pagat.com/whist/whist.html

05

nap

- for three to seven players, ideal for five
- easy to learn, quick to play
- nice balance of chance and skill

Nap, short for Napoleon, was a staple amusement of British family life before TV quiz programmes took over the world, since when it has lost ground. (My great-aunt was playing it until well into her nineties.)

Nap is more of a gambling than an intellectual game, but many players increase the 'think' factor by stripping the pack according to the number of players, as shown below.

The game

Cards. If not 52, then three players use 24 or 28 cards by stripping out all ranks lower than Nine or Eight, four use 28 or 32 by stripping out all lower than Eight or Seven, and five use 32 or 36 by stripping out all lower than Seven or Six.

The cards are shuffled before the first deal, and are cut before each subsequent deal, but are not shuffled again until a player has won a bid of Nap or higher.

Deal. Five cards each, either one at a time or in batches of 3+2 or 2+3, and stack the rest face down.

Bidding. Each in turn either passes or makes a higher bid than any gone before. A bid is an offer to win at least the number of tricks stated, using a trump suit of the bidder's choice, which is not yet announced. From lowest to highest, the bids and their scores or values are:

bid	object	value
two	win 2+ tricks	2
three	win 3+ tricks	3
miz	win 0 tricks at no trump	3
four	win 4+ tricks	4
Nap	win all 5 tricks	10
Wellington	win 5 for double score	20
Blücher	win 5 for quadruple score	40

Wellington may only be called over another player's call of Nap.

Blücher may only be bid over another player's call of Wellington, but not all schools allow it.

The Two-bid is really only appropriate to the original full-pack game. Players using the shortened pack usually omit it. The point is almost academic, as the short pack almost always gives at least one player a minimum bid of three.

Play. The highest bidder leads to the first trick, and the suit of that card is automatically trump, except when playing miz. Play as at Whist.

Score. The bidder, if successful wins from each player two, three or four units for the relevant bids, 3 for Miz, 10 for Nap, 20 for Wellington, 40 for Blücher. If unsuccessful, they pay to each opponent the amount they would have won, though penalties are usually halved for lost bids of five.

Optional Joker. If a Joker is added, it counts as the highest trump. In Miz, it is the only trump: it may only be played when its holder cannot follow suit and, if led, belongs to whatever suit its holder declares, which must be one in which they are otherwise void.

The play

Figure 5.1 illustrates some sample hands to show what sort of considerations are involved in the bidding. Five players are dealt the following from a 36-card pack:

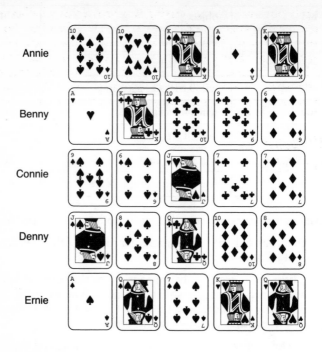

figure 5.1 Nap

If a call of 'Two' were allowed, Annie would certainly make it, holding the two top diamonds. Whether she will call 'Three' depends on whether or not she is prepared to take the slightly better than one-in-three chance of the ♠A being out of play. (Of the 31 cards she cannot see, 11 are undealt.) In fact it is undealt, and she would have won; but she decides against, and passes.

Benny calls 'Three', expecting to make the ♥A and two of his club trumps. This call would in fact make, as his lead would denude everyone else of trumps, leaving him with two of them and an Ace.

Connie calls 'Miz'. Her ♥J is an obvious danger, but she is prepared to bank on at least one opponent's having to overtake it with a higher heart, or on being able to discard to a subsequent lead in clubs or diamonds. In fact, this call would make.

Denny obviously passes, leaving Ernie to decide whether or not he can raise what would have been a safe 'Three' to 'Four' in order to overcall Connie's Miz. The question is not how many he can win, but whether or not he need lose more than one. He will lose one trick in trumps if any opponent holds the King and one lower spade, and he will lose a royal heart if the Ace is in play. In the event, he took the plunge, and went down protesting.

See also

http://pagat.com/trumps/nap

06

solo whist

- for four players (non-partnership)
- easy to learn
- a game of skill

Solo Whist crossed the Channel from Belgium (where its descendant Kleurwhist is still played) over 100 years ago and rapidly became one of the most popular of British card games. In its early days it almost rivalled Bridge as a potential successor to Partnership Whist in clubs, homes and 'polite society'. In the event, Bridge won out, but Solo went on to secure an alternative niche as a game of home and hearth, of public house and, up to the death of the railway system in the 1960s (in Britain), as the quintessential commuter game.

Solo shouldn't be thought of as an adaptation or perversion of Partnership Whist. It is a game in its own right and with its own pedigree. It has the rare merit of being one of the few trick games designed for four persons playing on their own account rather than in fixed partnerships. This makes it ideal for people who don't like partnership games and prefer to suffer for their own mistakes or bouts of creative experimentation.

Solo differs from Bridge in a number of other significant and related respects. The main one is that it has no overall structure. Each deal is complete in itself, and the result can be settled up immediately in cash or hard score, enabling players to cut in and out of a game without disturbing its flow, and a game can last for as many deals as there remain four people round the table, even though (as well befitted a commuter game) they may not be the same four that started the session going. For all these reasons, it is by nature a far less formal game than Bridge – chatting and ragging is not merely permitted but virtually required as an integral part of the proceedings. But don't let that fool you. It really is a game of skill and worth taking seriously.

The game

Preliminaries. Four players, 52 cards. The turn to deal and play passes clockwise around the table.

Shuffle and deal. Shuffle the cards thoroughly at start of play, but not between deals until a slam or an abundance has been played and won. Deal 12 cards to each player in batches of three at a time, followed by a single card to make 13. The final single card, which belongs to Dealer, is dealt face up to the table and not taken into hand until after the auction. Its purpose is to fix a suit of first priority for trumps.

Auction. There is a round of bidding to decide whether the contract to be played will be a partnership one or a solo against three opponents. The player at Dealer's left bids first, and each subsequent player must either pass or make a higher bid than any gone before. From lowest to highest, the bids are:

- **Proposal ('Prop')** An offer to win eight tricks with the aid of anyone willing to form a partnership, with the turned suit as trump.
- **Acceptance ('Cop')** An offer to partner the player who made a proposal, provided no higher bid has supervened.

The following are all higher and all independent (non-partnership) bids:

- **Misère ('Mis')** An offer to lose every trick, playing at no trump.
- **Solo** An offer to win at least five tricks, with the turned suit as trump.
- **Abundance ('a bunny', 'a bundle')** An offer to win at least nine tricks, with a trump suit of one's own choice, other than that of the turned card.
- **Royal abundance** An offer to win at least nine tricks with the turned suit as trump. This is actually announced as 'Abundance': at this stage it is only necessary to specify 'Royal' in order to overcall an earlier player's bid of abundance.
- **Misère ouverte ('Spread')** An offer to lose every trick, playing at no trump, and with one's hand of cards exposed on the table.
- **Abundance declared ('Slam')** An offer to win all 13 tricks, playing at no trump, but with the advantage of the opening lead. (Some schools allow slam with a personal trump suit, which may be overcalled by slam with the turned suit as trump. If this is followed, the soloist does not need the advantage of leading to the first trick.)

call	aim	pay-off
Prop and cop	win 8 tricks with partner	10 + 2
Solo	win 5 alone in turned suit	10 + 2
Misère	lose every trick (at no trump)	20
Abundance	win 9 alone in own suit	30 + 3
Royal abundance	win 9 alone in turned suit	30 + 3
Spread misère	lose every trick, open (NT)	40
Slam	win 13, NT, with opening lead	60

A contract is established when a bid is followed by three consecutive passes. The dealer then takes the turn-up into hand.

If the first player passes, and a subsequent player makes a proposal which no one accepts or overcalls, the first player (only) is allowed to accept the proposal, but not to make a higher call.

If the only bid made is a proposal, and no one accepts it, the proposer may raise their bid to a solo. The cards are gathered up and formed into a new pack without being shuffled and the next dealer deals them out. (Alternatively, some form of 'general misère' may be played. In the simplest form, all play at no trump and the winner of the last trick loses an agreed amount.)

Play. The opening lead is made (usually) by the player at Dealer's left. Players must follow suit if possible, otherwise may play any card. The trick is taken by the highest card of the suit led, or by the highest trump if any are played, and the winner of each trick leads to the next.

Particular contracts have particular rules as follows.

In *Prop and cop*, partners do not change positions or go out of their way to play alternately. If they are sitting next to each other, they play consecutively.

At *misère*, if the soloist wins a trick they lose the contract without further play.

In *abundance*, some schools do not require the soloist to name trumps until the first trick has been played and won.

In a *spread misère*, the soloist's hand is laid face up on the table only after the first trick has been played and won.

In a *slam* played at no trump, the soloist leads to the first trick, regardless of position.

Note. *Following a successful abundance or slam, the cards are thoroughly shuffled before the next deal.*

Hard score. Typical pay-offs in a British game are as follows (use similar small amounts in other currencies):

- prop and cop wins a basic 10p plus 2p per overtrick. One opponent pays this to one partner, the other opponent to the other partner. If lost, each partner pays an opponent 10p, plus 2p per under-trick
- solo pays the same as prop and cop, but to the soloist by each opponent, or, if lost, to each opponent by the soloist
- for abundance, the rate is 30p for the contract, plus 3p per over- or under-trick
- misère wins or loses a flat 20p, spread misère 40p, a slam 60p
- a general misère, if played, requires the loser to pay 10p to each opponent.

Some schools keep a separate kitty for slams and abundances. Everyone contributes an agreed amount to the kitty at start of play and after it has been won. The player of a slam or abundance wins the kitty if successful, or, if not, increases it by the amount of their original contribution.

Soft score. It's easy enough to keep scores in writing, as long as you remember that each row of the score-sheet should sum to zero. For example, if Annie and Connie win nine tricks at prop and cop they each score +12 (10 for the contract plus 2 for the overtrick), while Benny and Denny each lose –12. If Benny then wins a solo with seven tricks, the others each score –14 (paying 10 for the contract plus 4 for the two overtricks), giving Benny a plus score of 42. To convert the final result into hard score, each player with less than zero pays into a pot the amount of their deficit, and each player with more draws the equivalent of their win out of the pot. As long as each individual row sums to zero, so will the final totals.

call	aim	pay-off
Prop and cop	win 8 tricks with partner	10 + 2
Solo	win 5 alone in turned suit	10 + 2
Misère	lose every trick (at no trump)	20
Abundance	win 9 alone in own suit	30 + 3
Royal abundance	win 9 alone in turned suit	30 + 3
Spread misère	lose every trick, open (NT)	40
Slam	win 13, NT, with opening lead	60

The play

Solo Whist is a subtle game in which you can easily lose by being either too cautious or totally reckless. The over-cautious player never takes a chance on a reasonable but not foolproof bid which a more experienced or imaginative player will undertake promptly; the reckless player will undertake too many long-shot hands and come off worst.

If everyone is cautious, as usually happens with beginners, the game is dull because there are few bids. You can avoid this danger by playing a competitive misère when all pass, as those who lose by taking the most tricks may then learn to recognize strength in their hand when they see it. If one player is reckless, the game is dull because they hog the limelight, preventing others from taking a hand with their more reasonable bids, and the player's frequent losses will be a foregone conclusion. What makes any game exciting is the fight, not the defeat.

Before examining the possible calls more closely, we should first note one important respect in which Solo differs from Bridge, Whist and many other trick-taking games – namely, that cards are rarely shuffled and are always dealt in batches of three, with the result that a balanced distribution of cards among the four players is the exception rather than the rule. In Bridge and Whist you normally expect to find the cards of your own hand distributed 4–3–3–3 or 4–4–3–2 among the suits, so that any suit longer than five or shorter than two gives you a hand well worth thinking about. In Solo, a hand of the pattern 7–4–2–0 may well give you a good bid, but should not be regarded as anything out of the ordinary. Whether or not a given hand is biddable depends on its overall strength rather than on its distribution.

The difference between a slightly risky bid and an out-and-out long shot is therefore more marked. A slightly risky bid is one you can only lose against an unfavourable distribution of cards among your opponents. Such a call is worth making. A long shot is one you can only win if the remaining cards are favourably distributed. Such a call is rarely worth making.

When not the soloist, remember that you are playing as a member of a partnership of three, and not just for the pleasure of making as many tricks as you can yourself (or losing them, in the case of a misère). It is always to the advantage of the caller's opponents – who, in accordance with card tradition, but in defiance of logic, are known as the defenders – to lead through the caller rather than up to them. In other words, the lead to a trick is always best made by the player on the caller's right, so that they have to play second. Caller's preferred position to a trick is either first (leader) or fourth; the others should therefore play as far as possible to deny this advantage. When defending a positive (non-misère) bid, lead low through the caller, and try as much as possible to weaken their hand either by leading trumps or by forcing them out of the caller by leading suits in which they are void. If playing from a sequence (e.g. from Q J 10, etc.) always take with the lowest but lead with the highest – though, if you hold Ace, King, lead the King. By following these and other principles derived from Whist and Bridge your co-defenders will be able to deduce useful features of your hand and play accordingly.

Keeping track of the cards played is important. You don't have to remember them all, but at least try to count the trumps as they appear, keep track of the Aces and Kings, and note when anyone else has a void suit.

call	aim	pay-off
Prop and cop	win 8 tricks with partner	10 + 2
Solo	win 5 alone in turned suit	10 + 2
Misère	lose every trick (at no trump)	20
Abundance	win 9 alone in own suit	30 + 3
Royal abundance	win 9 alone in turned suit	30 + 3
Spread misère	lose every trick, open (NT)	40
Slam	win 13, NT, with opening lead	60

Proposal and acceptance

Some schools don't allow the bids of proposal and acceptance, admitting nothing lower than a solo, possibly on the grounds that 'it is too easy to make'. I think this view is debatable. If 'prop and cop' is found too predictably successful, it may mean that the players are calling too cautiously and passing up hands that more experienced players would think worth a solo. The whole point of aiming for eight tricks between two players is that both reckon they can win four but neither rates their individual hand good enough for five on its own.

It is conventional, not to say commonsensical, that somebody who proposes probably has strength in trumps, though not necessarily enough to justify a solo bid. It follows that a player who accepts a proposal doesn't necessarily need great trump strength but should be able to offer support in plain suits, either with a few high cards or with a void. If neither partner feels strong enough to lead trumps the bid was probably risky, and the defenders will take advantage of this reluctance to lead trumps themselves when they see what's going on.

Position is always important in the auction, but hardly more so than in 'prop and cop'. The best position to accept from is fourth hand (that is, as dealer), since the absence of an intervening solo call bodes well for the partnership contract. It's risky to accept eldest hand's proposal as second hand, as the third and fourth to callers may be tempted to let the contract stand for the sheer pleasure of beating it.

As first to bid, don't feel obliged to propose if your cards are only just biddable. If your hand isn't strong enough for an independent bid you can pass with confidence, since you will still be in a position to accept in the event that somebody else proposes, thereby suggesting that your hand may be stronger than you think. Alternatively, you may well propose on a hand that may border on playability as a solo. If a later player accepts, you then have a playable game; if not, and all pass, you may reasonably consider going for the solo, knowing that it cannot be overcalled.

Here's a hand that the first to call passed up, but subsequently found strong enough to accept a proposal (spades trump):

♠K Q 10 4 ♥K 2 ♣10 8 5 4 ♦8 5 2

The proposer's hand was:

♠ 8 7 6 5 3 ♥ A ♣ A 9 7 6 ♦ 10 9 6

This is the sort of combination that makes it criminal to abolish 'prop and cop'.

If you and your partner are sitting adjacently, the ideal position is for one of you to be leading to a trick when your partner is sitting to your right and so playing fourth. With presumed strength in trumps, you should lead them early in order to draw them from your opponents and so establish your plain suits. Against this, however, you should avoid forcing your partner to play trumps if you are weak in them yourself. As in Partnership Whist, note what suit your partner leads first, and return it when convenient to do so. Lead from strength – either trumps or from your strongest suit, whichever you want returned. It is not particularly desirable to lead a singleton.

Solo

For a solo you have to win at least five tricks with the turned suit as trump. This may sound obvious to a fault, yet in defiance of all probability, there are players who will quite happily bid a spade solo on a hand like:

♠ K Q 9 4 ♥ 8 ♣ A K Q J 3 ♦ 10 9 8

The idea is to make two trumps, one of them on a heart lead after the Eight has gone; at least the top two clubs; and one for luck, in either trumps or clubs. Without the lead, a probable outcome is the win of two trumps as anticipated, the possible win of ♣A when led and, if very lucky, the possible win of ♣K, for a final result of four or even only three tricks. 'Yes,' says one commentator, who shall be nameless; 'Solo is easy enough; just look for five near-certain tricks.'

At the other extreme, some players are so mesmerized by Aces that they will pass up a perfectly feasible solo bid for lack of them. Here's another hand with spades turned:

♠ K J 9 8 7 5 2 ♥ 5 ♣ J 9 4 ♦ Q 3

Given the lead, this is a good example of the 'slight risk' that's usually worth taking. With seven trumps, you can afford to lose two of them in the not unreasonable hope that those same two tricks will clear the defenders out of their three top trumps (Ace, Queen and Ten). A King lead should do it.

Even without the lead, you could safely bid solo (spades, again, for convenience) on:

♠ K Q 10 8 7 6 ♥ K 10 9 8 ♣ K 4 2 ♦ *none*

The non-trump Kings should produce two tricks, the void in diamonds brings in a low trump, and the other five trumps should be good for the outstanding two.

So what, in general, are the minimum requirements for a biddable solo? Obviously, to start with, you want length or strength in trumps, counting as part of this assessment any void or singleton plain suit that you ruff with a low one at the appropriate time.

On trumps alone, the borderline between a doubtful and a feasible solo is rather fine. For instance, a holding of A K Q 9 and a lower card is risky, whereas A K Q 10 and another might be expected to succeed without inducing gasps of astonishment. When holding five trumps, always calculate on the pessimistic assumption that at least one defender may hold five as well. Even a seven-card suit should be headed by nothing less than K J 9.

In plain suits, the chief merit is strength and shortness (not length). The expected failure of the first hand quoted above lies in the undue length of the club suit – A K Q J 3, five in all. The most favourable possible distribution of the outstanding eight is 3–3–2, which means that someone will certainly be trumping by the time you have drawn the odd two with the Ace and King. A more probable distribution is 4–3–1, giving you the Ace but not the King, while there is a strong chance (given the unbalanced distribution of your own hand) of one defender's being void, thus depriving you even of the Ace.

You may even dispense with strength in trumps if your hand contains strength and universal shortness – that is, an unusually even distribution of suits. The fact that spades are trump needn't inhibit you from calling a solo on:

♠ 5 4 3 2 ♥ A K 2 ♣ A K 2 ♦ A 3 2

Of course, it will be beaten if any defender is out of diamonds or holds only one heart or club, but the even suit distribution in your own hand lowers that danger to the acceptable level of 'slight risk'.

Some hands make acceptable solos only if you have the lead; others really require to be led up to. For example, consider the trump holding A K Q 10 2 in a hand that doesn't include a void or singleton. The problem card is the Jack. If you have the lead, you can play trumps from the top down and hope the Jack will fall by the time the Queen is out, leaving Ten high and a certain trick with the Two, and giving enough for solo even without side-suit support. Without the lead, the missing Jack is a permanent nuisance. By the time you have voided your short suit you run the danger of ruffing low with the Two and finding it overtaken by a higher trump. On the other hand, you're better off without the lead if you're short of Aces but rich in guarded Kings in short suits.

Playing as one of the defenders against a solo, you can safely lead a singleton to the first trick (which you should *not* normally do in playing against a prop and cop, or in partnership Whist). With a fairly even distribution, a low trump is also not a bad lead. Otherwise, lead your best card – from not too long a suit – and the highest of a sequence, unless you hold Ace, King, in which case play the King.

Abundance and royal abundance

An abundance is a solo, only more so. As before, you must have length and strength in trumps, but now you also need a strong, lengthy side-suit and at least one void. Because the dealing system easily (and deliberately) produces uneven distributions, double voids are not uncommon, and a strong two-suited hand is often a must for abundance.

Since your aim is to make at least nine tricks, one way of assessing the hand is to identify the four cards you can afford to lose, and to make sure there are not five of them. Otherwise, you make what is known as an 'eight-trick abundance', which comes expensive.

Given two suits of equal length, don't automatically entrump the stronger. Quite often the apparently weaker suit not only makes a better trump, but actually proves the only way of avoiding loss. For example, you can go a bundle on:

♠ A K Q J 10 9 ♥ 10 8 6 5 3 2 ♣ A ♦ *none*

but *only* in hearts, not in the apparently stronger spade suit. The reason is perhaps easiest to see if you examine the hand from the viewpoint of the four losers rather than the nine winners. If you make spades trump, how are you going to avoid losing more than four hearts? With hearts trump, however, you can afford to lose four for the sake of clearing out trumps and thereby safely establishing the spade suit. You will make one heart by ruffing a diamond lead, and a second either by a ruff in diamonds or clubs, or by finding your Ten high when the top trumps have gone.

Defending against an abundance, lead from your longest and strongest suit. Remember that the defenders need five tricks to win, and lose no opportunity to make five as soon as possible – that is, before caller can get in with their trumps and dictate the rest of the play. By all means lead suits in which caller is void, thereby forcing them to trump and so weaken their hand. Sometimes caller will be relying on a 'bum card' for a lucky trick: if you can spot this coming you can defend against it. They may, for instance, lead Ace, King of a side-suit, then switch to another line of attack in pretence of being void. By retaining the odd Queen, Jack or even Ten, instead of discarding at the earliest opportunity, you may well find it winning a low one at the thirteenth trick, led to by caller after extracting all the trumps. Again, if caller is banking on a risky King or Queen, they may be hoping to do so on a bad lead by the defenders. In this case they will be trying to lose the lead, so you can try to throw them back into it by forcing them to trump.

Declared abundance (Slam)

This is a bid to win all 13 tricks at no trump, and requires the sort of hand that's so unmistakable as to need no description, either of what it looks like or how to play it. You only declare abundance on a cast-iron hand, and if it really is cast-iron you simply lay it face up on the table and claim your winnings. If any defender can find a way of beating it then the game must be played, and if they are right you will have learnt a valuable lesson.

But it is worth explaining why a declared abundance is properly played at no trump, even though some players accept it as a trump game. The reason is, quite simply, that if you can safely make 13 tricks with a trump suit, then you can safely make 13 tricks without a trump suit. But don't you need a trump suit if you have a void? No. Take the following:

♠ A K Q J 10   ♥ A K Q J   ♣ A K Q J   ♦ *none*

Since the slam bid gives you the privilege of the opening lead, your void in diamonds is irrelevant.

Misère and spread misère

Beginners may be forgiven for imagining that a misère, the winning of no tricks at no trump, is what you bid when you have no good trick-winners but only a general miscellany of dribs and drabs. In fact, such a hand is precisely one that isn't worth bidding at all. The misère bid is a positive undertaking to successfully defend yourself against all efforts on the part of your opponents to force you to take a trick. For this purpose you need a very good hand – 'good', that is, from the point of view of beating off such attacks.

Many card-players, especially those who know nothing but Bridge, tend to look down on misère as a sort of jocular substitute round, played when no one has a good enough hand on which to make a 'real' bid. Nothing could be further from the truth. Both attack and defence at misère call for, and often receive, some of the best play to be seen at the card table.

In considering a misère, there are two good features to look for. One is low-ranking cards, and the other is a void suit. Note that the length of any suit you hold is irrelevant as long as it contains low cards. For example, in this hand:

♠ 5 3 2   ♥ A Q 10 8 6 4 2   ♣ 7 3 2   ♦ *none*

the hearts are just as safe from attack as the spades, as no one can force you to take a trick in either suit. As for low ranks, in a holding of five or more you must have the Two (you may escape without it, but the risk is great); with fewer, you may get away with nothing lower than Three or even Four. Note, too, that a holding of alternating low ranks is just as good as a sequence. In the hand quoted above, for instance, the A Q 10 8 6 4 2 of hearts is as good as 8 7 6 5 4 3 2. To prove it, imagine that the Three is led; you play the Two, and your Four is then the lowest of the suit. If the Five is then led, you play the Four and your Six is lowest, and so on.

The advantage of a void is obvious: when somebody leads it, you can throw out your potentially dangerous cards. Recognizing potential dangers can be a subtle affair. Because the hearts in the hand above are safe from attack, it contains no dangerous cards, so you needn't rush to throw out the Ace or Queen when diamonds are led. Clubs, however, are a different matter, for here your Seven is the most dangerous card in the hand. With three clubs out against you (6–5–4), you can only defend yourself against two of them (with your 3–2). By the time the third is led you may find the other two players void, thus forcing you to take the suit with the Seven. And this won't be just a case of bad luck, as experienced opponents will inevitably discover your weak suit and exploit it. In this case you need the diamond void as an escape hatch for your dangerous Seven.

In general, then, you can't bid misère with dangerous cards unless you have saving voids to accommodate them, and even then the device may only be expected to work once. Remember, too, to look at things from your opponents' viewpoint. If your hand is good enough for a misère but not good enough for an open misère, then by definition it contains a weakness, and the defenders' strategy will be to find out where it lies.

In defending against a misère a good lead is any singleton, or failing that, a middling card from a short suit. Don't play from a long suit, as the caller will probably have none of it so be able to throw out their most dangerous card. Don't play too low, as you must give your partners an opportunity to get rid of their own high cards in that suit. If you hold a Two, especially in a short suit, you may well hold the means to beat the contract. Save it until the top cards are out, then get the lead and play it. For this purpose you may need to hold back an Ace or other master card to make sure of getting the lead when you judge the time has come.

See also

http://www.pagat.com/boston/solowhist.html
http://www.pagat.com/software/solows.zip

07

oh hell!

- for three to seven players
- easy to learn, quick to play
- fun, but not without skill

> **The name of the game**
>
> Oh Hell! is undoubtedly named from the exclamation of disgust
> that accompanies taking an unwanted trick (or losing a wanted
> one). When it first appeared in the 1930s it was often bowdlerized
> into politer titles, like Blackout, Jungle Bridge, Botheration, etc.
> It's also known as Nomination Whist, though this better denotes
> an interesting variety of Solo.

The most distinctive feature of this fun game is that you bid to
take an exact number of tricks rather than a minimum number.
Oh Hell! may have been the first game to do this. The same
concept has since been explored more thoroughly in such games
as Ninety-Nine.

The game

Players. From three to seven. One of them must be appointed
scorekeeper, who will rule up a score sheet into as many columns
as there are players. A game consists of a number of deals with
one card fewer dealt each time, so the last is always a one-card,
one-trick hand.

Cards and deal. Whoever cuts the lowest card (from a standard
52-card pack) starts by dealing all the cards round until everyone
has the same number, which means (unless four play) a smaller
number will be left over. For example, if seven play, each receives
seven cards and three remain. The top card of the undealt batch
is faced for trump. If none remain, play at no trump.

Object. To win exactly as many tricks as you bid, neither more nor
fewer. The players look at their cards and each in turn, starting
with the player at Dealer's left, announces how many tricks they
propose to win. If seven are dealt on the first round, for example,
each player bids any number from none to seven. The scorekeeper
notes each player's bid in their column on the score sheet.

In some circles the Dealer, who bids last, is prohibited from bidding
a number which would bring the total of bids to the number of
tricks played. The purpose of this is to ensure that at least one player
will fail. Decide in advance whether or not to follow this rule.

Play. The opening lead is made by the player at Dealer's left, and
tricks are played to normal Whist rules.

Scoring. This varies from school to school. It has become much simplified with the passage of time, but the original schedule is as follows. Each player wins 1 point per trick taken, whether bid or not, and adds a bonus of 10 for fulfilling their bid. In any deal of five or more cards, a bonus of 50 is awarded for bidding and winning every trick played (grand slam) or 25 for bidding and winning all but one trick (small slam).

The winner is the player with the highest score at the end of the last deal, or the first to reach 100 points if this happens sooner.

In some schools the first deal is one card and each subsequent deal is one card more. In others, the number starts low and rises to the maximum, then goes back down to one again – or it starts high and goes down, then goes back up again. Both versions are also called Up the River, Down the River.

See also

http://www.pagat.com/exact/ohhell.html

08

hearts

- best for four, playable by three
- easy to learn
- a game of skill

Since it first appeared in America just over a century ago, this game has gained a new lease of life – a hearts transplant, so to speak – from its popularity as computer software. In its simplest form, the aim is just to avoid winning tricks containing hearts. Each player counts a penalty point for each heart taken in tricks, and the winner is the player with the lowest score when one player reaches a maximum of penalties. There are many local variations, but the following four-player game contains the best balance of common features and can now be regarded as standard. The three-hand game, described later, also works well.

The game

Cards. Standard 52-card pack ranking A K Q J 10 9 8 7 6 5 4 3 2 in each suit. Deal 13 cards each, in ones.

Object. To have the lowest penalty score when one player terminates the game by reaching 100 penalties. Penalties are scored for capturing penalty cards in tricks. The penalty cards are all the hearts, counting 1 each, and the ♠Q, counting 13. Alternatively, you may aim to capture all 14 penalty cards (known as shooting or hitting the moon), but need not announce this beforehand.

Exchange. Each player first passes three cards face down to their left-hand neighbour and receives the same number from their right. On the second deal, cards are passed to the right and received from the left. On the third they are passed between players sitting opposite each other. On the fourth, there is no exchange, the hands being played as dealt. The same sequence is repeated thereafter. Players may not pick up the cards passed to them until they have passed their own three on. There is no restriction on which cards may be passed.

Play. Whoever holds ♣2 leads it to the first trick. Players must follow suit if possible, otherwise may play any card. The trick is taken by the highest card of the suit led, and the winner of each trick leads to the next. There are no trumps.

Two special rules apply:

1 You may not play a penalty card to the first trick, unless you have no choice.
2 You may not lead a heart until the suit has been 'broken' by somebody having discarded one to a previous trick. (*Exception:* You may do so if you have nothing else, or when the only other card you hold is ♠Q.)

Unless otherwise agreed, it is acceptable to throw all non-penalty cards won in tricks to a common wastepile, and for players to leave the penalty cards they have won face up on the table before them so that everyone can see which are yet to come.

Score. At end of play each player counts 1 penalty point for each heart taken in tricks, and 13 for ♠Q. For taking all 14 penalty cards you may either deduct 26 from your total, or add 26 to everyone else's. The winner is the player with fewest penalty points when one or more players reaches 100. A tie-breaker may be played if necessary.

The play

Here's an amusing deal that demonstrates some of the problems and pitfalls the game can give rise to. Here are the hands as dealt, and each player's three discards:

N	♥10 9 3	♠10 9 7 3 2 ♦7 4	♣K 7 6	☞	♥10♦7♣7
E	♥K 7 6 4	♠A J	♦10 8 5	♣Q J 5 2 ☞	♠A♦10♦8
S	♥A Q 8 5 2 ♠K 6	♦Q J 9 6	♣10 8	☞	♠K♣10♣8
W	♥J	♠Q 8 5 4	♦A K 3 2 ♣A 9 4 3 ☞		♥J♦K♣9

North's idea was to get rid of some indeterminate cards and keep their safe run of spades. (A long runs of spades is always good, though I would have attempted to void either clubs or diamonds.) East certainly had to get rid of their high spade, as did South. West's four spades to the Queen is not comfortable, but the Queen is nearly always better in one's hand than out, and they can reasonably hope for an extra spade from North to make the suit safer.

After the pass, the players' hand are:

North	♥J 9 3	♠10 9 7 3 2	♦K 4	♣K 9 6
East	♥K 10 7 6 4	♠J	♦8 7 5	♣Q J 7 5 2
South	♥A Q 8 5 2	♠A 6	♦10 Q 9 6	♣–
West	♥–	♠K Q 8 5 4	♦A J 3 2	♣A 10 8 4 3

East duly leads ♣2 and the game goes as follows:

	E	S	W	N	Comment
1	♣2	♠A	<u>♣A</u>	♣K	North would have kept the King had South not shown out of clubs.
2	♦7	♦Q	<u>♦A</u>	♦K	North seems unnecessarily cautious about diamonds.
3	♦5	<u>♦J</u>	♦3	♦4	
4	♠J	♠6	<u>♠K</u>	♠10	By playing ♠K second to the trick, West makes it pretty clear he holds the Queen safe.
5	♥10	♥10	♥2	<u>♥J</u>	East hangs on the ♥K in case it encourages anyone to shoot the moon.
6	<u>♥K</u>	♥8	♣10	♥9	Now East can play it and lose the rest.
7	♥7	<u>♥A</u>	♣8	♥3	
8	<u>♥6</u>	♥5	♣4	♣9	
9	<u>♣5</u>	♥Q	♣3	<u>♣6</u>	North beats West in spades.

At trick six, North 'sacrifices' with ♥9, planning to win the trick and lose the rest, thus preventing anyone from shooting the moon. East, however, with the same object in view, 'over-sacrifices' with the King.

At trick four, West could (and perhaps should) have unloaded ♠Q before it was too late. He reckoned, however, that his five-card holding would save him from being forced to take a trick with the Queen, and embarked on the not infrequent dodge of letting everyone know he held the Queen and winding up the suspense by withholding her for the last trick. Unfortunately for him, however, North also held five spades and got rid of the King early on. Coming in at trick nine, North plays from ♠ 9 7 3 2 against West's ♠ Q 8 5 4, and West finds himself, at the last trick, hoist by his own petard.

Result: North 2, East 5, South 6, and West 13 penalty points.

The play

In passing cards on, don't automatically discard hearts or high spades. The longer a suit, the safer you are from having to win tricks in it, especially if you have a few low cards including the Two. The advantage of keeping high hearts and the spade Queen is that you have more control over when they get played to tricks. In particular, be chary of passing on the Ace of hearts, for fear of giving your neighbour a chance of shooting the moon. The bad Queen is usually good for you if guarded by at least four other spades (though not in the game described above!). Holding the Queen as one of three or fewer spades, you won't do much good by throwing them all out in case you get passed the Ace or King, which of course are the most dangerous cards in the pack.

Don't discard with a view to being able to shoot the moon yourself. For one thing, you can't expect canny opponents to pass you helpful cards such as top hearts and, for another, it usually becomes obvious when someone is deliberately aiming for it, which usually makes it easy to circumvent. Normally, you won't expect to go for the moon until about half way through the play, when the possibility of doing so will have had a chance to manifest itself.

In play, lead a low spade whenever you are safe in spades and the Queen is in someone else's hand. Conversely, note carefully when other players on lead fail to do this, as it usually means that that is where they are weak.

Variations

A common variation on the game is to play with a positive score of 10 points awarded for capturing ♦10. Four can also play in different kinds of partnership as follows:

Fixed partnerships. The players facing each other across the table are partners for the whole game, and the passing cycle is left, right, across, none.

Rotating partnerships. In the first deal, North-East oppose South-West, and each player exchanges three cards with their neighbouring opponent. In the second, North-South oppose East-West, and each exchanges cards with their partner. In the third, North-West oppose South-East and each exchanges with their neighbouring opponent. In the fourth, there is no exchange and the first two players to win a trick become partners. Shooting the moon requires all penalty cards to fall to one player, not just to one partnership.

Ad hoc partnerships. The passing cycle is left, right, across, none. The first two players to win a trick – whether or not either trick contains a penalty card – become partners for the rest of the hand, and the other two play in partnership against them. If only one player wins tricks they will, of course, score alone for a shoot.

Hearts for three

Remove the ♦2, deal 17 cards each, and play as described above. In the first deal you pass three cards to your left, in the second to your right, in the third not at all, and then repeat the cycle. In a variant recorded in some older books under the name Black Maria there is a penalty of 10 for capturing ♠K and of 7 for capturing ♠A.

In a version called Widow Hearts, the full pack is used, four cards are dealt face down as a widow, each player receives 16 cards, there is no passing of cards, and the player at Dealer's left leads to the first trick. The widow is added to the last trick, and any penalty cards it may contain count against the player who wins it.

See also

There is an embarrassment of riches when it comes to Hearts on the net, probably due to the fact that probably everyone in the world who uses Windows™ also uses the Microsoft™ Hearts program that comes with it. As usual, the best starting-point for exploring all the possibilities is the Pagat website:

http://www.pagat.com/reverse/hearts

09

ninety-nine

- for two to five players, best for three
- easy to learn
- a game of skill

Ninety-Nine is an extension of the 'exact bid' principle of Oh Hell!, in that everyone bids to win a precise number of tricks, neither more nor less. Compared with other bidding games it has the advantage that most hands can be bid in several different ways, and that everyone can bid and even win their contracts in every deal, so you don't have to hang around waiting for a good hand to come up before you can bid. In this respect, at least, it beats even Bridge.

I invented Ninety-Nine (in 1968) with the deliberate intention of producing a skill-demanding game for three players that should be easier to learn than classic three-handers such as Skat – something that has long been absent from the repertoire of British card-games. It was first published in *Games & Puzzles* magazine in 1975 and has since been reproduced in so many other card-game collections as to have become something of a classic.

Though originally designed for three, Ninety-Nine plays quite well with other numbers. Versions for two, four and five players follow the main description.

The game (for three players)

Cards. Thirty-seven, ranking A K Q J 10 9 8 7 6 in each suit, plus one Joker.

Game. A game is 100 points over as many deals as it takes. It is possible for more than one player to win a game. A match is won by the player with the highest total when at least one player has won three games.

Deal. Deal 12 cards each, one at a time, face down. Place the last card face up on the table to establish a trump suit.

Joker. If the turned card is the Joker, the deal is played at no trump. If not, then the Joker represents the turned card, and whoever holds it uses it exactly as if it were that card, either for bidding or for trick-play. They are not obliged to say that they have it.

Object. Each player discards three cards face down and plays out the other nine to tricks. Your three discards are called 'bid-cards', and by means of a code explained below they are selected to represent any number from nought to nine. This number constitutes your bid, and your aim is to win exactly the number of tricks your bid-cards represent.

Bidding. Herein lies the point of the game. You can bid anything from nought to nine tricks by discarding three bid cards in accordance with the following code (see also Figure 9.1):

Any ♣ represents	3 tricks
Any ♥ represents	2 tricks
Any ♠ represents	1 trick
Any ♦ represents	0 tricks

For example, you can represent a bid of three by any of the following discards: ♣♦♦ (3 + 0 + 0), ♥♠♦ (2 + 1 + 0), or ♠♠♠ (1 + 1 + 1). Similarly, there are three different ways of bidding 3, 4, 5, 6 or 7 tricks, two ways of bidding 2 or 8, and one of bidding 0 (♦♦♦) or 9 (♣♣♣).

Note. *Only the suits count for bidding – it makes no difference what their ranks are. If the Joker is used as a bid-card it represents the suit of the turn-up.*

Having decided on your bid-cards, lay them face down on the table before you, slightly spread so as not to get confused with won tricks. Normally, bids remain secret and are not revealed until the end of the game. But you do have the option of making a premium bid for a higher score, which involves giving certain information about your cards, as follows:

- Declaration: Before play, you can turn your bid-cards face up so the other two players know how many you are aiming for.
- Revelation: For this, you not only reveal your bid but also spread your hand of cards face up on the table before the first trick is led to.

Each of these bids carries a bonus, which goes to the bidder if successful, otherwise to each opponent (regardless of whether or not they succeed).

Only one player may make a premium bid in any round. If more than one player wishes to declare or reveal, priority goes to the revelation over the declaration. If equal, the player at Dealer's left has greatest priority and Dealer least.

figure 9.1 Ninety-Nine

Each suit represents a number of tricks related to its shape. Thus a club has three bobbles, a heart has two cheeks, a spade has one point, and a diamond is a zero with straight sides (more or less).

Tricks. The first lead is always made by the player left of Dealer. Normal rules of trick-taking apply. Follow suit to the card led if possible; if not possible, either trump or discard from side suit. The trick is taken by the highest card of the suit led or by the highest trump if any are played. The winner of a trick leads to the next.

Score. When the last trick has gone, anyone who succeeded in their bid must turn their bid-cards face up before being credited with a bonus. A failed player, however, is not obliged to do so. Each player scores 1 point per trick won, regardless of their bid, plus (if applicable) a bonus for succeeding.

This bonus depends on how many players succeeded, as follows:

- if all three succeeded, they each add a bonus of 10
- if two succeeded, they each add a bonus of 20
- if only one succeeded, that player alone adds 30.

A declaration carries an additional bonus of 30, and a revelation one of 60. This goes to the bidder if successful, otherwise it is credited to each opponent, in addition to any other score they may have made on their own account.

Examples:

	A	B	C		A	B	C	
bid	4	3	1	dec.	4	3	2	rev.
took	5	3	1		5	3	1	
success bonus	–	20	20		–	30	–	
premium bid	–	–	30		60	60	–	
total	5	23	51		65	93	1	

The highest possible score is 99, attained when the only player to succeed also gains the bonus of 60 for a revelation, whether played successfully by themselves, or unsuccessfully by somebody else.

Game score. A game ends when one or more players reaches or exceeds 100 points. Anyone who does so adds a game bonus of 100, provided that they succeeded in their last bid. For example, if A and B reach 100, and A and C succeed in that deal, then only A gets the game bonus – not B, who failed to make their last contract, nor C, who failed to reach 100.

When one or more players have won three game bonuses, the match ends and the winner is the player with the highest score.

Variation 1. Here's a more interesting way of fixing trumps if you haven't got a Joker or prefer not to use one. The first deal is played at no trump. Thereafter, the trump suit is determined by the number of players who succeeded in their bids in the previous deal as follows: clubs if all three succeed, hearts if two, spades if only one, diamonds if none.

Variation 2. You may prefer to play a fixed number of deals rather than up to a target score. If so, try the following 18-deal system. Separate a 54 card-pack, including two Jokers, into 36 playing cards (Ace to Six inclusive) and 18 trump indicators. The latter consists of the four Twos, Threes, Fours and Fives, plus the two Jokers. Shuffle the trump indicators and stack them face down. After each deal, but before anyone bids, turn the top card of the stack face up. The suit of this card is trump for the deal, or no trump if it is a Joker. The winner is the player with the highest score at the end of the eighteenth.

The play (for three players)

The most challenging aspect of Ninety-Nine is that by removing three cards for the purpose of bidding you inevitably alter the hand you are left to play with. This often gives you a good deal of choice. Almost any hand of cards at Ninety-Nine is biddable, since there are ten different numbers of tricks to bid and no fewer than 220 different ways of discarding three cards from 12. It's true that not all the possibilities make sensible bids, but more often than not you will find yourself confronted with a choice of two or three different bids to make and two or three different ways of representing each bid. Deciding between them is where the basic strategy of the game comes in. You have to take into account who has the lead, what the trump suit is (a factor that has more bearing on the play of Ninety-Nine than on any other card game), what the other players are likely to bid (for which purpose it helps to note which cards are lacking from your own hand), and, above all, which of your cards are to be regarded as trick winners and which as trick losers.

The first thing to remember is that, since you are aiming to win an exact number of tricks, you are at the same time aiming to lose a corresponding number of tricks. For example, a bid of three is the same as a bid to lose six. Your first job must therefore be to estimate which of your cards are probable winners (certain Aces, Kings and trumps), which are probable losers (Sixes and Sevens), and 'incalculables' – those of middling ranks, and especially Jack, Ten, Nine, any one of which is likely to win a trick when you want it to lose, or lose when you want it to win.

That done, you will aim as far as possible to retain extreme cards (winners and losers) and get rid of incalculables by using them to represent the bid. Choosing between several likely bids will often be controlled by the suit-bidding values of the cards you can most do without. You must enter the play with a clear idea of the intended role for each and every card: whether it is to win a trick, or to lose or be discarded to a trick, or to be played early on with a view to seeing what happens, and adjusting your subsequent play accordingly.

Curious imbalance of suits

The fact that suits have bidding values is unique to Ninety-Nine, and has a unique effect on the relative strength in play of the four different suits. In most card games there is a trump suit and three side suits. Apart from the fact that they have different symbols, there is no essential playing difference between one side suit and another. Similarly, one trump suit is as good as another. A game with spades as trump may be more highly valued than one with clubs (as in Bridge), but this has no effect on those suits' relative strength as trumps once the game is under way. Ninety-Nine is different, however, in that clubs are nearly always a strong suit, hearts less so, spades relatively weak, and diamonds totally unreliable. Here's why.

With three players and nine tricks, the commonest bid is, naturally, three. In fact, a fundamental principle of Ninety-Nine is 'If in doubt, bid three'. Three tricks, you will remember, can be represented in three different ways: ♣♦♦, ♥♠♦, or ♠♠♠. It is therefore obvious that spades and diamonds are *more likely* to be laid aside as bid cards than hearts or clubs. Statistics compiled from actual games confirm that – again, *on average* – the nine cards out in bids, and therefore missing from play, are three diamonds, three spades, two hearts, and one club. In fact, there is a slightly greater tendency for diamonds to be out than spades, as zero is the second commonest bid.

It follows that, in play, clubs and hearts tend to be long suits (eight and seven respectively), spades and diamonds short (six and five). Players are more frequently void in diamonds than any other suit, but only rarely void in clubs. In plain suits, therefore, given a normal distribution of cards, you can usually expect ♣A and ♣K to be trick winners, and probably also ♥A; but ♠A is not certain, and ♦A is positively risky, standing the most chance of being trumped.

Similarly, at the opposite extreme, if you have the lead and want to lose it, ♣7 is a much safer card than ♦7, as the diamond can so easily be undercut by ♦6 and followed by a discard when the third player is void.

Thus in assessing your hand you are concerned not only with the suit of cards, in deciding which to keep and which to use as bidders, but also with their ranks. From every point of view the most unreliable card of all, and so the likeliest candidate for discarding, is ♦10 – the most incalculable rank of the most unreliable suit.

This imbalance of suits also has its effect on trumps. For example, a player dealt ♦A K Q when diamonds are trumps will often discard them for a certain bid of nought. In which case the player holding ♦J has the top trump and may well be forced to take an unwanted trick with it. Should they therefore count ♦J as a probable winner? Not necessarily, for an opponent dealt ♦A K Q might equally well keep them in hand and void spades for a bid of three.

At the other extreme, clubs are reliable as trumps. If clubs are trumps and your highest trump is the Jack, you can be pretty certain that it's the fourth highest in play. The upper trumps are unlikely to be out in bids, because they imply bids of high numbers of tricks, for which purpose they would need to be kept in hand.

A further consequence of suit imbalance is that premium bids (declarations and revelations) tend to be safer in reliable suits (clubs, hearts) than in the others.

Playing for tricks

You will normally go into play with most cards already earmarked as winners and losers. Inevitably, you will have one or more of middle ranks or weak suits which may be either. What you need to do is get the lead as early as possible and lead out the incalculables to see what happens to them. If they win, you can work out in advance which probable winners you must now reclassify as losers. If they lose, you must do the reverse.

With incalculables out of the way, or if you have none to start with, it's usually right to cash your most reliable non-trump winners, and then lose the lead. Trumps normally play their role as leads at the end of the round, though of course circumstances occur in which they are better led early on.

Note carefully what cards others are playing. It's often possible to work out what they've bid from what they play; even if not, a great deal of scope exists for playing thwarting tactics.

For example, if ♦7 is led, and followed by ♦6, you can be sure that neither wants the trick. If you have no diamonds you may do well to discard rather than trump, even if you want a trick, solely to discomfit the first player, who probably counted it as a sure loser. On the whole, if you're uncertain whether or not a particular lead means a player wants the trick, it often proves best to duck it. The fact is (and it's a fact I can't explain) that in Ninety-Nine players tend to underbid rather than overbid, and therefore more often find themselves trying to lose unwanted strong cards than win with weak ones.

If one player has declared or revealed, it's always more profitable to spoil their game (working in collaboration with the other player) rather than make your own bid. If you can do both, of course, so much the better.

Length of suit

Long suits are weak; voids are strong. If you can bid in such a way as to create a void, you have splendid opportunities for either trumping or losing unwanted cards when that suit is led. This point often determines which of several possible bids is best to make.

A long suit is bad unless it contains safe low cards. Suppose you hold ♣ A Q 9 8 6 when some other suit is trumps. Normally you expect to be dealt three of each suit, given an even distribution. Here you have five. This could mean that an opponent who was dealt only one or two succeeded in voiding clubs with a view to bidding high and trumping them. It's therefore wise not to regard the Ace as a winner. Much safer is to treat all five as sure *losers* and bid accordingly. This particular holding is quite safe: you can never be forced to take with a club. The situation would be different, however, if your holding were ♣ A Q 10 9 8, for now you have neither a sure winner (the Ace may be trumped) nor a sure loser. Leading the Eight would be a sure signal of your intentions, and the others would, on principle, force you to take the trick.

Premium bids

For a declared bid you should have extreme cards in at least three suits and a void if possible. Remember that your bid-cards will be revealed, and that opponents can learn something from them. For example, if you bid three with three spades they may assume you have a void in that suit, and will probably refrain from leading it. This could be awkward if you were relying on the void as a means of making your trumps or losing some risky cards.

In order to reveal, you must be absolutely certain of the future destination of every card in your hand. Extreme cards or voids are necessary in every suit.

Unbiddable hands

Some hands look unbiddable at first sight. And so they may be, in the sense that you need the same cards for bidding as for making the tricks you bid. For example:

(trump ♦) A 6 ♣ J 10 ♥ K J 9 7 6 ♠ Q 10 7

Here the only sensible bid, of one trick, can only be made by throwing out the very card (♦A) you need to make it with. You could bid two, by throwing two spades and ♦6, but would then stand little chance of taking a trick in hearts.

In this example, it is impossible to make a 'sensible' bid – that is, one that you can be sure of fulfilling. What you do instead is adopt the Technique of the Meaningless Bid (TOMB for short), which involves throwing out bid-cards solely for the surprise value of their absence from play. In this case the throw-outs are ♦A and both clubs. Your chances of making six tricks are remote, but the likelihood of spoiling your opponents' bids is most promising. See the first player's surprise when you trump their ♣A with ♦6, and the second player's astonishment when they find you out of trumps and are forced to win it with ♦7!

Fortunately, few hands are completely unbiddable in this way, and it is better to avoid the meaningless bid. But laying aside a card for its surprise absence is always good tactics. Strong Aces and high trumps are ideal candidates for this practice.

Sample game

With spades as trump, the following hands are dealt:

Annie	♠ A J 10	♦ J 9	♣ Q 10 8 6	♥ K Q 7
Benny	♠ K 7 6	♦ K 10 6	♣ A J 7	♥ A 9 8
Connie	♠ Q 9 8	♦ A Q 8 7	♣ K 9	♥ J 10 6

A fairly even distribution. Annie can safely classify her clubs as losers, and expects to make one trick in hearts. Spades is an unreliable trump suit and there is a chance that both King and Queen are out in bids, leaving her ♠J second highest. She bids three, discarding ♣Q ♦J ♦9, making a void in diamonds and getting rid of two highly indeterminate cards.

Benny's hand is tricky. There seem to be three winners (Aces and ♠K) and four losers (Sixes and Sevens), giving a sensible bidding range of three to five tricks. One possibility is to discard ♣J, getting rid of a difficult middling card, together with the two high diamonds for a bid of three. This leaves ♥9 and ♥8 as nasty incalculables, as whichever of them is left after the Ace has gone is vulnerable to a low lead in the suit. Another possibility is to discard ♥9 ♥8 ♦10 for a bid of four. This gets rid of the problematical hearts and calls for a fourth trick from either the ♦K or a low trump to a heart lead once the Ace has gone. In the event, Benny goes for a 'surprise' bid, throwing out his three spades for a bid of three and putting his trust in his three high cards.

Connie's hand looks most unpromising at first sight, as it is full of middling ranks, especially in the unreliable trump suit. Her only sure loser is ♥6, and the nearest approach to a winner is ♣K. Her most sensible bid is two, discarding ♥J♦A♦Q, and intending to win with ♣K and ♠Q.

The playing hands are now:

Annie	♠ A J 10	♦ *none*	♣ 10 8 6	♥ K Q 7
Benny	♠ *none*	♦ K 10 6	♣ A J 7	♥ A 9 8
Connie	♠ Q 9 8	♦ 8 7	♣ K 9	♥ 10 6

And the play runs as follows:

Annie	Benny	Connie	
♥K	**♥A**	♥10	Annie leads the King to draw the Ace
♣10	**♣A**	♣9	Benny leads the second of three intended winners . . .
♣6	**♦10**	♦8	. . . and leads an incalculable Ten, which makes the third
♣8	♦6	**♦7**	Benny gets off play with the lowest diamond, which Connie is not pleased to take
♥Q	♥9	♥6	Connie escapes with the lowest heart, voiding the suit and hoping to be able to throw her unwanted King to it. Annie makes one of her intended winners
♥7	**♥8**	♣K	Benny takes an unwanted excess trick, and Connie throws her now unwanted King
♠J	♣7	♠9	Annie takes the second of her three proposed tricks . . .
♠10	♣J	**♠Q**	. . . and, as intended, loses the trump Ten to the Queen
♠A	♦K	♦8	Connie leads her last unwanted card to Annie's wanted Ace
3	4	2	tricks
20	0	20	success bonus
23	4	22	score for the deal

Ninety-Nine for two

Deal three hands of 12 cards each face down. Separate the top three cards of the dummy hand as its 'bid'. These remain face down and unseen until end of play. Each player bids in the usual way. Either or both players may declare, but neither may reveal. After the bids and any declarations have been made the dummy is turned face up and sorted into suits. The first deal is played at no trump, thereafter the trump suit is determined as in the three-hand game.

Non-dealer leads to the first trick, waits for the second to play, then plays any legal card from dummy. If a live player wins the trick, they lead first from hand and third from dummy. If the dummy wins a trick, the person who played from it then leads first from dummy and third from hand.

At end of play, the dummy's bid-cards are turned up and both live players score as in the three-hand game. However, because the dummy rarely makes its bid exactly, consider it to have failed if it wins more tricks than bid, succeeded if it wins fewer, and declared if it made its bid exactly. If one live player declares and fails, the other two score the bonus of 30. If both declare and fail, neither gains it but the dummy scores 60 extra.

Ninety-Nine for four

Deal 13 cards each from a 52-card pack. Use three bid-cards to bid up to ten tricks. A bid of three diamonds represents nought or ten tricks, and either number of tricks automatically fulfils the contract. The contract score is 30 if one player succeeds, 20 if two, 10 each if three, zero if all four either succeed or fail in their contract. If all four succeed, the next deal is played at no trump, otherwise the trump suit is determined as in the three-hand game. The premium score is 30 or 60 as before.

Ninety-Nine for five

This is ideally played with a 60-card pack, which you can buy at specialist games shops for playing Five Hundred. (Not surprisingly, it's called a '500' pack.) In fact it contains 63 cards, but you won't need the two red Thirteens or the Kookaburra (Joker).

If you can't get hold of a 500 pack, you can make a 60-card pack by adding to a 52-card pack extra Eights and Nines (for example). Each player then receives 12 cards and lays aside three cards to bid up to nine. The contract bonus is 10 if all five succeed, 20 if four, 30 if three, 40 if two, 50 if only one. No one may reveal, but any number of players may declare for a bonus of 50 points, or minus 50 if they fail. If four or five players succeed, the next deal is played at no trump.

If you're using a 52-card pack plus duplicates, and duplicate cards are played to the same trick, then the first one played outranks the second.

See also

http://www.davidparlett.co.uk/oricards/ninety9.html

http://www.pagat.com/exact/99.htm

10

euchre

- best for four players in partnerships
- fairly easy to learn
- a game of skill

> **The name of the game**
>
> Euchre is pronounced *yooker*, as is the first half of its ancestor, the Alsatian game of Juckerspiel. *Jucker* means 'young man', and, by extension, 'Jack' (at cards). It is therefore the 'Jack's game'. The bizarre spelling 'Euchre' may have resulted from an attempt to represent its pronunciation by someone who, having no German, was influenced (perhaps unconsciously) by the word 'eucharist'.

Originating in 18th-century Alsace under the name *Jucker* or *Juckerspiel*, Euchre is now widely played throughout the English-speaking world, especially in southern England and the American mid-west. There are versions for numbers of players from two to seven, but its most common format is that of a four-player partnership game.

In the West Country of England Euchre is played on a highly organized league and championship basis in an area including Bristol, Taunton and Exeter, where its popularity is equivalent to that of Cribbage in other parts of England. It also has many followers in America, Canada, Australia and New Zealand. In the 19th century it was one of the most popular home and social games of the United States and Australia. Nowadays, the Australians more often play a hybrid of Euchre and Bridge known as Five Hundred (see next section), itself developed in America, where it is also still played.

Euchre's chief claim to fame is the fact that it is the game for which the Joker was invented. Here's how it came about. In Euchre, the two highest trumps are the Jack of the trump suit and the other Jack of the same colour, known respectively as the Right Bower and the Left Bower. (Bower rhymes with *power* and derives from another German word for Jack, literally 'farmer'.) In the 1860s American players started adding to the game the blank card that was customarily included in every pack, counting it as the highest trump of all, or Best Bower. Playing-card manufacturers responded to this use by overprinting this card with the phrase Best Bower, accompanied by an arbitrary pictorial design, such as an eagle. The design that eventually won out was that of a jester, and it seems quite likely that the word Joker was suggested by the name of the game. In short, the Joker amounts to a highly glorified Jack.

In England, the Best Bower is often represented by one of the black Twos, which in that capacity is called (the) 'Benny'.

The following description is of the English West Country game, which differs in slight respects from the American game recorded in most card-game books. Even then, it remains to add that not all schools follow exactly the same rules, so be prepared for local variations.

The game

Players. Four, in fixed partnerships.

Cards. Twenty-five, consisting of A K Q J 10 9 in each suit plus one Benny, which may be a Joker or the ♠2.

Game. In home play, a game is won by the first side to reach a previously agreed target score, traditionally 5 points. In tournament play, the first side to reach 21 points wins a leg, and a match is won by the first side to make two legs.

Shuffle and deal. The cards are shuffled before each deal and cut by the player at Dealer's right. Deal five cards each in two rounds of three and two respectively. Place the undealt five face down to one side and turn the top card face up. The suit of this card is the suit of preference for trumps.

Object. Players bid for the right to go for game with the turned suit as trump or, if all pass, with a trump suit of their own choice. Game is three or more tricks. Winning all five scores double, and losing the contract loses double. The bidding player has the further option of playing 'alone', without any contribution from their partner, for a double score.

Rank of cards. The three highest trumps are:

1 The Best Bower, or Benny (Joker or ♠2 or ♣2)
2 Right Bower (Jack of trumps)
3 Left Bower (other Jack of the same colour as trumps)

followed by Ace, King, Queen, Ten, Nine. In non-trump suits the cards rank A K Q (J) 10 9. Note that the suit of the same colour as trumps will be one card short because its Jack belongs to the trump suit and not to its nominal suit.

figure 11.1 euchre
the five top trumps in spades

Bidding. Each in turn, starting with the player at Dealer's left, must either pass or 'order it up', i.e. go for three or more tricks using the turned suit as trump. Ordering it up is so termed because, regardless of who makes it trump, the dealer is entitled to take the turned trump into their own hand in exchange for any unwanted card, which they discard face down. A player intending to play alone must announce 'Up, down' without a pause. Ordering up ends the auction.

If all pass, the faced card is turned down and there is another round of bidding. This time each in turn has the right to bid game by announcing a different trump suit, and Dealer does not have the privilege of taking the originally turned card. The first to make trumps ends the auction. If the maker intends to play alone they must announce this as part of their bid, e.g. 'Alone, spades', or 'Spades, down' without a pause.

If all pass again the cards are bunched and the deal passes to the next player in turn.

If the faced card is the Benny, Dealer announces what suit they wish it to represent *before* looking at their own hand. The auction proceeds as normal, except that there is only one round. If all pass, the cards are bunched and the deal passes on.

Going alone. If the maker announced 'alone' or 'down', their partner lays their hand of cards face down before the first trick is led and takes no part in the play.

The maker's partner may turn their partner down and play alone themself, but Dealer cannot be turned down if they have taken the turned trump.

If the maker (or their partner) plays alone, either member of the opposing side may then also elect to turn their partner down and attack the contract alone. As before, Dealer cannot be opposed alone if they have taken the turned trump.

Play. The opening lead is made by the player to the Dealer's left, unless anyone is playing alone, in which case the lone player leads first. Normal rules of trick-play apply. Follow suit if possible (remembering that the Benny and left bower belong to the trump suit), otherwise play any card. A trick is taken by the highest card of the suit led, or by the highest trump if any are played, and the winner of each trick leads to the next.

Score. The maker's side, if successful, scores:

- for winning three or four tricks   1 point
- for winning all five tricks   2 points
- for winning all five alone   4 points

The score of 4 does not apply if the originally turned card was the Benny. The maximum score is then 2 points.

If the maker's side wins fewer than three tricks it is 'euchred', and the opposing side scores 2 points if both played, or 4 points if one played alone.

Revoke. A revoke (and, in tournament play, a misdeal) incurs a penalty of 2 points.

The play

Euchre takes some getting used to if you approach it from Nap, Whist or Bridge. The main point of difference is the fact that the trump suit is longer than any individual non-trump suit, and in assessing your hand you can count Jacks as potential trumps. For example, suppose the turn-up is ♠9 and your hand is:

♠ A Q ♥ A J ♦ J

If spades are trump your hand is worth about two half-tricks. You might win a trick by trumping a club lead, but your trump Ace is only fourth highest in its suit, being covered by three bowers. You might win a trick with the red Ace, but, with only four outstanding hearts against you, it is more likely to be trumped. Your Jacks and Queen are pretty useless.

If the turn-up were ♥K, your hand would be stronger. Your red Jacks are now second and third best trumps, and, if you dealt, you can take the trump King in exchange for the weak Queen. The hand is now worth at least three tricks.

If the turn-up were a heart, your hand would be strong enough to play alone, as you have the second, third and fourth highest trump, the turned trump itself, and an outside Ace. Whether it is worth playing alone is debatable. It only nets a worthwhile bonus if you win all five tricks, which is unlikely as you lack the Benny. The chances are normally 50–50 of its being either with your partner's hand or in the undealt cards, but if your partner has already passed you had better reckon without it. You might just play it as a loner on the off-chance that it lies among the four unknown cards.

With a club turned, your hand is hopeless unless everyone turns the preferred trump down and you are able to choose your own suit. Obviously you will go for hearts, hoping to make three trumps, or two trumps and the ♠A, or two trumps and a trick from your partner.

As may now be obvious, skill at Euchre lies almost entirely in the bidding: in deciding whether to order up the turned suit, whether to name one of your own, and whether to play alone. With so few cards in play, it is hardly possible to exercise much strategy, as even the opening lead of a singleton Ace stands a good chance of being trumped. There is also little opportunity for communication between your own and your partner's hand.

Position is of particular importance in Euchre. In first or second position you should order it up if you have two good tricks and a possible third in your own hand, and have no especially strong suit that you would wish to call in the event that all should pass. In third position you need three good possibilities, as your partner has already shown weakness by passing. The same applies in fourth position, except that, as Dealer, you will reassess your hand more favourably by reference to the turn-up and the effect of your discard. In a second round of bidding, the non-dealing side should prefer to entrump the suit of the same colour as the turn-up ('make it next', in traditional terms), and Dealer's partner one of the opposite colour ('cross it'), for reasons which, if not obvious, should emerge from the following deal:

West deals and turns up ♠Q. (B is for Benny):

North	♠ *none*	♣ Q J 10	♥ A	♦ Q
East	♠ K	♣ A	K	♦ A 10
South	♠ B 10 9	♣ *none*	♥ Q 9	♦ *none*
West	♠ A J	♣ K	♥ *none*	♦ K J

North passes, having nothing but the left bower (third highest). East passes, knowing that successful bids require trumps rather than the Aces and Kings which pass for strength in other games. South hesitates: she has three trumps, of which the Benny is unbeatable but the other two feeble. We will suppose she passes. West, also with three trumps after the exchange, orders it up and discards ♦J. North leads ♥A, and, although this is trumped by West, North-South defeat the contract by three to two. Post mortem examination shows that South, though right to hesitate, could have bid and made the contract.

Let's change the turn-up to ♣9. North, now with three good trumps and a singleton Ace, orders it up. West takes the turn-up in exchange for his red Jack, giving him three trumps including third best. By most lines of play, North-South win.

Change the turn-up, again, to ♥J. North and East unhesitatingly pass. South holds three trumps, including the Benny, and orders it up, though not without hesitation. West takes the red Jack turned up in exchange for his black Jack, and leads it to force out the Benny and weaken the contracting side in trumps. This deal could go either way. So far as I can make out, differing lines of play variously enable either side to win by one trick.

Finally, let's make the turn-up ♦9. The first three players again unhesitatingly pass. In West's position I would do the same. In the event, he would almost certainly win four-one by ordering it up, but he couldn't be expected to know about his partner's two helpful trumps. Suppose instead he also passes (by 'turning it down'). Has anyone now got a biddable hand? West's pass suggests weakness in red suits, so North and South will be looking to their red cards and East to her black. North and East will pass again. We have seen above that South could successfully bid hearts. Whether or not she would do so in actual play is more a question of psychology than strategy.

See also

http://www.pagat.com/euchre/euchre.html
Euchre is one of the most popular and widespread games
available for on-line play.

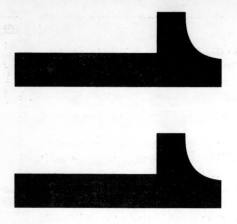

five hundred

- best for four players in partnerships
- fairly easy to learn
- a game of skill

> **The name of the game**
>
> You will be surprised to learn that the game of Five Hundred is played up to a target score of 500. The same name has been applied to other card games using the same target. For example, Cinq Cents is a variety of Bezique.

Five Hundred, devised around the turn of the 20th century as a cross between Euchre and Bid Whist, is a good game for three. It is also a good game for two, four, five and six. It was invented in the USA and is still played there, widely if patchily; but its real home has since become Australia, of which it may now be said to be the national card game. For this reason the following description is that of the Australian version rather than the American, which has since developed along lines of its own, exhibiting different rules of play in different localities.

Five Hundred involves tricks and bidding. It was originally played as a three-hander with the 32-card Euchre pack plus Joker, each player receiving ten cards and three being laid aside as a widow. As this basic format applies regardless of the number of players, it follows that four play with 43 cards, five with 53, and six with 63. For the latter purpose, the Australian '500' pack contains ten extra cards in the form of Elevens and Twelves in each suit, Thirteens in hearts and diamonds, and one Joker, known as 'the Bird', since it depicts a kookaburra. You can get genuine '500' packs outside Australia from specialist games shops, and they are well worth having if you like tinkering about with card games for peculiar numbers of players such as five and six.

However, they are not absolutely essential to your enjoyment of Five Hundred, as I am told by the natives that very few people bother to play the game six up – in fact, it is most often played by four in partnerships. Nevertheless, I will start with the three-hander and progress to the others, largely because there is no shortage of partnership games, but there are few good three-handers that do not involve complicated card-point counting. In any case, all the Internet sites concentrate on the partnership game.

As noted in the article on Euchre, 'Bower' rhymes with 'power' and derives from a German word for Jack.

The game (for three players)

Cards. Thirty-three, consisting of one Joker plus A K Q J 10 9 8 7 in each suit.

Game. Scores are noted at the end of each deal and kept accumulatively. They may be plus or minus and it is possible for a score to sink below zero. The game ends when one or more players reach 500 points, either plus or (more rarely) minus, and the winner is the player with the highest score.

Deal. The turn to deal and play passes to the left. Deal cards in batches as follows: three to each player, three face down to the table, four to each player then three again all around so that each player has ten cards. The undealt cards form the 'kitty'.

Object. The highest bidder takes the kitty, discards three in its place, and aims to win at least as many tricks as stated in the bid after declaring a trump suit or no trump. A player may also bid misère, i.e. to lose every trick, playing at no trump. Opponents also score for any tricks they take individually.

Rank of cards. When there is a trump suit, cards rank from high to low as follows:

- Joker (best bower)
- Jack of trumps (right bower)
- other Jack of same colour as trumps (left bower)
- A K Q (J) 10 9 8 7 in each suit (except where Jack promoted).

Note that the left bower is the third highest card of the trump suit and does not necessarily belong to the suit marked on its face. The trump suit is therefore one card longer (nine) than plain suits of the opposite colour (eight each), while the suit of the same colour as trumps is one card short (seven).

In a so-called no-trump game, all Jacks revert to their normal position between Ten and Queen, and the Joker is the only trump.

Auction. Starting with the player at Dealer's left, each in turn must pass or make a higher bid than any gone before. Passing does not prevent you from bidding again later. (It did originally, forcing players to make their highest bids immediately; but this restriction has largely been dropped.) When two players pass in succession, the third becomes the declarer and the last-named bid is the contract. (It may not be increased.)

If all pass without bidding the game is played at no trump and each player aims to win as many tricks as possible.

The lowest bid is 'six spades', i.e. an offer to win at least six tricks with spades as trump. This can be overcalled by bidding six in a higher suit, for which purpose they rank spades, clubs, diamonds, hearts, no trumps (or 'no-ees'), or by increasing the number of tricks. Alternatively, bids may be made by announcing their scoring values as shown in the table. Thus a bid of 'six spades' may be announced simply as '40'.

trumps	6	7	8	9	10
♠ spades	40	140	240	340	440
♣ clubs	60	160	260	360	460
♦ diamonds	80	180	280	380	480
♥ hearts	100	200	300	400	500
NT no trump	120	220	320	420	520
misère (NT)	250		mis open:		520

Misère is a bid to lose every trick at no trump. Though worth 250, it is overcalled by any bid of eight or more tricks, including eight spades for 240. Open misère, played with Declarer's cards face up on the table, overcalls everything, including the equally valued ten no trump.

Kitty. The highest bidder takes the kitty and adds it to their hand without showing it. They then throw out any three cards face down in its place. If everyone passed, so there is no highest bidder, the kitty is left out of play face down and untouched.

Play. The opening lead is made by the Declarer, or, if all passed without bidding, by the player at Dealer's left. If playing open misère, Declarer lays their cards face up on the table before leading.

Suit must be followed if possible, otherwise any card may be played. A trick is taken by the highest card of the suit led or by the highest trump if any are played. The winner of each trick leads to the next. Everyone keeps their own won tricks separate from everyone else's.

In any no-trump contract, including misère, the Joker is a trump and belongs to no suit of its own. Its holder may not play it if able to follow suit to the card led. If they lead it, they name a suit which others are required to follow if possible. This must not be one in which they have already shown themself void.

Score. If you make your contract, you score its value. There is no bonus for overtricks, unless you win all 10, in which case you score either 250 or the value of your contract, whichever is higher. If you lose, you deduct the contract value from your current total. The opponents each score 10 for each trick they won individually, or, in a failed misère, 10 for each trick taken by Declarer. (Misères must therefore be played through to the bitter end.) If all passed without bidding, each player scores 10 per trick won.

The winner is the player with the highest score when someone reaches 500 points, whether plus or minus. If two or more players reach 500 simultaneously, and one of them is the Declarer, Declarer wins the game.

The play

The first thing to be aware of in Five Hundred, if you are already used to other trick-taking games with bidding, is that of the 30 cards in play no fewer than ten are trumps – that is, one-third of the pack as opposed to only one-quarter in other games. Usually, five or six of the ten tricks are won by a trump (whether to a trump or a plain suit lead).

Assessing your hand

There being ten trumps and only two 'sides' to the game – you versus them – your minimum requirement is five trumps, together with strength in at least one other suit. You can consider bidding with only four trumps, provided that at least two are in the top three. And don't forget that the top three are the Joker and Bowers: the Ace of trumps is only the fourth highest of its suit.

Strength in side suits means at least an Ace or a high-guarded King. The high guard (Queen, or either Jack or Ten depending on the bower situation) is necessary for you to be able to make the King by leading from below and forcing out the Ace. A side suit headed by a guarded Queen is unlikely to win a trick; in any case, the three cards involved in a guarded Queen are better discarded to the kitty to leave a void in hand. This brings us to the second indicator of strength in a side suit, namely, a void or the possibility of creating one by means of the discard. Finally, a long side suit, one with four or more cards, is very desirable.

No-trump hands don't turn up very often, and can hardly be missed when they do. You shouldn't attempt a no-trumper without the Joker, as that is the one and only way of getting back into a suit in which you have a high gap. You will need strength in all four suits besides, since once you allow someone else to establish their suit your good cards will simply be whisked out of your hand before you get back in.

The kitty

The main purpose of exchanging through the kitty is not so much to draw good cards from it as to improve the balance (or imbalance) of your suits by creating either a void or a long suit. This is not to say that it will contribute nothing useful to the hand – you can often rely upon it to produce an extra trick if you are already sure of seven, and perhaps two if you are sure of six. But the important thing is not to rely on it to provide a single specific card (such as the Joker) without which a risky bid may be lost as a foregone conclusion. Holding four of a suit, the chances of finding a fifth in the widow are 5 to 3 in favour; holding five, the chances of finding a sixth drop to 5 to 4.

Bidding

The method of bidding allows no room for manoeuvre. With most hands you will have only one potential trump suit; only occasionally will you have the luxury of switching to another suit in order to overcall on the same number of tricks. Furthermore, once you have made your bid you must lie on it – you can't increase it for a higher score. If, therefore, you have a probable eight hearts don't bother to sneak up on it by starting at six. That being the highest suit, neither of the others may wish to raise you to seven, in which event they will pass and leave you to make a certain 100 instead of a probable 300. You must start by bidding the highest you dare, and know in advance whether or not you will allow yourself to be forced up.

Note carefully what the others bid, as this can give you a good idea not only of their strong suits but also of the distribution of the Joker and Bowers.

Discarding rarely presents problems. Retain all trumps, consecutive top cards, and a suit of four or more – in that order. Create a void if possible. And do make sure to keep the kitty separate from your win tricks, just in case you mistake it for a trick.

trumps	6	7	8	9	10
♠ spades	40	140	240	340	440
♣ clubs	60	160	260	360	460
♦ diamonds	80	180	280	380	480
♥ hearts	100	200	300	400	500
NT no trump	120	220	320	420	520
misère (NT)	250		mis open:		520

Trick-play

As declarer you will want to lead trumps first in order to draw your opponents' teeth, so that you can later succeed in establishing a long suit of four or more. If you have no long suit, you will gain greater control over potential trick-winners in other suits by letting the player on your left gain the lead rather than their partner. In other words, if not leading, your best position is playing third to a trick. At no trump, lead from your longest rather than your strongest suit, and return to it whenever possible.

As an opponent of the Declarer, your primary objective is normally to defeat the contract rather than make tricks of your own. (Unusually, you might find yourself playing to the score. Thus, if Declarer is unable to make game – that is, reach 500 points – on succeeding at their contract, but your temporary partner is not only well ahead of you but also only 10 or 20 points off target, you will obviously prefer to prevent your partner from taking tricks wherever possible.)

When Declarer leads trumps, prefer to play low if your partner will win the trick, since Declarer's chief preoccupation is to leave themselves holding the highest trumps in play. In fact, you can nearly always afford to duck their lead as second player if it is obvious that Declarer is trying to force out a higher trump, since, if it isn't in your own hand, it must be in your partner's.

When leading, generally try to avoid opening up new suits, and stick by preference to your own longest or strongest.

Sample game

Connie deals the following hands:

Annie	♠ 7	♥ A 10 7	♣ K 10 8 7	♦ J 10
Benny	♠ K J 9 8	♥ K 9	♣ J 9	♦ 9 7
Connie	♠ Q 10	♥ Q J 8	♣ A	♦ A K 8 Joker

Annie starts by making an optimistic bid of six hearts. Her ♦J would be the Left Bower with that suit as trump, making a better set of four trumps than the unbiddable alternative in clubs.

Benny, strong in spades and holding both Bowers, overcalls with seven spades, hoping to improve his scrappy side suits by taking the kitty.

Connie bids seven of her higher-ranking diamond suit, which is well supported by the Joker and ♥J (Left Bower).

Annie and Benny pass, and Connie takes the kitty, consisting of ♠A ♣Q ♦Q. This excellent draw increases her trump holding, adds a side-suit Ace, and enables her to void a suit by throwing out three hearts. Her playing hand is now:

Joker ♥ J ♦ A K Q 8 ♠ A Q 10 ♣ A Q

She leads the Joker and the Left Bower, thus drawing all the outstanding trumps. Annie, who had the Right Bower (♦J), returns ♥A, believing Connie to be more probably void in clubs than hearts. Not so. Connie ruffs it, cashes her ♣A, plays her remaining trumps, and loses two spades to Benny.

Result: Connie scores 180 for her contract of seven diamonds, leaving Annie and Benny to score 10 and 20 respectively.

trumps	6	7	8	9	10
♠ spades	40	140	240	340	440
♣ clubs	60	160	260	360	460
♦ diamonds	80	180	280	380	480
♥ hearts	100	200	300	400	500
NT no trump	120	220	320	420	520
misère (NT)	250		mis open:		520

The game for two to six players

The cards used for each number of players, in addition to the Joker, are as follows:

Two players 25 cards = Joker plus A K Q J 10 9 in each suit.

Four players 43 cards = Joker plus A K Q J 10 9 8 7 6 5 in each suit, plus both red Fours.

Five players The standard 52-card pack plus Joker.

Six players The full 63-card Australian '500' pack, with Elevens and Twelves in all four suits, Thirteens in red suits, and the Kookaburra (Joker).

In each case each player receives ten cards and three form a kitty, though in serious four-hand partnership play it is common to omit the Joker and make only a two-card kitty. Four and six players play in respectively two or three partnerships, the members of each partnership sitting opposite each other. For example, if six play, the rotation of players around the table is A–B–C–A–B–C.

In all partnership versions, it is only the declarer who takes the kitty. Five play on an 'optional call' basis. That is, after taking the kitty and discarding, the declarer must either announce that they are playing alone against four, or else call for a partner by naming a card not in their own hand. Whoever holds that card becomes Declarer's partner and immediately identifies themself. The plus or minus score made by the partnership is awarded equally to both members of it.

There is no reason why four should not also play on the optional call basis.

American Five Hundred

American Five Hundred is usually played by four in fixed partnerships, with a 45-card pack consisting of A K Q J 10 9 8 7 6 5 4 in each suit, plus Joker. Deal ten each and a five-card kitty called the 'middle' as follows: 3–(3)–2–(2)–3–2, the figures in brackets being those of the middle.

See also

http://www.pagat.com/euchre/500.html

12

spades

- best for four players in partnerships
- fairly easy to learn
- a game of skill

This relatively recent American Whist derivative is sufficiently popular and widespread to have become the subject of numerous clubs, tournaments and websites, so it is probably only a matter of time before it sweeps the rest of the English-speaking world. It is usually played by four in partnerships, but is easily adaptable for other numbers. It is full of variations and not subject to universally accepted 'official rules'. There are versions for two to four players, all playing on their own account, but here I will restrict myself to the partnership game for four.

The game

Preliminaries. Four play crosswise in fixed partnerships, using a 52-card pack ranking A K Q J 10 9 8 7 6 5 4 3 2 in each suit. Deal 13 each in ones.

Trumps. Spades are always trumps.

Object. Each side's object is to win at least as many tricks as it bid.

Bidding. There is no competitive auction. Instead, each partnership contracts to win a certain minimum number of tricks.

First, the members of the non-dealing partnership discuss how many tricks they think they can win between them, with the player at Dealer's left speaking first. You and your partner, in this situation, may tell each other how many tricks you can certainly win and how many you think you might win, but you're not allowed to specify which cards you hold in any particular suit, or to say anything about distribution (such as holding a void or singleton) – your information must be restricted to numbers of tricks.

When you have agreed on how many tricks you are prepared to contract to win between you, this number is noted down, and the dealer's partner begins a similar discussion for their own side.

Note that in Spades, unlike other partnership trick games, it is both sides that establish a contract, not just one.

Variation. Some players prohibit the dealer's side from bidding the number of tricks that would make the total bid by both sides exactly 13.

Bidding 'nil'. If you think you can avoid winning a single trick in your own hand, you may declare 'Nil'. In this case your partner announces how many tricks they propose to win. This establishes your side's contract. If you bid nil and fail, any tricks you win will be added to your side's contract and may be counted for overtricks, which means it is possible for your side to make, in the same deal, a plus score for the positive contract and a minus score for the failed nil.

Note 1. *Only one member of a partnership may bid nil, unless by prior agreement you are playing the so-called Double Nil variant (see later).*

Note 2. *If in assessing the amount of your side's contract you say that you probably won't win any tricks, this does not commit you to making a nil bid. Some, however, insist on either a nil bid or a minimum assessment of one trick.*

Play. The dealer's left-hand opponent leads to the first trick and may not lead a spade.

Variation. *Everybody must play their lowest club to the first trick. In this case, it is best if the opening lead is made by the holder of ♣2.*

You must follow suit if you can, but otherwise may play any card. The trick is taken by the highest card of the suit led or by the highest trump if any are played. The winner of each trick leads to the next.

No one may lead spades (unless they have no other suit) until the suit is 'broken' – that is, until at least one player has trumped with a spade when unable to follow suit.

Score. A side that takes at least as many tricks as its bid scores 10 times its bid, plus 1 per overtrick. There is a penalty, however, for consistent underbidding. When, over a series of deals, a side's overtricks total 10 or more (as witnessed by the final digit of their cumulative score), their score is reduced by 100, and any overtricks above 10 carried forward to the next cycle. This is called sandbagging.

Example. *Your side's current score is 178. You bid five tricks and win eight. You score 50 for the bid plus three overtricks, making 231. Your score is reduced to 131. Next time the final digit of your cumulative score runs beyond 9, you lose another 100.*

Variation. *Each overtrick counts minus 1 point and there is no sandbagging.*

For a failed contract, a side loses 10 points per trick bid.

A nil bidder, if successful, adds 50 to their side's score, in addition to the score won (or lost) by their partner for tricks made. If not, nil bidder's side loses 50 points, but any tricks taken by the nil bidder may be counted towards the fulfilment of their partner's contract.

Game. Play up to any agreed target, typically 500 or 1000.

Blind Nil variant. This bid is open only to a side that is trailing by 100 or more points. It permits a player to bid nil *before* looking at their hand of cards. They then take up and examine their hand and pass two cards face down to their partner. Their partner adds those two to their hand and similarly passes two cards face down to the blind bidder. The score for this feat is double that for an ordinary nil, that is, plus or minus 100 points.

Double Nil variant. This variant allows *both* partners to bid nil in the same round and, again, is restricted to a side that is trailing by 100 or more points. If successful it scores 500 points. The penalty for failure is 250 if one partner wins any trick or 500 if both do.

Sample game

Here's a sample deal to show how the bidding works and how the game might go. Denny deals the following hands:

Annie	♠ K 9 7	♥ 6 4	♣ A Q 10 6 4	♦ K J 3
Benny	♠ Q 8 5	♥ K 9 8	♣ K J 3	♦ Q 9 7 4
Connie	♠ A J 3 2	♥ Q 7 3	♣ 8 2	♦ A 8 5 2
Denny	♠ 10 6 4	♥ A J 10 5 2	♣ 9 7 5	♦ 10 6

Annie announces 'Two tricks, maybe three.' She expects to make the ♣A, ♠K, and perhaps a high diamond, but has probably underestimated the potential of her long club suit. Connie, expecting to make both Aces, probably a club ruff and possibly ♥Q, replies 'Three or four – shall we say six?' Annie agrees, and they settle on a cautious bid of six.

Benny declares himself the proud holder of possibly three half-tricks. Denny, seeing only an Ace and a possible ruff in diamonds, says 'Maybe one-and-a-half for me, too. Call it three?' To this, Benny replies: 'That only makes nine bid altogether, leaving four floaters. Let's go for at least four.' They do.

As they are playing the 'low clubs first trick' variation, Connie leads ♣2 and the game proceeds thus:

	A	B	C	D	
1	♣4	♣3	<u>♣2</u>	♣5	
2	♥6	♥9	♥7	<u>♥A</u>	Cashes the Ace before it can be trumped.
3	♥4	<u>♥K</u>	♥3	♥5	Returns the highest of partner's suit.
4	♣6	♥8	<u>♥Q</u>	♥2	Annie would have trumped if Connie hadn't played the Queen.
5	<u>♣A</u>	♣J	♣8	♣9	Connie voids clubs; Annie doesn't want to risk the Queen or Ten.
6	♣10	♣K	<u>♠2</u>	♣7	Now spades are broken and can be led.
7	♦J	♦7	<u>♦A</u>	♦10	But Connie first tests diamonds, which Annie's Jack encourages.
8	<u>♦K</u>	♦4	♦5	♦6	
9	♦3	<u>♦Q</u>	♦2	♥10	
10	<u>♠K</u>	♦9	♦8	♠10	
11	♠9	♠5	<u>♠J</u>	♠4	
12	♠7	♠8	<u>♠A</u>	♠6	
13	♣Q	<u>♠Q</u>	♠3	♥J	

Annie and Connie, bid six, made eight, score 62, instead of the 80 they would have scored for bidding eight in the first place. Benny and Denny bid four, made five, score 51.

The play

Spades is a great new game (relatively speaking) with many subtleties. One of the best is the sandbagging score system, which forces players to become increasingly accurate in their bidding so as, on the one hand, not to win too many overtricks, with the risk of losing 100, or, on the other, not to overbid to such an extent as to risk losing ten times the value of their bid. An example of the sort of situation that can arise can be illustrated as follows.

Playing up to 500, we stand at 367 to their 478; they bid eight between them and we bid three. We might logically have bid five instead of the three we seem unconfident of exceeding, but if we did so we would only just make it and they would inevitably win. Since we can afford the two overtricks that a bid of five might make without being sandbagged, we stick to three. To stop them winning, we want either to stop them short of eight tricks, for which purpose we need at least six, or we want them to take at least two overtricks for a sandbagging penalty, for which purpose we need not exceed our proposed three. To put it another way, we need any number of tricks except four or five.

My experience suggests that beginners tend to underbid. You may find it helpful to use hand assessment practices common in Bridge, such as counting quick tricks, and to employ such playing conventions as encouraging your partner to lead the same suit again by playing an otherwise unnecessarily high card, as Annie did at trick seven in the sample game.

See also

http://www.pagat.com/boston/spades.html
Spades is one of the most popular and widespread games available for on-line play.

13

contract bridge

- for four players in partnerships
- easy to learn the basics
- a game of great skill

Bridge – properly known as Contract Bridge to distinguish it from its ancestors – is basically Whist but with trumps established by bidding rather than by turning the last card. This seemingly small difference is actually tremendous. It means that most of the information about the lie of cards which, in Whist, you have to deduce from the play is, in Bridge, largely conveyed before any card is played by means of the auction – a period of play in which players communicate with one another in a highly condensed code. While Whist will serve you in good stead when it comes to the actual play of the hand, a sound grasp of bidding requires much concentrated study and lots of practice before you can safely sit down with regular players. For this purpose it is desirable, first, to study at least one reputable book specifically devoted to Bridge for learners; second, to take a course and get some assisted practice at a local adult education centre; and third, to join a local Bridge club and do your learning from the experience of experienced practitioners. There are also private tutors, of course, if you can afford them.

Here it is only possible to offer a general introduction to the game, sufficient to give you some idea of whether or not you are going to find all the above worthwhile. Before you start, you should know that Bridge is played in several different formats. For home and informal play there are two possibilities: Rubber Bridge and Four-deal Bridge, or Chicago. In Rubber Bridge, a rubber is the best of three games, and a game is won by the first side to reach 100 points below the line over as many deals as it takes. As a rubber may take anything from ten minutes to over an hour to complete, traditional Rubber Bridge is best if there are just four of you.

Chicago, on the other hand, consists of exactly four deals and therefore consistently lasts about 20–30 minutes. This makes it more suitable if you have enough players for two or more tables and wish to change partners or opponents after each game, or if you have an odd number of players so that one or more is sitting out at any one time. The third format, Duplicate Bridge, is a club or tournament game, in which pairs of players compete with one another by playing the same hands at different tables. The effect of this is to cancel out the 'luck of the deal' as far as any one team is concerned, thus producing (theoretically) a win for the team that played, overall, with the greatest skill.

The game

Four players, sitting crosswise in partnerships, each receive 13 cards from a well-shuffled 52-card pack. An auction is held to determine what contract shall be played. A contract is an undertaking made by one partnership to win a stated number of odd tricks in return for naming the trump suit, or specifying 'no trump' if preferred. Odd tricks are tricks in excess of six. Thus a bid of 'one club' is an offer to win at least seven of the 13 tricks with clubs as trump, and a bid of 'seven no trump' an offer to win all 13 without a trump suit.

When no one will bid any higher, the last-named bid becomes the 'contract'. The player who first named the contracted trump suit is the 'declarer', and the members of the opposing partnership are called the 'defenders'. Declarer's partner, after the opening lead, lays their hand of cards face up on the table as a dummy, and Declarer plays from both hands.

If successful, Declarer's side scores 'below the line' (towards game) for the number of odd tricks contracted and won. Any overtricks earn 'premiums' (bonuses) above the line. Premiums for honours and slams also go above the line. If unsuccessful, the defenders make appropriate scores above the line, i.e. not counting towards game.

A game is won by the first side to reach 100 points below the line. This can only be done by winning a contract, not beating one. The rubber is won by the first side to win two games, and the winners score an additional premium which is larger if the losing side failed to win one game. A side that has won one game is described as 'Vulnerable', and is subject to certain extra premiums for success, or extra penalties for failure. The effect of vulnerability, if not its purpose, is to discourage a side that has won a game from deliberately seeking high but unsound contracts for the sole purpose of preventing the other from winning a game.

As befits its social status, Bridge tends to be played with great formality and is accordingly equipped with a multiplicity of procedural niceties amounting almost to ritual. The beginner should learn these from the outset in order to avoid potential embarrassment when playing in formal situations – in other words, as a form of social self-defence.

Preliminaries

Bridge is played with a single 52-card pack, but it is customary to use two such packs distinguishable from each other by the colour or design on the reverse. Both are shuffled, one is spread out face down on the table and each player draws a card from it. The two drawing the highest cards become partners (unless partnerships were agreed in advance), the highest having first choice of seats, right of first deal, and choice of which pack to deal from. For the purpose of drawing and playing, cards rank high–low A K Q J 10 9 8 7 6 5 4 3 2 in each suit. Of drawn cards equal in rank, spades beat hearts beat diamonds beat clubs.

Shuffle and deal

On the first deal, the player at Dealer's left 'makes' (shuffles) the pack to be dealt from while Dealer's partner makes the other. The pack when made is set face down at the maker's right, as their right-hand opponent will be next to deal. Dealer takes the shuffled pack from their left and sets it face down for their right-hand opponent to cut. Having completed the cut, Dealer distributes the cards face down one at a time in clockwise rotation starting with the player at their left and finishing with themself.

The auction

Each in turn, Dealer first, must do one of the following:

- Pass, which in the UK is normally done by saying 'No bid'. (because, in British pronunciation, it can be misheard as 'Hearts'). This does not of itself prevent a player from bidding later.
- Make a bid, which must be higher than any previous bid. The lowest bid is 'one club'. A higher bid is made by increasing the number of tricks bid or offering the same number but in a higher suit. For this purpose suits rank upwards thus: clubs, diamonds, hearts, spades, no trump. Thus 'one club' can be

overcalled by 'one' anything else, but 'one no trump' only by raising the level to 'two' or more. The highest possible bid is 'seven no trump'.

- Announce 'Double' if the previous bid was made by an opponent. This offers (or threatens) to double whatever score is won or lost if the last-named bid is established as the contract.
- Announce 'Redouble' if the previous announcement was an opponent's 'Double'. This offers (or threatens) to quadruple the scoring value of the proposed contract.

A double or redouble is automatically cancelled if followed by another bid, whether or not in the same suit as the one doubled.

The auction ends when a bid, or a double or redouble, has been followed by three consecutive passes.

The last-named bid becomes the contract, and its suit, if any, is trump. The member of the contracting side who, in the auction, first mentioned the eventual trump suit, or who first bid 'no trump' if such is the contract, becomes the declarer.

If all four pass immediately, the cards are thrown in and the next deal made by the next player in turn to do so.

Play

Declarer's left-hand opponent leads to the first trick by playing any card face up to the table. Declarer's partner then lays their hand of cards face up on the table in four columns, one for each suit, each running from high to low towards the declarer, and spread just sufficiently to enable each card to be identified. The trump suit (or clubs, if none) should be placed at dummy's right, i.e. Dealer's left as they face it.

Declarer plays second to the trick from dummy, and fourth to the trick from their own hand. Normal rules of trick-taking apply. Follow suit if possible, otherwise you may play any card. A trick is taken by the highest card of the suit led, or by the highest trump if any are played, and the winner of each trick leads to the next.

Declarer, upon winning a trick, leads from whichever of their side's two hands furnished the winning card. Their partner not only takes no active part in the play but may not communicate anything to Declarer by way of advice, suggestion, criticism, query, appeal, horror, apoplexy, etc. The most they may do is call attention to errors of procedure, such as Declarer's failing to follow suit from dummy when able to do so, or leading from the wrong hand upon winning a trick.

The defenders keep all their won tricks together, customarily in front of the partner of the first defender to win one.

Revoke

A player who fails to follow suit though able to do so has committed a revoke. What happens then is too complicated to detail here, and if you are going to play the game seriously you will need a copy of *The International Laws of Contract Bridge*. Briefly, however, if neither the offender nor their partner has yet played to the following trick, the offender may retract the wrong card and play a correct one, and anyone who played after it may retract their card and play another. Furthermore, if the offender was one of the defenders, their incorrect card becomes a penalty card and is laid face up on the table, and so does that of their partner if it is retracted and replaced. If a penalty card is an honour, it must be played at the next legal opportunity; if not, it must be played in preference to any other card of that suit below the rank of an honour. (That is, when that suit is led again, the offender is allowed to play an honour, if they wish, and to leave the penalty card in abeyance.)

If the offender or their partner plays to the next trick without correcting it (other than to the thirteenth, when it can still be corrected), the revoke is established. In this case, the offending side must concede two tricks to the opposition if they won the trick of the revoke, otherwise one trick. (There are further complications and provisos, but this will suffice for home play.)

Scoring

Each player keeps a score sheet divided into two columns, one for each side, and divided into an upper and a lower half by a horizontal line. Scores are recorded below the line for tricks contracted and made, and above the line for overtricks, bonuses and penalties.

All scores are recorded individually, not cumulatively. When one side's below-line scores total 100 or more (as can readily be seen 'by inspection'), a second horizontal line is drawn beneath their last score and across both columns. A new game begins, with both sides scoring below this line as before. The side that has won one game is now 'vulnerable', and subject to certain increased rewards and penalties. Another line is drawn when a second game has been won. If it is won by the same side, the rubber ends, and the side with two games gets a bonus before scores are totalled. If not, a third game is played, both sides now being vulnerable, and the rubber ends when either side has won its second game. This carries a smaller bonus.

The rubber ended, each side totals all the scores made above and below the line in its column. The difference between the two side's totals is the margin of victory. The rubber bonus is usually (but not inevitably) sufficient to ensure that the side that won two games will win overall, regardless of above-line scores. Slam bonuses, however, are so great that the scores they attract above the line are capable of outweighing a rubber bonus made by the opposing side. Details of scoring are presented in the table opposite. The following notes explain and amplify it.

If the contract makes, the declaring side scores below the line a number of points for each trick bid and won. For example, if the contract was 'two' and they made three, they score only for two below, the third counting as an overtrick and so being scored above the line. The actual score per trick depends on which suit was trump, if any, and is affected by doubling or redoubling. Note that a successful contract of three no trump suffices for game, the score being 40 + 30 + 30 (= 100). Any overtricks they may make are scored above the line. In normal circumstances (undoubled) they score at the same rate as those scored below the line. If doubled or redoubled, however, they each score 100 or 200 respectively, and twice this if the declarers were vulnerable. In addition, any successful contract that was doubled scores a flat bonus of 50, or 100 if redoubled – 'for the insult', as my bridge tutor called it.

CONTRACT MADE: Declarers score below the line for each trick bid and won:

in a minor suit (♠♥)	20	40 D	80 R
in a major suit (♣♦)	30	60 D	120 R
at no trump, for the first trick	40	80 D	160 R
at no trump, for each subsequent trick	30	60 D	120 R

D = Doubled, R = Redoubled, V = Vulnerable, tv = trick value (20, 30 or 40)

Declarers may also score above the line:

for each overtrick (if not vulnerable) *or*	tv	100 D	200 R
for each overtrick (if vulnerable), *plus*	tv	200 D	400 R
for making a doubled/redoubled contract, *plus*	–	50 D	100 R
for making a small slam, *or*	500	750 V	
for making a grand slam	1000	1500 V	

CONTRACT DEFEATED: Defenders score above the line:

	if declarers not vulnerable			if declarers vulnerable		
undertricks	*und*	*dbld*	*rdbld*	*und*	*dbld*	*rdbld*
one	50	100	200	100	200	400
two	100	300	600	200	500	1000
three	150	500	1000	300	800	1600
four	200	800	1600	400	1100	2200
five	250	1100	2200	500	1400	2800
six	300	1400	2800	600	1700	3400
seven	350	1700	3400	700	2000	4000

HONOURS: Scored above the line by either side holding in one hand:

any four of A K Q J 10 of trumps	100
all five of A K Q J 10 of trumps	150
all four Aces at no trump	150

PREMIUM AT END OF PLAY

for winning the rubber, if opponents won no game	700
for winning the rubber, if opponents won one game	500
in an unfinished rubber, for winning the only game	300
in an unfinished rubber, for having the only part-score in an unfinished game	100

A successful small slam (contract of six) carries a flat bonus of 500, increased to 750 if made when vulnerable. A grand slam (contract of seven) scores twice these amounts. They are not in themselves affected by doubling or redoubling. Note that slam bonuses accrue only if the relevant number of tricks has been bid – if you win six when you only bid five, you don't score for the small slam. By way of compensation, there is no extra penalty for failing a slam bid: one trick down is one trick down, regardless of the size of the contract. If the contract goes down (fails), the defenders score above the line a certain amount for each trick by which the declarers fell short of their contract (undertricks). The actual amount per undertrick does not depend on the trump situation, but does vary according to doubling and vulnerability. The rarely occurring bonus for the fourth and each subsequent undertrick applies only in the case of a doubled or redoubled contract, and is additional to that of previous undertricks. Thus, if the declaring side, vulnerable, bid five spades and was doubled, the possible range of scores according to the actual number of tricks taken is then as follows:

13 Declarers: 300 below, 200 above, 50 above ('for the insult')
12 Declarers: 300 below, 100 above, 50 above
11 Declarers: 300 below, 50 above
10 Defenders: 200 for first undertrick
 9 Defenders: 500 (= 200 for the first + 300 for the second)
 8 Defenders: 800 (= 200+300+300)
 7 Defenders: 1100 (= 200+300+300+400 . . .)

and so on.

The score for honours is credited above the line to the side of whichever of the four players was dealt the four or five honours concerned. (Yes, honours *can* be scored by either side, not just the declarers.) As it is lost if not claimed before the next deal, it is advisable for their holder (if not dummy) to announce 'honours' upon playing the last of them to a trick. The scores are minimal and are not affected by doubling or vulnerability. A rubber can be won only by the declaring side and upon winning its second game. This carries a bonus of 700 if they won two games straight off, or 500 if three were played. If, for any reason, the rubber was not finished, but one game was completed, the side winning that game scores 300 for the rubber. If play ended before a game was completed, and if only one side has made a part-score (less than 100) in that game, then they score a bonus of 50. This is not of itself sufficient to carry an incomplete rubber bonus of 300, but may be made in addition to it if play ended during the second game.

Where settlements are made on the basis of the final score, it is usual to round them to the nearest 100. The winners of the rubber illustrated in the sample score sheet therefore win 12 units from the opposing partnership. (A score ending in 50 is rounded down to the nearest 100 in the UK, and rounded up in the USA.)

	WE	THEY	
g	50		
g	200		
f	500	150	c
e	100	60	c
a	30	100	b
a	60	100	c
f	120	80	d
g	80		
h	60		
h	500		
	1700	490	
	-490		
	1210		

Example of scoring

(a) We bid 2♠, made 3♠, scored 60 below for the bid of two and 30 for the overtrick.

(b) We bid 3♥, were doubled, and made only two. They scored 100 above for the doubled undertrick.

(c) They bid 3NT, made 5, scored below the line 40 for the first and 30 for each of the other two contracted tricks, plus two overtricks for 60 above. One of them held four Aces, scoring 150 for honours. They win the first game. Another line was drawn to mark the second.

(d) They bid and made 4♣ for 80 below.

(e) They bid 2♠ and made one, giving us 100 above for the undertrick (they being vulnerable).

(f) We bid and made a small slam of 6♦ for 120 below the line, giving us a game and making ourselves vulnerable. We also counted 500 above for the slam. Another line was drawn and a new game started.

(g) We bid 1NT, were doubled, and made three. This gave us 2 x 40 below the line, plus 200 above for the doubled overtrick (we being vulnerable), plus 50 'for the insult' (making any doubled game).

(h) We bid and made 2♥ for 60 below the line, giving us the second game and 500 for the rubber. Our margin of victory computes to 1210.

The play

Bridge is essentially a partnership game and this is nowhere more apparent than in the auction. In the play of the cards, Declarer becomes the lone and star performer, and, while there is scope for co-operation between the defenders, much of that is founded on information co-operatively exchanged during the auction – whether their own if they had a chance to bid, or if not, by inference from that of the declaring side.

Bidding is a means of communication between partners. Its primary purpose is to ensure that they reach the best possible contract for the 26 cards held between them. This involves conveying as much information as possible to each other about their respective hands. The potential of bidding as a language derives from the fact that specific information can be conveyed by means of artificial bids, or 'conventions'. Whereas a natural bid is one you would be quite happy for the partnership to engage in as a contract, a conventional bid merely requests or conveys information. It rarely represents a serious contract, which could well be disastrous if played.

The standard British bidding system, called Acol, is used widely by both home and tournament players, and has considerable currency outside its country of origin. It has the advantage of being based on natural bids, but easily incorporates conventions and bidding sequences devised originally for other systems. It is important to note that the laws of the game forbid either partnership to use any system or individual convention which is unknown to the other side. Before play, both partnerships must state which system they are using (Acol, etc.) and with what artificial bids and conventions.

Strength and distribution

The most basic information you want to communicate about your hand is its *strength*, in terms of high cards such as Aces and Kings, and its *shape*, or relative distribution of the four suits.

Strength is measured in 'high card points', abbreviated to hcp. For this purpose each Ace in your hand counts 4 hcp, each King 3, Queen 2, and Jack 1.

As there are 10 hcp in each suit, and 40 in the whole pack, a hand counting 10 hcp is about average.

Shape, or distribution, denotes the relative numbers of cards you hold of each suit. If your 13 cards are divided 4–3–3–3 or 4–4–3–2, your hand is described as balanced, even, or 'flat', and suggests a no-trump bid. If it contains a long suit of five or more, your hand is unbalanced, and suggests a bid in the longest suit. Distributions of 4–4–4–1 and 5–3–3–2 are borderline cases. The first is not balanced but contains no obvious long suit. Whether it better suits a trump or no-trump contract depends on its hcp and how it fits in with your partner's hand. The pattern 5–3–3–2 contains a long suit, but if this is a minor suit you may consider it as potential no-trump material. This is because, at lower bidding levels, you score more for a no-trump contract than for a minor suit contract requiring a greater number of tricks.

High card points should not be counted too rigidly, as they can be affected by distribution. For example, a hand consisting of all 13 cards of one suit counts only 10 hcp, but is as good as 40 since it will win every trick in a contract based on that suit. Similarly, you should deduct a point if your hand contains a singleton King, or has no Aces. When you and your partner have agreed a suit, you can also add points for short side suits of two or fewer cards. But distributional points must be considered with caution, as they don't become a fixed quantity until a suit is agreed. Once added, you may subsequently have to remember to subtract them again.

Bidding

The aim of the auction is for the side with the best potential contract to discover and bid it. What you and your partner are looking for is a fit, which means either the suit in which you hold between you the greatest number of cards, or a complementary distributional pattern between both hands more suited to a no-trump contract. The minimum comfortable trump requirement for a one-in-suit contract is eight cards of that suit between you. Seven is feasible and even fewer may be playable, though with fewer than seven you will certainly be in the wrong contract. For no trumps, a fit means having all four suits stopped between you. A suit is stopped if headed by an Ace or a guarded honour – that is K x, Q x x, or even, at worst, J x x x. ('x' means anything lower than a Ten, its precise numerical rank being irrelevant to the point at issue.)

In bidding towards a contract, you will be considering whether to aim for a part-score, a game, or a slam. A part-score is one that is not enough to win you the current game. 'Game' denotes a contract that brings your score to 100 or more below the line from a score of zero – that is, 3NT (100), four of a major suit (120), or five of a minor (100). If five in a minor looks probable, you will prefer to test the possibility of reaching 3NT instead, as this requires you to win only nine tricks for game, as opposed to 11 in a minor suit.

It helps to know that a game at NT or in a major suit normally requires 26 or more points between you, and in a minor suit at least 28. Standing at zero, your first concern will be to go for game if possible. If you already have a part-score, you will be looking for another part-score sufficient to complete the 100 points, and need not bid any higher than absolutely necessary to achieve this object and overcall your opponents' bids.

The following table of points actually scored by all possible contracts, including slam bonuses but disregarding the effects of doubling and vulnerability, is worth examining for the light it throws on their relative values.

	♣	♦	♥	♠	NT
1	20	20	30	30	40
2	40	40	60	60	70
3	60	60	90	90	100
4	80	80	120	120	130
5	100	100	150	150	160
6	620	620	680	680	690
7	1140	1140	1210	1210	1220

This makes it very clear that at lower levels, where the bidding mostly takes place, minor-suit contracts are hardly worth pressing if there is any chance of a major-suit or no-trump fit, even at a lower level, except for the purpose of overcalling the other side's bids. It is only at slam levels that this discrepancy is wiped out and minor suits come into their own.

The time to be more ambitious is when you gather from the early auction that a slam may be in the offing. A slam brings huge rewards if successful but does not lose any more than usual if unsuccessful – unless you are vulnerable, when you must bid more cautiously. A small slam normally requires about 31–33 points in a suit or 33–34 at no trump, and a grand slam 37 points.

This leaves a dead zone of rather unrewarding contracts between the levels of game and a small slam, i.e. four or five no trumps and five of a major suit. As we shall see later, this dead zone offers a patch of bidding space in which to exchange useful information about the possibility of attempting a slam.

We must, however, start at the beginning, which means with mundane low-level bids designed to convey preliminary information to one another about the nature of your hands. Here it is necessary to distinguish four types of bid as follows:

- An *opening bid* is the first one of the auction. Dealer has the first opportunity to make the opening bid, but, if they pass, the right to do so passes round the table until someone exercises it. Beginners sometimes fail to grasp the fact that the opening bid is by definition the first one of the whole auction, regardless of who makes it.
- A *responding* bid, or response, denotes, for our present purposes, the first bid made by the partner of the player who opens the bidding.
- A *rebid*, apart from its obvious general meaning, specifically denotes the second bid made by the opener in the light of their partner's response.
- An *intervening bid*, or overcall, is one made by either opponent of the opening bidder. Most significantly, it denotes the first bid made by an opponent of the opening bidder. It may intervene between the opening bid and the response, or between the response and the opener's rebid.

We can ignore intervening bids to start with and assume that the opening bidder and their partner make all the running. This does happen often enough to be realistic – perhaps not half the time, but not far off.

The first thing you and your partner need to discover is how many points you hold between you. If it's around 26 points, you should expect to make a game contract (that is, worth 100 below the line). If the points are divided 13–13, it is the responder's responsibility to make sure game is reached (for example, 1♠–4♠, or 1NT– 3NT). If they are divided 16–10, the opener will make an intermediate rebid to show that their hand is not minimum and responder will then bid game (for example,

1♦ – 1♠, 3♦ – 3NT). When the points are divided 19–7, it will be the opener's responsibility to make sure game is reached once their partner makes a response (1♦ – 1♠, 4♠) or (1♦ – 1♠, 3NT).

Opening one in a suit

The commonest opening bid is one in a suit. You make it with a hand containing 13 to 21 points and a reasonable rebid in case your partner responds by bidding in your weakest suit. If you have six or a good five of the suit you bid, you can reduce the minimum requirement to 12 or even 11, but you must have a sensible rebid available because of the 'unlimited' nature of this opening – that is, your partner won't know whether you have as few as 12 or as many as 21, or something in between, and whatever it is makes a big difference to how your partner assesses their hand. The very fact of opening invites your partner, if strong enough, to respond in their best suit, and your sensible rebid will be necessary in case their best suit is your worst.

Given the minimum requirement, open with your longest suit. For example, in the left hand, below, open one diamond. This gives you a sensible rebid of two diamonds over any response except one heart, which you can raise to two. With two five- or six-card suits start with the suit higher in bidding value, for example, hearts in the right-hand example. This enables you to show your lower suit (clubs) at the 2-level, thereby conveying useful information about your hand and keeping your options open.

♠ x x   ♠ x
♥ Q J x x   ♥ K Q J x x
♦ A Q J x x   ♦ K x
♣ K J   ♣ A K x x x

Which to open of two four-card suits depends on whether or not they are 'touching', i.e. adjacent in bidding value, such as hearts and diamonds. Textbook procedure is to open the higher suit first. This enables you to name the lower suit if your partner responds, leaving either of you the possibility of going back to the first suit without having to raise to the level of three. Naming the lower first, then the higher at the next level, is a 'reverse' bid suggesting a high point-count (16+) and demanding a response. Some players now tend to bid the lower suit in any case. Either way, the important thing is that you and your partner should stick to whatever system you have agreed upon.

Of non-touching suits, bid clubs first if the other is spades. Otherwise, the choice is less easy. You may want to bid spades before diamonds in hope of finding a major suit fit first, or clubs before hearts in order to keep your exploratory opening bids at a safe level. If in doubt, the mechanical answer is to bid the four-card suit ranking immediately beneath the shortest suit held. A more creative guideline is to consider all the probable responses to either bid and make whichever of them will not give you a rebid problem. If you want a rule for two four-card suits that is both easy to remember and likely to be safe whether the suits are touching or not, I suggest the following: bid hearts first if this is one of them, otherwise diamonds, otherwise clubs.

With three four-card suits, bid the one below the singleton, or hearts if the singleton is clubs.

Responses to one in a suit

Now swap positions and suppose you are responding to an opening bid of one in a suit.

- With fewer than 6 points, pass. Your partner could have a minimum 13, and will not thank you for your support if you turn out to have 18 or fewer between you. If they have substantially more, they can always bid again.
- With four or more cards of the suit bid, raise it to two on 6–9 points, three on 10–12, four on 13–15.
- Without a fit, but with a biddable suit of your own and up to 15 points, bid it at the lowest possible level. If the lowest level is one, 6 points will do; if two, at least 8 are needed. With 16 or more points, jump to one level higher than necessary. This is forcing to game: it shows you have enough strength between you for a contract worth at least 100 and possibly a slam, and tells your partner not to pass before reaching game level at least. You may also jump with slightly fewer points if your suit is six or more cards long.
- With neither a fit nor a distinctive suit of your own, but with a balanced hand suitable for no trump, offer one no trump on 6–9 points, two on 10–12, three on 13–15.

Opening two clubs

The two-club opening is (in Acol) a convention that bears no necessary relation to your actual holding in clubs but denotes any hand counting at least 23 points and 5 quick tricks (qt).

Quick tricks are ones you can expect to make in the first two or three rounds of each suit. A suit headed by:

A K = 2 qt
A Q = 1½ qt
A = 1 qt
K Q = 1 qt
K x = ½ qt.

It forces partner to keep bidding to game (unless you yourself stop it at 2NT).

The following hand, counting 23 points and a total of 5 qt, demands a two club opening:

♠ K Q x ♥ A K J x x ♦ A Q x ♣ K J

Your partner must respond positively to this opening if they have at least 1½ quick tricks or a good 8–9 points, and can offer a major suit or no trumps at the two level, or three of a minor suit. As it is a forcing bid, however, which prevents them from passing, they must have access to a conventional negative response in case they have nothing to declare. In this case the negative reply is (logically enough) the lowest they can possibly make, i.e. two diamonds. If then you see no prospect of game, as here, you can sign off by bidding a perfectly acceptable 2NT.

If your partner does respond, however, you can start developing the auction in other directions. For example, a response of two hearts would offer prospects of a slam in hearts, which you would explore by methods of slam bidding (see below). Two spades would be worth raising to four for an immediate game, and two of a minor suit would give you a safe rebid of three no trump. Either of these might then prompt your partner to start looking for a slam.

Opening two in a suit other than clubs

The so-called 'strong two' opening also has a special meaning, but, unlike two clubs, it is natural rather than conventional, in that you name a genuine prospective trump. It doesn't require any particular number of points, but indicates strength in one of the following respects:

Eight or more playing tricks and a long major suit headed by at least A–Q, such as:

♠ A Q J x x x x ♥ x ♦ A J ♣ A x x

Two long suits, worth exploring for a possible fit, such as:

♠ – ♥ A Q J x x x ♦ x ♣ A K Q x x x

A point-count almost high enough to open 2♣ but lacking the requisite 5 quick tricks, such as:

♠ K Q J ♥ K Q x x x x ♦ Q ♣ A K x

You must be prepared to bid again, as a strong two opening is forcing for one round. The negative response, in case your partner has nothing to offer, is 2NT, which you can leave as the final contract.

What happens if you feel your only natural suit bid is two clubs, which you can't make because it doesn't qualify for the two-club convention? Well, you only have two choices. If the suit is long enough, open three clubs as described below. If not, open one club, and hope the auction stays open so you can repeat the suit at a higher level next time round.

Opening three in a suit

Open three on a weak hand containing one suit of at least seven cards, which, so far as you can see, is useless for anything but a bid in that suit, such as:

♠ x ♥ J x x ♦ K Q J x x x x ♣ J x

A three-bid is 'pre-emptive', in that you don't normally expect to make such a contract, but would rather try it and go down than allow the other side to open up communications and possibly make a high-scoring contract cheaply. The main requirement is that you should expect to win six tricks in your own hand, or seven if vulnerable. It is best made from third position after two passes, thus discouraging the fourth player, who probably has a biddable hand, from opening except at a dangerously high level. You don't make it from fourth position yourself, of course, as you have no one to pre-empt. In this case a bid of 'one' will suffice after three passes. It isn't usual to open more than three in a suit, since strength is indicated by opening at the two level, and a three-bid specifically implies weakness in all but one quarter. An opening bid of four may be regarded as the same as three, but stronger by one trick.

One no-trump opening and responses

No-trump openings are made on balanced hands (4–3–3–3, 4–4–3–2, or 5–3–3–2 with a long minor suit), with stops (defensive tricks) in at least three suits, and, unlike one-in-suit openings, falling into a precise and narrow range of high card points. The main reason for this is that if your partner has an unbalanced hand, with a good prospective trump, they will want to know early on how much support they can expect from you in side suits in order to judge how far to go with their own suit in case a slam is on. Alternatively, they may also have a balanced hand, in which case, since no-trump contracts earn more points for fewer tricks, it is particularly desirable to bid to the most accurate level. For these reasons it is essential that you open in no trumps only within the agreed range of points for the level at which you bid, never so much as 1 point below that range or, even more importantly (since the temptation is greater), above it.

One no trump may be opened 'weak' on 12–14 or 'strong' on 16–18 points. Which it is must be agreed between you and your partner beforehand. Some partners agree to play a 'variable' no trump, opening strong when vulnerable and weak when not. Some prefer a strong no trump regardless of vulnerability, but the modern tendency is to prefer 'weak' throughout. A weak no trump has the advantage – except after three passes – of a pre-empt, in that it prevents the other side from opening communications below the level of two. At the same time, its limited nature enables your partner to assess more accurately how safe it is to respond at that level themself.

The following hands may be opened at 1NT (weak):

♠	A K x	K x x x	x x x
♥	x x	A Q x	K J x x
♦	Q x x x	K x x x	K Q J x
♣	Q J x x	J x	Q J x

The following should *not* be opened at 1NT:

♠	x x x	K J	A x x
♥	K J x x	A J x x	K x x
♦	J x	x x	K Q J x
♣	A K J x	K x x x x	Q x x

The first should be opened one club, having two weak suits but the possibility of a major suit fit. The second should also be opened one club, being wrong in shape: 5–4–2–2 is acceptable for no trump, but not when one of the doubletons is unstopped and the other ill-headed against a bad break (of A–Q). The third counts 15, which is too many. Open one diamond and switch to no trump next time round.

In responding to a NT opening, your options are to pass, to raise the NT bid, or to try a suit take-out.

Given a balanced hand, raise 1 NT (weak) to 2NT on 11–12 points, 3NT on 13–17, 4NT on 18–19, 6NT on more. The 4NT response invites opener to go for the small slam (6NT) if they bid on not less than the maximum 14 points. However, points are not everything, especially at low levels, and hands counting less than 13 should be passed if they contain an obvious weakness. Raise 1NT (strong) to 2NT on 10–12 points, 3NT on 13–18, 4NT on 19–20, 6NT on 21–24.

Given an unbalanced hand with a long major suit in the range of 0–7 points (or 0–10 if vulnerable), bid two of that suit. This is a 'weak take-out': it means 'I can't support no trumps, but your hand will support a contract in this suit, so pass and leave me in it' – which your partner is then obliged to do. You can take-out into diamonds, but as two of a minor suit scores no more than 1NT, only do this if you are sure the suit contract is safer than one in no trumps. As for two clubs, this has a special meaning.

A response of 2♣ to an opening 1NT is the Stayman convention. It means 'I have enough points to look for a game, but would prefer it in a major suit, as I hold at least four cards in both of them. Which one can you best support?' If your partner cannot support either, they give the (equally conventional) negative response of 2♦, enabling you to remove to 2NT if need be. If they can, they will bid two of their major suit, and you can take it from there, in whatever direction seems best. The Stayman convention can be extended into a response of 3♣ to an opening 2NT. Stayman may be useful if you play a lot. If not, the appropriate situation may occur so infrequently that you forget to use it, or don't recognize it when you partner does.

Two no-trump openings and responses

Open two no trumps on a balanced hand containing 20–22 points. Your partner should pass with 0–3 points, but with a balanced hand should reply 3NT on 4–10, 4NT on 11–12, 6NT on 13–14, leaving you to raise any of these if your count was maximum. Alternatively, they may take you out into three of a suit in which they hold at least five cards.

There is no point in opening a balanced hand at more than 2NT. If the hand is worth 3NT, indicate your strength by opening with a conventional two clubs. This is forcing to game level anyway, while allowing you plenty of bidding space in which to explore the possibility of a slam.

Intervening bids

We have so far taken it for granted that only one side is doing the bidding, their adversaries meanwhile respectfully murmuring 'no bid' and touching their forelocks from time to time. What often happens, however, is that one side starts the auction, the other side immediately intervenes, and a period of interaction at the one and two levels (or even higher, given freakish distributions) eventually results in one of the partnerships dropping out of the auction. An intervening bid is what you may make if the bidding has been opened by the player on your right, or on your left followed by two passes.

An intervening suit bid at the one level requires length rather than strength. A 10-point count suffices with a five-card suit, and you can deduct a point for each card in excess. Thus:

♠ x   ♥ K Q x x x x   ♦ x x x   ♣ A x x

while not qualifying for an opening bid in first position, would rate a bid of one heart over a minor-suit opening from your right. With 13–15 points you can overcall at the two level. For example, change a minor-suit 'x' to a King on the above hand and you could overcall an opening one spade. With no long suit but 16 or more points you could overcall with 1 NT.

Informatory or 'take-out' double

An intervening bid may take the form of a purely conventional double. This is typically made when the player on your right deals and opens one in a suit. A double in such a position cannot possibly arise from a genuine expectation that the auction will stop there and the contract be beaten. It therefore has a special use, indicating (in effect) 'My hand is strong enough to open but weak in the suit bid. Show me a suit and I will support it or make some other constructive response.' Your partner should then respond as they would do if you had opened the bidding.

Slam bidding

When you obviously hold between you a lot of points and have agreed a suit with a good fit, the player who took the initiative will want to find out whether their partner has enough of the outstanding Aces and Kings for a playable slam. They will usually do this by means of the Blackwood convention, whereby bids of 4NT and 5NT ask about Ace and King holdings respectively.

Suppose you deal and find yourself with this:

♠ K Q ♥ A Q J x x ♦ A K x ♣ K J x

With 23 points, you open two clubs. Your partner replies two hearts. Good! They have at least 1½ tricks and you have a fit in hearts. Translating their tricks into at least 6 or 7 points, you have at least 29–30 between you and will be thinking of a slam. The quick way of doing this is to bid a 4NT immediately. Since 3NT would suffice for game, 4NT should be interpreted as agreeing the heart suit and seeking further information by means of the Blackwood convention.

Blackwood asks your partner to say how many Aces they hold by responding to 4NT as follows:

5♣ shows no Aces held (or all four)

5♦ shows one Ace

5♥ shows two Aces

5♠ shows three Aces

Suppose your partner replies five hearts, showing two Aces. With four between you, a small slam is likely. Whether or not you can bid a grand slam depends on who holds the heart King. You therefore launch into phase 2 of Blackwood by bidding 5NT, asking for Kings on the same scale (except that four Kings is indicated not by six but by seven clubs). If your partner replies six diamonds, they have the King, and you can finally call seven hearts – not 7NT, as you could lose a trick in a minor suit.

If they replied six clubs, you would know the trump King to be off-side and would therefore sign off at six hearts. Similarly, if in response to your 4NT your partner had shown only one Ace, you would have left it at five hearts. To have asked for Kings with 5NT, and got a negative response, would have left you in the impossible situation of having to bid the small slam lacking both an Ace and the trump King.

Blackwood need not be employed as precipitously as this. Given an agreed suit and the chance of a slam, bidding space can often be used to convey information to prevent the uncertainty described in the preceding paragraph. But this takes us beyond our brief and into books devoted specifically to Bridge, of which there are more than a few.

Declarer's play

The unique challenge of Bridge lies in planning, and then putting into operation, the line of play which will yield all the tricks you need from the two hands you can see. Even when it is obvious that there are enough trick-winners between them, it is not always obvious without careful examination exactly how the cards should be played and in what order. One permanent occupational hazard of Declarer is that of taking a trick in the wrong hand so as to make it impossible to get back into the other hand to win subsequent tricks. The other is that of not having enough obvious tricks, and having to work out ways of gaining the one or two extra you may need to make the contract.

In a trump contract it is usually right to attack and draw trumps as soon as possible, especially if you haven't as many of them as you would like and therefore need to establish winners in your long side suits without risking their being ruffed. As to side suits, it is often important to avoid cashing your immediate winners, but to keep them as defensive strongholds while you attack the suit or suits in which you have top card weakness. In other words, hang on to the suits headed A–K until you have driven out the adverse cards from those headed K–Q, Q–J–10, and so on. Always calculate how many tricks you can afford to lose, and lose them earlier rather than later as part of a constructive strategy to establish future winners, trusting that those you were dealt originally will not have walked away in the meantime.

Let's apply this to the following grand slam in hearts with dummy sitting west and yourself east.

♠	K Q	A x x
♥	A Q J x x	K x x x
♦	A K x	J x x x
♣	K J x	A x

First, count your tricks. In spades, three, but remember to keep back the Ace until the King and Queen have made. In diamonds, two, and you must find a way of losing the 'x' in dummy to a trick won in hand, perhaps by ♠A. In clubs, two. In trumps, assuming the worst case that they fall two to a trick, five. Total 12. One missing. Where is the thirteenth coming from? The only safe answer is to ensure that one of the trumps from the shorter holding – the one in your own hand – can be used to ruff a lead from dummy. At some stage in the proceedings, you will want to lead ♣A from hand, followed by a low club to the King, followed by dummy's third club for you to ruff.

How is this hand likely to go? If clubs are led, which seems likely, you will take with the Ace, return a club to the King, lead your last club, and ruff it in hand, leaving you three tricks up with ten to go and clubs safe. Next, draw some trumps by leading a low one to the Jack followed by a low one to the Queen. At this point, being in dummy, win tricks six and seven with the spade King and Queen. Now get back into hand with dummy's last low trump to the King, and play off the ♠A, to which you can now discard the dummy's useless diamond. This leaves you with only diamonds in hand, enabling dummy to take the remaining four tricks with the two top diamonds and two outstanding trumps.

Sometimes, when your initial survey reveals a trick short, you may find the only chance of developing another trick is to risk a finesse, which may be defined as an attempt to win a trick with a lower card when a higher one is held (or accessible). Suppose, in the above contract, dummy's diamond holding were A–Q–J and yours 10–8–6–3. You might decide that the only way of getting home is to go for a second trick in the suit against the King. A finesse always depends upon the critical card lying in one rather than another of the adverse hands. For it to work here, the King must be in South's hand and you approach it by leading low. If South plays the King, you win with the Ace; if not, you hope they held it up and go for a win with the Queen. If North has the King, the Queen will lose, and the finesse will fail. Situations do occur in which you can theoretically finesse against either defender, but you still have to choose which one to attack, as you can't take on both at once. Whichever way you look at it, a finesse is a 50–50 chance, and should be avoided if there is any safer way of winning the trick you need.

Defenders' play

Experience of Whist and other partnership trick games will be of value to your play as a defender. The main problem is knowing what to lead first before the dummy has gone down. It's usually desirable to avoid leading a suit mentioned by either opponent in the auction, and to lead one mentioned by your partner, unless you have a long suit of your own headed by the Ace, which you will want to make before it can be ruffed.

If your partner hasn't mentioned any suit, a standard opening lead is the fourth highest card (i.e. fourth from the top) of the longest non-trump suit in your hand. (This can give your partner maximum information about the lie of the suit by applying the old 'rule of eleven' – see Partnership Whist.)

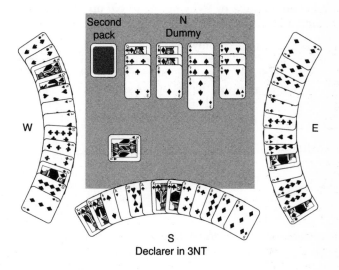

figure 13.1 Bridge

South, with 17 points and long clubs, opens 'one' of that suit. West intervenes with 1♥. North, after some thought, rejects no trump and spade responses in favour of three clubs. East passes. South now counts at least 27 points between the two hands which is borderline for a game in clubs, but safer at no trump. This is duly bid; North passes, West attacks hearts by leading the King, dummy goes down, and the situation is as illustrated. It is usual for trumps to be set out to the left of dummy as seen by Declarer, or clubs in a no-trump bid, as here. Declarer will probably make five clubs, one diamond, three spades and a heart, scoring 100 below the line and 30 above for the overtrick.

Another satisfactory lead is an honour heading a sequence of three or more, such as Jack from J–10–9, etc. or a low singleton so that you can trump that suit when your partner returns it.

Four-deal Bridge ('Chicago')

As a home game, Chicago has two advantages. One is that a rubber is always four deals, so if two or more tables are operating it is possible for players to swap tables and partners without too much hanging around. The other is that its scoring system, essentially that of Duplicate (Tournament) Bridge, encourages players to bid up to the full value of their hands, so there is no question of 'Why bother to bid up to five clubs if we only need 20 for game?'.

The score sheet needs only five rows divided into two columns, one for each side. There is no distinction between above- and below-line scoring: if a partnership makes its contract it scores in its own column; if not, the defenders score in theirs. Part-scores are not carried forwards from deal to deal (though they were originally, and many Americans still play this way).

In deal 1, neither side is vulnerable. In deals 2 and 3, non-dealer's side is vulnerable. (A modern development. Originally, dealer's side was vulnerable.) In deal 4, both sides are vulnerable. If a deal is passed out, the cards are gathered and (after the shuffle and cut) re-dealt by the same dealer, instead of being passed round to the next as in Rubber Bridge.

The score for a successful contract is the sum of two parts:

- The natural score for the number of tricks actually made, including overtricks, and with any doubling taken into account.
- If the contract value was less than game (100), add 50 for a part-score. If it was 100 or more, add for game 300 if not vulnerable, 500 if vulnerable.

The defenders' score for defeating a contract is the same as in Rubber Bridge. There is no score for honours, nor extras for the rubber.

Mini Bridge

Learning card games that involve an auction and a contract is a tricky affair because, whereas the auction comes before the play, you have to understand how the play goes before you can bid intelligently. Mini Bridge, developed during the 1990s, is not only an excellent way of enabling learners to follow the practice of play before having to get involved with the finer points of bidding, but also is a sufficiently interesting game in its own right to be played on a tournament basis. At the time of writing, there is no universally accepted version of Mini Bridge, but the basic essentials run along these lines.

Deal 13 cards each in the usual way. Everybody counts the high-card point value of their hand, and each in turn, starting with the dealer, announces what that value is. If both sides have 20 points, the hands are thrown in and a new deal made.

The side with the higher point-count becomes the declaring side, and the actual declarer is the member of that partnership holding the greater number of points – or, in case of equality, the first of them to announce it. Declarer's partner then lays their hand of cards face up as a dummy, and Declarer, after examining both hands, announces either 'Game' or 'Not game' in clubs, diamonds, hearts, spades, or no trump.

With a combined point-count of 26 or more between both hands, the declarer is obliged to bid 'Game'. This means that they must win at least as many tricks as necessary to make a 'game' score of 100 – that is, three or more at no trump, four or more in a major suit, or five or more in a minor.

With a combined point-count of 25 or less, declarer may bid 'Not game'. In this case they must play to win at least one odd trick – that is, at least seven of the 13 played. They are permitted to bid 'Game' if they think it worth the attempt.

The contract established, the opening lead is made (as usual) by the declarer's left-hand opponent, and play proceeds as in the standard game.

Scores are made without reference to above or below a line.

- For a successful non-game contract, the declaring side scores the actual value of tricks made above six (20 each in a minor suit, 30 in a major, and 40–30 at no trump), plus a part-score bonus of 50.

- For a successful game contract, the declaring side scores for tricks as outlined above, and adds a game-score bonus of 300.
- For a failed contract, the defending side scores 50 per undertrick.

See also

http://www.pagat.com/boston/bridge/html
A beginners' introduction

http://www.math.aau.dk/~nwp/bridge/laws/rlaws-e/
The International Laws of Contract Bridge

http://www.worldbridge.org/
The website of the World Bridge Federation

Bridge is one of the most popular and widespread games available for on-line play.

14

twenty-five

- for three to ten players, best for five
- tricky to learn
- nice balance of chance and skill

Ireland's national card game sometimes appears in books under the name Spoil Five, as your aim is to prevent anybody from winning three of the five tricks played if you can't win three of them yourself. It was renamed Twenty-Five when the habit developed of scoring points in fives instead of ones. The game is also played by Gaelic descendants in Canada and Nova Scotia, with the target score raised to 45, producing a partnership variety called (believe it or not) Auction Forty-Fives.

Newcomers may find it initially daunting because of the peculiar rank of cards and rules of play, which obviously derive from the ancient Spanish game of Hombre, and take a little getting used to. But it is well worth the effort, as much for its intrinsic interest as for its cultural and historic significance – not to mention the fact that it is one of the very few games for which five is the best number of players.

The game

Preliminaries. From three to ten can play. Four may play in two partnerships of two, and six in two partnerships of three or three of two. For non-partnership play, five is ideal. Each starts with 20 chips or counters, but scores can easily be kept in writing.

Cards. Fifty-two. There is always a trump suit, and three or four cards are always the highest trumps, namely (from the top down):

Five of trumps (traditionally known as 'Five fingers')
Jack of trumps
Ace of hearts (♥A)
Ace of trumps (if other than hearts)

The others rank from high to low according to colour:

in ♥ and ♦ : K Q [J] 10 9 8 7 6 5 4 3 2 [A] ('high in red')
in ♠ and ♣ : K Q [J] [A] 2 3 4 5 6 7 8 9 10 ('low in black')

The bracketed cards only occupy those positions when they are not among the four top trumps.

Deal. Everyone chips one to the kitty. Deal five cards each in batches of two and three, or four and one. Stack the rest face down and turn the top card for trump.

Object. Primarily, to sweep the kitty by winning at least three tricks, and preferably all five. Failing this, to 'spoil five' by preventing anyone else from winning three, thereby increasing the size of the kitty for the next deal. If played for written scores, each trick counts 5 points and the target is 25.

Robbing the pack. If dealt the trump Ace, you may declare that fact and then 'rob the pack' by taking the turn-up and discarding an unwanted card face down. You needn't declare it if you don't intend to rob, but if you do, you must rob before playing to the first trick. If the turn-up is an Ace, Dealer may rob the pack by exchanging it for any unwanted card.

Play. The player at Dealer's left leads to the first trick, and the rules of trick play are:

- To a plain-suit lead, you may freely either follow suit or play a trump, but you may only play anything else if unable to follow suit.
- To a trump lead, you must play a trump if possible, unless the only one you hold is one of the top three trumps (Five, Jack or ♥Ace) and it is *higher* than the one led. In this case, you may 'renege' by discarding from another suit. In other words, you can't force a player to disgorge one of the top three trumps by leading a lower trump, but only by leading a higher one of the top three, and then only if that player has no lower trump.

Example. *If the trump Six is led and you hold the trump Five, trump Jack, or ♥A, but no lower trump, you needn't play it but may discard from any other suit. But you can't renege against a higher trump. For example, if the trump Jack is led, you needn't play the trump Five, but must (if you have no alternative) play ♥A, as it is lower than the Jack.*

The trick is taken by the highest card of the suit led, or by the highest trump if any are played, and the winner of each trick leads to the next.

Jinking. If you win the first three tricks straight off, you sweep the kitty without further play. If instead you 'jink' by leading to the fourth trick, this counts as an undertaking to win all five, and you will lose your stake if you fail to get them all.

Score. A player who wins three or more tricks wins the kitty, and for winning all five gains an extra chip from each opponent. If nobody wins three, or a jinker fails to win five, the tricks are said to be 'spoilt'. The kitty is then carried forward to the next deal, and is increased by one chip per player.

Game. The game ends when somebody runs out of chips (hard score) or reaches 25 points (soft score).

The play

You should decide almost from the outset whether to go for three tricks or to spoil the five. Most hands are run-of-the-mill, and spoiling is the safest bet. One way of doing this is to refrain from playing a top trump to an early trick – by legally reneging – thus saving it for subsequent use against a player who has won a second trick, or is threatening to do so, with a view to a third.

To go for three you generally need three trumps, one of them a top trump. You can't count a plain-suit King as a winner from the outset because the rules of play allow it to be trumped even by a player who can follow suit. But it becomes more promising if you can retain it while trumps are being drawn in early tricks. Many a third trick is won by leading to the last trick a plain suit that no one can either follow or trump.

In the following illustration, the turned card is ♦Q, making diamonds trump, and the hands are:

Ardal	♥10 6 2 ♠3 ♣7
Bernadette	♠J 8 ♣9 6 2
Caitlin	♦5 ♥A K ♠5 ♣A
Déidre	♦9 4 ♠Q 7 4
Eamon	♦A ♥J 4 ♣Q 10

Only two players can reasonably go for three tricks: Caitlin has two top trumps and a King, while Eamon's ♦A entitles him to take the turned Queen in exchange for his most worthless card, ♣10. With ♥10 led, the play might go:

	A	B	C	D	E
1	♥10	♣9	♥K	♦4	<u>♦Q</u>
2	♥6	♠8	<u>♥A</u>	♦9	♥4
3	♥2	♣6	<u>♦5</u>	♠7	♦A
4	♣7	♣2	♣A	♠4	<u>♣Q</u>
5	♠3	♠J	♠5	♠Q	<u>♥J</u>

1 Déidre is obliged to trump, Eamon elects to do so and wins the trick. He leads a low heart, expecting to force out trumps so that he can come in later with his Queen and win the last trick with the Jack.
2 Caitlin, unable to follow suit, is forced to trump (♥A is third highest).
3 Caitlin now leads the unbeatable Five, which must force out any top trumps still in play, as well as (she hopes) the trump Ace known to be in Eamon's hand. Eamon reluctantly complies.
4 Unfortunately for Caitlin, her ♣A falls to Eamon's Queen. Eamon, having now re-entered by another route, leads the ♥J as originally intended, and sweeps the kitty.

Had Caitlin led ♣A to the third trick, Eamon would still have won by leading ♥J to the fourth. Caitlin would have been obliged to trump, and Eamon would have won with the last remaining trump.

Auction Forty-Fives (for four or six players)

This is a partnership version of Twenty-Five for four or six players. Six play in two partnerships of three, each player being flanked by an opponent on either side.

The deal, rank of cards, and play of tricks, are as at Twenty-Five.

Auction. After the deal but before the play there is an auction.

Each in turn, starting with the player at Dealer's left, may pass or make a higher bid than any that has gone before, except that the dealer has the privilege of 'holding' the previous bid. (That is, making it their own by privilege of position.)

Bids are made in multiples of 5, starting at 5 and going up to a maximum of 30. The maximum is greater than 25 because, in addition to the score of 5 points per trick won, another 5 is credited to the side that was dealt the highest trump in play.

Bidding continues until three pass in succession. The last-named bid is the contract.

Discards. Before play, each in turn, starting from the left of the dealer, may make any number of discards, face down, and be dealt the same number of replacements from the top of the stock.

The opening lead is made by the opponent sitting to the left of the highest bidder.

Scoring. As stated, each trick counts 5 and the highest trump counts another 5 points. The non-bidding side always scores what it makes. So does the bidding side if successful; if not, they lose the amount of their bid.

For bidding and making 30, the score is doubled to 60.

Game. Play up to 120 points. A side standing at 100 or more points may not bid less than 20.

See also

http://www.pagat.com/spoil5/25.html

This describes a simpler form of the game based on local contributions. There is no 'jinking'; each won trick scores 5 points; and the game ends the moment one player or team reaches 25 points (even if this happens in the middle of a hand). I suspect that jinking may be an old feature now on the way out. Pagat also describes a version with bidding, known as '55', or '110', or '220', depending on the target score.

part two

two

plain-trick games

15

piquet

- for two players
- tricky to learn
- a game of great skill

Piquet is one of the oldest and greatest of card games for two. It was one of the first card games I ever learnt and I still never tire of playing it. Unfortunately, it is now something of a rarity (one author says it is now played only by 'card gourmets and snobs'), possibly because it is, frankly, not as easy to pick up from scratch as the positively childish Gin Rummy, or even the disarmingly deceptive Cribbage.

Piquet is very easy to follow once you have got the basic idea, but the rules are subject to so many niceties of detail as to make it look at first reading far more complicated than it really is – a classic case of not being able to see the wood for the trees. You may therefore find it helpful to go through the following introductory exercise, either alone or with a prospective partner, before plunging into a thicket of detail.

A sample hand

Take a 32-card pack, or make one by discarding all ranks below Seven from a 52-card pack. Construct two hands consisting of the following 12 cards:

	Elder (non-dealer)								*Younger (dealer)*							
♠	-	-	Q	-	-	-	8	7	A	K	-	-	-	-	-	-
♥	A	-	-	J	-	-	-	-	-	K	-	-	10	9	-	-
♣	A	-	-	-	-	-	8	7	-	K	Q	J	10	-	-	-
♦	A	-	Q	J	-	9	-	-	-	-	-	-	10	-	8	7

Arrange the remaining 12 cards in the following order:

♥Q ♥8 ♥7 ♠9 ♦K ♣9 ♠J ♠10

Spread them face down in a row, overlapping one another, with the back of the ♥Q on top. This row is called the talon. In real play, of course, no one knows what these cards are.

What will happen is this. Elder (non-dealer) will first discard up to five cards and draw the same number of replacements from the top of the talon. Younger (dealer) will discard as many as remain (typically three) and also draw replacements. They will then seek to score points for declaring certain card combinations in their new hands, and finally seek to win a majority of 12 tricks, which are played at no trump. The purpose of the draw is therefore partly to compose winning combinations and partly to ensure a good playing hand. Before you can do this, you have to know what the scoring combinations are. They fall into three classes.

- **Point.** This is scored by the player who holds the greatest number of cards in any one suit. If equal, it goes to the player whose longest suit has the highest point-value. For this purpose an Ace counts 11, courts 10 each, and numerals their face value. If still equal, neither scores.
- **Sequence.** This is scored by the player who holds the longest suit-sequence. If equal, it goes to the player whose longest sequence runs from the highest top card. If still equal, neither scores. If one player does score for holding the best sequence, they may then score for any other sequences contained in the hand.
- **Set.** A set is three or four Aces, Kings, Queens, Jacks or Tens. Lower numerals don't count. A *quatorze* (set of four) beats a *trio* (three). Whoever holds the highest quatorze or, if none, the highest trio, is entitled to score for it and any other sets held in the same hand.

Now examine the two hands with these combinations in mind. Elder's best chance of making point and sequence lies in keeping all his diamonds. He therefore discards his Sevens, Eights and ♥J, drawing in their place ♥Q ♥8 ♥7 ♠9 and ♦K.

Younger will obviously keep her high cards and club sequence, and will hope to draw the fourth King or Ten, either of which would give her a winning quatorze since she has one of each Ace, Queen, Jack. Making the obvious discard of three low numerals, she draws in their place ♠J ♠10 ♣9.

The playing hands are now:

	Elder (non-dealer)									*Younger (dealer)*								
♠	-	-	Q	-	-	9	-	-		A	K	-	J	10	-	-	-
♥	A	-	Q	-	-	-	8	7		-	K	-	-	10	-	-	-
♣	A	-	-	-	-	-	-	-		-	K	Q	J	10	9	-	-
♦	A	K	Q	J	-	9	-	-		-	-	-	-	10	-	-	-

Both players have a 'point of five', elder in diamonds and younger in clubs. But elder's five comprise 50 card-points and younger's only 49, so elder scores 1 per card, 5 points in all, for holding the better point.

For sequences, elder's four to the Ace is beaten by younger's five to the King. Younger therefore scores for the sequence, and would be entitled to score for any other sequences if she had any. Sequences also score 1 per card, but those of five or more carry a bonus of 10, so in this case younger scores 15.

For sets, elder's trio of Aces is beaten by younger's quatorze of Tens, which also entitles her to reckon her trio of Kings. Quatorzes count 14 and trios 3, so younger scores 17 for sets.

Elder now leads to the first trick with the scores so far at 5 to 32. He cashes his seven winners immediately – there is no point in messing about – and scores a bonus of 10 for winning a clear majority of tricks.

There is far more to it than that, of course; but if you take this sample deal as illustrating the wood you will find it much easier to pick your pathway through the following trees.

The game

Piquet has been played in so many countries and for so many centuries that each one has developed its own 'national' version over the course of time. The one described here is designated English Rubicon Piquet. 'Rubicon' denotes the target score of 100 points which the loser must reach in order to avoid being more heavily penalized. (It's like the lurch in Crib.)

Note. *Most books follow a traditional way of explaining how the game is played. The traditional way, however, is more complicated than it need be. The following description is therefore worded in what I have found in practice to be more easily comprehended. This does not mean that the game plays any differently from that usually described in English-language games books.*

Game. A game, properly called a partie, consists of six deals, each dealing alternately. The winner is the player with the higher cumulative total, and wins extra if the loser is 'rubiconed' by failing to attain 100 points.

Cards. Use a 32-card pack ranking A K Q J 10 9 8 7 in each suit. Whoever cuts the higher card chooses which player shall deal first. Dealing first can be an advantage, and is never a disadvantage.

Deal. Shuffle the cards lightly, have them cut, and deal 12 each. You may deal in batches of two or three, but whichever you choose you must stick to it throughout the partie. Spread the remaining eight face down to form a talon.

Carte blanche. A dealt hand devoid of court cards is called a *carte blanche* (or 'blank', if you prefer English), and may be declared for 10 points. If you have one, you must declare it immediately, and (if you are elder) prove it by rapidly dealing your hand of cards one by one face up to the table. If you get one as younger, you declare it immediately but don't prove it until after elder has drawn cards from the talon.

The draw. Elder must discard from one to five cards (he may not stand pat) and draw the same number of replacements from the top of the talon downwards. If, as elder, you take fewer than five, you may peep at those you did not take, other than the last three, without showing them to younger.

When elder has drawn, younger may discard up to as many as remain – usually three – and similarly draw replacements from the top of the remaining talon. Like elder, younger is obliged to exchange at least one card. If after the exchange you, as younger, leave any card or cards untaken, you may either reveal them to both players, or leave them face down if you prefer; but you may not look at them yourself without showing them to elder.

Declaration of point. Elder, if he wishes to score for point, states the number of cards in his longest suit – for example, 'Point of five'. Younger replies 'Good' if she cannot match it, 'Not good' if she can beat it. If equal, she asks 'Counting?', and elder then states the total value of its constituent cards, reckoning Ace 11, courts 10 each, and numerals at face value. Again, younger replies 'Good' if she cannot match it or 'Not good' if she can beat it. If she says 'Equal', neither scores for point; otherwise, the better point-holder scores 1 per constituent card.

Declaration of sequences. Elder, if he wishes to score for sequences, now states the length of his longest, e.g. 'sequence of four'. Younger replies 'Good' if she cannot match it, 'Not good' if she can beat it.

If equal, she asks 'To?', and elder then states the top card of the sequence. Again, younger replies 'Good' if she cannot match it or 'Not good' if her top card is higher.

If she says 'Equal', neither scores for point. Otherwise, whoever holds the best sequence scores for it and any other sequences held in the same hand. Sequences of three and four score 3 and 4 respectively, of five to eight 15 to 18 respectively.

Declaration of sets. Elder, if he wishes to score for sets, now announces his highest-ranking quatorze or trio, e.g. 'Fourteen Queens' (etc.), 'Three Tens', or whatever. A higher-ranking set beats a lower, but any quatorze beats a trio. Younger replies 'Good' or 'Not good', as the case may be. Whoever has the best set scores for it and any other sets in the same hand. Trios score 3 points each, quatorzes 14.

table of scores at piquet

scoring combinations		
carte blanche	10	a hand devoid of face cards (K, Q, J)
point	3–8	1 per card of longest suit
sequences	3	three in suit-sequence (*tierce*)
	4	four in suit-sequence (*quart*)
	15	five in suit-sequence (*quint*)
	16	six in suit-sequence (*sixième*)
	17	seven in suit-sequence (*septième*)
	18	eight in suit-sequence (*huitième*)
sets	3	three of A, K, Q, J or 10 (*trio*)
	14	four of A, K, Q, J or 10 (*quatorze*)
premium scores		
repique	60	either player reaches 30 for combinations alone before opponent makes any score
pique	30	elder reaches 30 for combinations and tricks before younger makes any score
score for tricks		
for leading	1	to elder for leading to first trick
per trick won	1	if led by self
	2	if captured from opponent's lead
cards	10	bonus for winning 7–11 tricks
capot	40	bonus for winning all 12 tricks

Leading to the first trick. All such declarations having been made, elder plays a card face up to the table, saying, and scoring, 'One for leading'. Before younger responds, however, the scores that have so far been announced verbally may be noted down, together with any bonus scorable for *pique or repique*.

Pique, repique. If either player reaches a score of 30 or more for declarations before the other has scored anything at all in the deal, that player adds a bonus of 60 for *repique*. Here it must be noted that scores accrue strictly in this order: blank, point, sequence, set. If, therefore, either player scores for blank or point, the other cannot score repique for reaching 30 on sequences or sets. Conversely, scoring for sets alone offers no protection from repique if the other player reaches 30 while scoring for sequences.

Note: *Some books claim that declaring equality for point or sequence prevents the opponent from claiming repique, but this was never part of the official rules drawn up by the Portland Club.*

Pique is a similar bonus, but can be scored only by elder. If elder, by adding to his declarations points made in the play of tricks, reaches 30 before younger has made any score at all, then elder counts an additional 30 for pique. Younger cannot make it because elder's point for leading to the first trick takes effect before younger's score for combinations.

Tricks. Tricks are played at no trump. You must follow suit if you can, otherwise may play any card. The trick is taken by the higher card of the suit led, and the winner of each trick leads to the next. You score 1 point for winning a trick to which you led, or 2 for winning a trick led by your opponent. A convenient way of recording this is to store 1-point tricks face down and 2-point tricks face up on the table.

Note: *The trick-scoring rule is usually stated '1 for leading to a trick, 1 for capturing the lead, and 1 for winning the last trick'. This comes to exactly the same thing.*

For winning a majority of tricks – that is, seven or more – you score an additional 10 'for cards'. For winning all 12 tricks, you add 40 for *capot* instead of 10 for cards.

Game score. Scores are cumulated at the end of each deal ready for the next. Whoever has the greater total at the end of the sixth deal normally scores 100 plus the difference between the two final totals. If, however, the loser fails to reach the rubicon of 100 points, then the winner scores 100 plus *both* players' totals.

Example. If you win by 160 to 110, you score 100 + (160 – 110), making 150; but if you win by 160 to 90, your score is 100 + (160 + 90), making 250.

Note that the rubicon bonus applies even if the winner also fails to reach 100. If both players have the same score at the end of six deals, another two deals are played to break the tie.

Illustrative deal

Let's follow a sample hand played by (for the sake of argument) Napoleon and Josephine (see Figure 16.1). Josephine deals, making Napoleon elder hand, and the cards are:

Nap: ♠ A K J ♥ A Q J 8 ♣ J 8 7 ♦ 9 8

Jos: ♠ 10 7 ♥ 10 9 7 ♣ K Q 10 ♦ A Q J 10

Napoleon has up to five exchanges, and hopes to draw more hearts and the (so-called) fourteenth Jack. He therefore discards ♠K and the two low clubs and diamonds.

Josephine must keep her fourteen Tens, as it is obvious from her own hand that Napoleon cannot have a higher-ranking quatorze, and discards ♠7 ♥9 ♥7.

After the draw, the hands are:

Nap: ♠ A J 9 8 ♥ A K Q J 8 ♣ J 9 ♦ K

Jos: ♠ Q 10 ♥ 10 ♣ A K Q 10 ♦ A Q J 10 7

Declarations proceed as follows:

> *Nap.* Point of five.
> *Jos. (also having a point of five)* Worth?
> *Nap.* 49.
> *Jos. (with 48)* Good.
> *Nap.* In hearts. And a quart major. *(Meaning a sequence of four to the Ace.)*
> *Jos.* Good.
> *Nap.* That's five for point, four for the sequence, making nine . . . *(Looks for another sequence to count, but fails*

to find any. His next call is somewhat tentative.) Three
Jacks?

Jos. Not good.

Nap. (leading ♥A) And one's ten.

Jos. I count fourteen Tens and three Queens, seventeen.

Tricks are played as follows.

Napoleon leads out all his hearts from the top down, to which
Josephine plays her ♥10 and four diamonds to the Queen.

Having made five 1-point tricks, Napoleon leads ♦K for
Josephine to take with her last remaining diamond, the Ace. This
gives her a 2-point trick. She then leads her four clubs from the
top down, for 4 points. This leaves her with ♠ Q 10 to
Napoleon's ♠ A J, so whichever she leads gives Napoleon a 2-
point and a final 1-point trick.

Final scores: Napoleon 28 (10 for declarations, 8 for tricks, 10
for 'cards'); Josephine 23 (17 for combinations, 6 for tricks).

Napoleon did right to lose the lead after his first five tricks. Had
he led spades immediately, he would only have divided the
tricks, and failed to score 10 for cards. Josephine's 'fourteen
Tens' served her in good stead. Usually, elder's average score is
about 28 to younger's 18 or so.

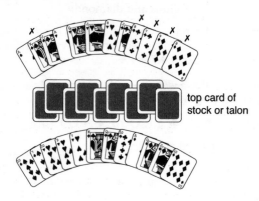

top card of
stock or talon

figure 15.1 piquet

Napoleon, as elder hand, can discard and draw five cards. Wishing to keep
his point in hearts and to draw the fourth Jack, he discards those marked
with a cross. This leaves three for Josephine, whose main aim is to retain the
diamond point and four Tens.

The play

The difference in strategy as between dealer and non-dealer is more marked in Piquet than in any other two-hand game with the possible exception of Cribbage. Elder starts with all the advantages:

- being able to draw up to five cards
- having the opening lead and
- being the only player able to score for pique.

Younger can usually only draw three cards, which is rarely sufficient to rescue a bad hand from disaster, since it is quite possible for her to hold all eight of a suit and yet lose every trick. For this reason elder is usually in a position to take chances and play an attacking hand, while younger should look first to keeping guards in all suits and not take chances that might weaken them.

Discarding as elder hand. To start, then, elder should always seek to exchange his full entitlement of five cards, for to take fewer is to waste his overwhelming advantage and to give younger considerably more room to manoeuvre. If he takes only four cards instead of five, he has reduced his advantage by 20 per cent but increased younger's by 33 per cent. Cards taken in excess of those he feels necessary to his hand are not wasted, as younger does not merely fail to get them but does not even know what they are.

As elder hand, which five cards should you throw out? The beginner's temptation is to throw out low cards that look useless for tricks, and with only three or four of them may prefer to take fewer than his entitlement. What you should do, however, is to look at it the other way: decide which cards you must retain for the best chances of combining, and throw out the rest.

The most important ones to keep are usually those of your longest suit, your potential 'point'. Given two of equal length, keep the suit with the higher point-value or the best chance of turning into a sequence. The point in this hand, for example, is hearts:

♠ A K J 10 ♥ Q J 10 9 ♣ A Q ♦ K 9

since there are twice as many chances (King or Eight) of converting it to a quint than there are of drawing the Queen necessary for a quint in spades. Furthermore, this quint is 'good against the cards' – meaning that it is obvious from your own cards that younger could not possibly draw an equal or better sequence. The discards from this hand, therefore, are ♠J ♠10 ♣Q ♦K ♦9.

You may also discard with a view to completing a quatorze, but problems can arise because this combination tends to conflict with the discarding requirements of a point or sequence. The hand above was not complicated by this factor because (a) it contained two each of the valid ranks, thus preventing younger from scoring anything for sets, and (b) it offered much better chances of filling to a quint in hearts.

By contrast, the following hand, though superficially similar, is not so easy:

♠ A K J 10   ♥ J 10 9 8   ♣ A K 7   ♦ K

Again, there are almost twice as many chances of making a quint or better in hearts (5 to 4 against, or 44 per cent) as a quint in spades (3 to 1 against, or 25 per cent). This time, however it is not good against the cards, as younger might fill an equal or better sequence in diamonds, or even have been dealt it. Furthermore, you have three Kings and would prefer to keep them with a view to drawing the fourth, especially as younger may wind up with fourteen Queens. Since it is vital to restrict younger's entitlement to not more than three cards, you are faced with two or three possible ways of discarding from this hand.

1. Keep the heart sequence and the Kings, neither of which is at present good against the cards, and discard ♠A ♠J ♠10 ♣A ♣7.
2. Keep the Kings and the potential spade quint, discarding the hearts and bottom club and drawing to ♠A K J 10 ♣A K ♦K.
3. Forget the Kings and keep both spades and hearts in the hope of making two quints and repique. However, the chances of doing so are very remote, since you can only draw four cards.

The chances of drawing the fourteenth King are the same in both cases. In the first case there's a 1 in 4 chance of making the quint; in the second there is 4 in 9. But although the latter gives better odds, it would lose if younger had a sequence of six in diamonds, and might tie if she has a quint, whereas the quint major in the former would be good against a diamond quint.

Further, if younger gets only five diamonds instead of six, the retention of spades here stands a better chance of scoring for point because the cards held are higher in value (as it stands, worth 31 against only 27). On the whole, then, case 2 is the safer holding against younger's possibilities, even though case 1 gives better chances on the face of it.

To summarize, elder should nearly always exchange the maximum of five cards, unless the hand dealt is so strong as to contain a quint or quatorze and the chance of (re)pique or capot. You should keep the longest suit intact for point, or, with suits of equal length, the one with the higher count or longer sequence.

You should keep a trio with a view to filling a quatorze, but may reasonably break a trio of Tens or Jacks if the cards show that younger may hold a higher ranking quatorze, or if you find other pressures for discarding from them. If you really are forced into a choice of discard between point and trio, keep the point with a view to winning the majority of tricks.

Having classified cards into those that must be kept for combinations and those that need not, prefer to discard unneeded Aces and Kings rather than discard fewer than five, unless this spoils the chance of capot. If discarding requires it, don't hesitate to unguard Kings or Queens. Discard from as few different suits as possible. Unless a suit contains a card needed for a combination, it is often as well to throw the whole of it out as just a part, and sometimes even better.

Discarding as younger hand. As younger hand your approach is quite different. Having normally only three cards to exchange, you have considerably less opportunity to draw to high combinations. The question of tricks is also of greater importance, since – to take an extreme case – you can be capoted though holding a handful of high cards, if they're in suits of which elder has none. Whereas elder can usually expect to take more tricks with an average hand and proper play, younger must usually discard and fight to at least divide them.

Your first concern, then, after looking for carte blanche, is to ensure adequate coverage in all suits to avoid the danger of capot. A hand such as this:

♠ A K J 9 8 7 ♥ J 10 9 ♣ Q 9 ♦ 8

will lose every trick if elder has no spade in hand, which seems very likely. Here it is vital, before thinking about combinations, to cover the three weak suits by discarding spades. You should even keep the pathetic ♦ 8 to act as a guard in case you draw the

King. Of course, the probability of drawing one card in each of the three suits is very low, but at least two should be drawn to defend against capot. Even then it may be hard to find the right discards to elder's winning leads. Quite apart from tricks, the potential combinations are not worth much. From the cards, there is every chance that elder will hold seven diamonds, and even six clubs would be worth more than your six spades. (Assess this quickly by noting that your spade suit lacks cards counting 20 in face value, whereas his six clubs would lack only 19.) And if you draw ♠Q for a quart major, he is just as likely to hold at least a quint in diamonds.

This hand, however, is an extreme case of weakness for tricks, and is introduced only to point out that a good-looking hand at first sight must be looked at very closely before any discarding decisions are made. As far as combinations are concerned, judge your discards in much the same way as for elder hand. Two points must be noted, though.

1 Don't aim for a particular combination if it means unguarding a suit or losing a vital trick.
2 Don't hesitate to discard only two, or even one, if drawing more would just mean throwing good cards after bad. In this case (unlike elder's situation) any cards you leave remain out of play instead of going into your opponent's hand. This is the reverse of elder's best practice.

To summarize: as younger, discard defensively with a view to retaining coverage in sufficient suits to avoid capot. Don't take all cards available if this means throwing out guards or trick-winners, and don't waste good cards in going after high combinations which are not good against the cards. Other things being equal, always keep your point suit, as it is your best and cheapest defence against pique/repique.

Declaring combinations. The next important part of the game is not the playing of tricks but the announcement of combinations. Here it is necessary to understand that, in Piquet, you can only score for a combination if you declare it, and, if you do declare it, you must specify exactly what it is. That is, if you score for point you must say which suit it's in, and you must similarly specify the suit and top card of any sequence if so requested. The only exception to this is that if you declare a trio, you needn't specify which suit is missing from it. More often than not it will be unnecessary to announce such details, as each player can see from their own hand and discards what their opponent is holding. For this reason it is permissible, and in some cases can be advantageous, to avoid declaring a combination, or to declare a smaller combination than you actually do hold, in order to withhold some information which might be vital to your opponent's play. This is called 'sinking'.

Practised players therefore usually enter the play with a pretty shrewd idea of their opponent's holding, gleaned from what they have announced in declarations together with an estimate of which of the other cards are more likely to be out of their hand than in it. For this reason it is important not to say more about your holding than you really need in order to establish whether or not your declaration is 'good'.

Suppose, as elder, you hold:

♠ Q J 10 9   ♥ A Q J 10   ♣ A K 10   ♦ 10

You call a point of four; younger asks its value, and replies 'not good' to your 40. Your next declaration is 'fourteen Tens', with not a word about the sequence. Why? Because if point of four is not good at 40, younger must have a point of four worth 41, and from your own holding you can see this to be ♦A K Q J. Your sequence of four is bound to be not good, so to mention it at all would only be to give younger gratuitous information about your hand.

Again, if as elder you held fourteen Kings after exchanging five cards, but had seen neither hair nor hide of an Ace, there would be no point in announcing them unless younger took fewer than three cards, as she would certainly not have thrown an Ace with Kings against her.

Similar considerations apply to younger. Suppose you hold:

♠ A Q J 10 7   ♥ 8 7   ♣ Q J 10   ♦ K 9

Your discards were two diamonds and a club. Elder calls a point of five. Without hesitation you should immediately announce 'good'. Since his point can only be in hearts, it must be worth at least 49 to your 48 in spades, and there is no point in giving away free information.

Playing to tricks. It is because so many of the opposing cards are known by the time tricks are played that it has been said, in reference to this part of the game, that 'in Piquet, there are no surprises' – which is not quite true, but worth bearing in mind.

As elder you should normally lead your point suit from the top down, unless it is headed by a tenace (A–Q or, more especially, K–J). This will force younger, when no longer able to follow, to start discarding from the bottom of her point, unless she is confident of gaining the lead and winning tricks with the whole of her point. A time when *not* to lead your point, as elder, is when it lacks the top card and there is pique to be made by leading a non-point winner. For example:

♠ K Q J 10 8 ♥ A K Q ♣ A K ♦ K Q

Elder has scored nothing for point (younger having 48 in diamonds), but has made 25 from a quart, a tierce, fourteen Kings, a trio of Queens, and 1 for leading. Leading hearts and clubs, instead of spades, gets him to 30 for tricks and 30 for pique.

As younger, defending against elder's point lead, you must do everything to avoid unguarding suits, even to the extent of throwing out winners from your own point. For instance, suppose you hold:

♠ Q 8 ♥ Q J 9 ♣ K 7 ♦ A K J 10 8

Elder has counted point six and three Aces, and then leads his six spades. You'll have to discard diamonds from the bottom up after clearing your two spades, for if elder's sixth card is a heart or club you may well be capoted. If possible, of course, you should keep your point and throw low cards from other suits if you can do so without losing the guard.

More on 'sinking'. The addition of the rubicon has added much interest and excitement to the strategy of the game by sometimes making it vital to play to the score. If your opponent is well in the lead by the sixth deal, while you are still short of the rubicon, you are faced with a nice problem: whether to go all out to reach it, taking chances and playing boldly if need be, or, instead, to go for as few points as possible, by seeking equalities in combinations and playing to divide the cards. (If you are rubiconed, remember, your opponent adds your own score to theirs, plus 100 for game.)

If elder is trailing at the last deal and feels unable to reach 100, he will do best to sink everything he holds, even if (especially if!) this includes a quint or quatorze – in other words, declare nothing and let younger count whatever she holds as good. There is no point in trying to equalize. As elder, you may be convinced that younger has point five and quint major as well as yourself, but if you declare either of them, younger will simply announce good and let you make the score, since it will ultimately be credited to her own account. In trying to divide the cards, elder must not allow younger to manoeuvre him into taking the majority by 'suicide' play to tricks. Younger does not mind who wins the cards, as long as they are not divided.

If the positions are reversed, younger is somewhat better placed for declaring equalities, since elder has to announce first, and younger can sink as much as may be necessary to equalize. For example, suppose you hold a point consisting of K–Q–J–10–7, worth 47. Elder declares a point of four. You ask its value; he replies 'thirty-nine'. You announce 'equal', sinking nine from your face value, and neither scores. Elder next announces a tierce to the Queen. Again, you equalize. By sinking the King, you also have a tierce to the Queen.

(Some players only allow whole cards to be sunk, thus making it illegal to sink nine from K–Q–J–10–7 since that value does not correspond to a card held. This debatable point, not covered by the Portland Club Laws, should be agreed beforehand.)

While it's easy to see the value of sinking for the purpose of keeping one's score low when certain of being rubiconed, some other advantages are rather less obvious. The author of the following extreme example, 'Cavendish', pointedly adds: 'It is useless to practise this stratagem against an indifferent player who does not count your hand.' In other words, you can't bluff someone who is half asleep. Elder holds:

♠ A K Q J 9 8 7 ♥ K ♣ A K ♦ A K

After equalizing on point (younger having seven hearts), elder could next call fourteen Kings. But this would give his hand away. If younger knows about the singleton ♥K, she will play everything except her red Ace to be sure of taking at least one trick. Elder therefore sinks one King, knowing from his own hand and discards that younger cannot possibly beat it. Younger asks him which King he doesn't count, and elder (of course) replies 'hearts', which younger may believe or not, as she wishes. This puts younger in the unenviable position of choosing whether to throw all her hearts to elder's lead of spades in order to retain a guard in clubs or diamonds, or to hold back ♥A until the last trick in case elder hasn't discarded the King. By sinking, elder drops 11 points (counting 3 instead of 14 for Kings), but has a good chance of making capot – except (as Cavendish says) 'against a very acute or very stupid player'.

See also

http://www.pagat.com/notrump/piquet.html
An excellent description by Noel Leaver, with sample hands and notes on play.

66

sixty-six

- for two players
- complicated, but easy to learn
- nice balance of chance and skill

This snappy little ancestor of the more sedate and elaborate games of Bezique and Pinochle is one of the most delightful and varied two-handers ever devised. It has been popular in Germany for some 200 years, and, under the name Schnapsen, is one of Austria's most extensively played national card games.

The game

Preliminaries. Use a shortened pack of 24 cards ranking and counting as follows:

A	10	K	Q	J	9
11	10	4	3	2	0

Note that Tens count more than Kings, and beat them in trick-play. The point-value cards are called counters.

Deal six each in two batches of three and stack the rest face down. Turn the top card of the stock for trump and slip it half under the pack, face up, for reference.

Object. The overall winner is the first player to win seven game points, each deal being worth one, two or three game points. In each deal the aim is to be the first to claim (correctly) to have reached a cumulative score of 66 card-points. Card-points are reckoned for:

1 Winning counters in tricks, according to the schedule above.
2 Declaring 'marriages' – a marriage being the King and Queen of the same suit and counting 40 in trumps, 20 in each plain suit.
3 Winning the last trick (if the play gets that far without someone claiming 66) counts 10 points.

The significance of 66 is that, disregarding marriages, it is one more than half the total number of points available in play, since 30 for the card-points in each suit, plus 10 for last, makes 130.

Throughout play, you must count and remember the total number of points you have gained so far, as the deal is not necessarily won by the first player to *reach* 66 but by the first to *correctly claim* to have done so. The hefty scores for marriages make it possible for both players to pass this total, hence the importance of announcing it. It is not permitted to keep count in writing or with mechanical scorers.

Play. Non-dealer leads to the first trick, and the winner of each trick leads to the next. Any card may be led, and in the first part of the game any card may be played second – there is no obligation to follow suit or trump. The trick is taken by the higher card of the suit led, or by the higher trump if any are played. The winner of each trick draws the top card of the stock, waits for the other player to draw the next card, then leads to the next trick.

The turn-up. If you hold the Nine of trumps, whether you were dealt it or drew it in course of play, you may exchange it for the trump turn-up provided that:

1 You have just drawn a card from stock.
2 The next trick has not yet been led.
3 The turn-up is still covered by at least two cards.

Note: *Merely winning the lowest trump in a trick does not entitle you to exchange it for the turn-up.*

Marriages. If at any time you hold a King and Queen of the same suit, whether dealt or drawn from stock, you may declare and score for the marriage upon leading to a trick. You do this by showing both cards, announcing 'Forty' if it is in trumps or 'Twenty' otherwise, and leaving one marriage partner on the table as the lead to the trick. Since you may only do this upon leading, it follows that, when you are the dealer, you will have to win a trick before you can declare a marriage.

Phase two. The first half of the game ends when the loser of the sixth trick draws the trump turn-up, which will be the trump Nine if it has been exchanged. (Or when one player calls 66, in which case there is no second half; or when one player fore-closes, in which case see below.)

The last six tricks are played to different rules. The second to a trick must now play:

1 A higher card of the suit led, if possible; otherwise
2 A lower card of the suit led, if possible; otherwise
3 A trump, if possible; otherwise
4 Any losing card.

Note. *In this phase of the game marriages may no longer be declared.*

Winning the last (twelfth) trick counts an extra 10 'for last'.

Quite often, however, the game never gets as far as the last trick, for the following reason.

Shut-out (foreclosure). If, before the stock runs out, you think you can reach 66 from the cards left in hand, you may shut the stock out by turning the trump turn-up face down. (Which does not prevent your opponent from exchanging it for the lowest trump before the next trick is led.) You may do this before or after drawing a sixth card, but, if you do draw a sixth, you must allow your opponent to do so as well. The last tricks are played to the same rules as described above for Phase Two, except that there is no score of '10 for last' (because it applies specifically to the twelfth trick).

Score. The first player to claim correctly to have reached 66 scores 1 game point, or 2 if the other player is *schneidered* ('snipped') by failing to reach 33; or 3 if the other player is *schwarz* ('blackened') by not having won a single trick.

The following conditions also apply:

1 If non-dealer declared a marriage upon leading to the first trick, but failed to win that trick or any other, the marriage is annulled, and the winner scores 3 for schwarz.
2 If one player claims to have reached 66 but is proved wrong, the other scores 2 game points, or 3 if he or she had not yet won a trick.
3 If one player shuts the stock and fails to win, the other scores 2 game points.
4 If both players make 65, or neither claims to have reached 66 by end of play, the game point is held in abeyance and goes to the winner of the next deal.

Schnapsen. The Austrian game of Schnapsen is almost identical, but is played with a 20-card pack omitting the Nines. Five cards are dealt to each player in batches of 2+3 or 3+2, and the trump turn-up may be taken in exchange for the Jack of trumps.

The play

For a game based on so few cards and simple material, Sixty-Six offers extraordinary scope for tactical and strategic skill.

The most important strategic requirement is to decide whether and when to shut the stock and foreclose the game. Between experts, few games are played out to the bitter end. The time to foreclose is when you have a majority of the trumps remaining in play, including the Ace and Ten (unless either has already gone), and can be sure of reaching at least 60 from the winners in your own hand. You can reckon on gaining an average 2–3 card-points from each losing card played by your opponent, but don't expect to capture an Ace or Ten that you've not yet seen in play, as it could well be lying in the undrawn stock.

Before the shut-out, or the last six tricks, an average safe lead is the Nine or Jack of a plain suit, especially if you hold the Ten, as your lead may force the Ace out and leave your Ten high. If, however, you hold the Ace, keep it for as long as the Ten remains unseen, as you may thereby manage to catch it with the Ace in the play of the last six.

Don't lead plain-suit Aces in the first half of the game unless you want them trumped in order to weaken your opponent's trump holding. You might do this, for example, if you know you have three trumps each and want to enter the end-game with a majority of trumps. More often, it can be a good move when you yourself are weak or void in trumps and want to prevent the other player from enjoying a clear run of trumps in the end play. If you find yourself short of trumps and holding such a long suit that it is unlikely your opponent can follow, lead low from that suit as often as possible. Either you will pick up points from castaways thrown to them, or you will force out trumps with little loss to yourself.

Obviously, you will keep single Kings and Queens in the hope of marrying them. But if your opponent plays to a trick the partner of a King or Queen in your own hand, you will know there is no point in keeping it and thus be given a spare discard or good lead.

Sixty-Six calls for much concentration to be played successfully. Always be aware of how many of the six trumps you have, and how many have been played to tricks, so that by the time the last six are played you will know pretty well what the trump division is between you and play accordingly. It is a tremendous advantage to go into the last six with one trump more than your opponent.

Keep track of Aces and Tens, in order to assess your chances of capturing a Ten with an Ace, and how to avoid losing a Ten to an Ace. Keep track of Kings and Queens, so that you will know whether or not it is safe to discard an unwed marriage partner.

Finally, keep count not only of your own point-score to date but also of your opponent's. This takes practice, and you will probably have to start by just concentrating on your own.

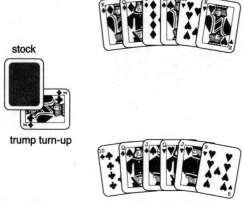

figure 16.1 Sixty-Six

The turned King makes clubs trump. North will start by showing the diamond marriage, announcing 'Twenty to score', and leaving the Queen on the table as the opening lead. North's 20 does not come into effect until he has actually won a trick. South, having nothing to declare and seeing no reason to cash the trump Ten so early in the game, will pass this by throwing a worthless card (Nine) from her longest suit. North then draws from stock and will lead again when South has also drawn.

See also

http://www.pagat.com/marriage/schnaps.html

17

bezique

- for two players
- complicated, but easy to learn
- a fast game of skill

The classic game of Bezique is a more substantial elaboration of Sixty-Six and has been played in many different forms. In the 19th century it was the high-class gambling game of the Parisian clubs and popular in that capacity throughout Europe. And from its German equivalent, Binokel, arose the quintessentially American game of Pinochle in all its own varieties.

The version described below is for two players using two 32-card packs shuffled together. Other versions were invented for various numbers of players and involving greater numbers of cards, but are not now much in evidence – probably because few people nowadays are likely to keep out of circulation eight, six, or so much as four 32-card packs shuffled together for the rare occasions on which they have the time and inclination to embark on such exotic extravaganzas.

The game

Equipment. You need two 32-card packs shuffled together, neither containing any card lower than a Seven. It doesn't matter if they are of different back designs or colours, as long as they are the same size.

Scores are made continually throughout the game, and can be kept on paper, though some sort of mechanical scorer is useful. Patent Bezique markers, of the same design as Whist and Piquet markers, are now antiques, but dial-type scorers are still produced from time to time. Even a Cribbage board will do. All Bezique scores are in tens, so twice round the crib board at 10 per hole gives a maximum of 1210 points, enough to be getting on with.

Rank. In each suit, cards rank: A 10 K Q J 9 8 7. Note the position of the Ten. It counts higher than King both in play and in cutting for the deal.

Deal. Whoever cuts the higher-ranking card may choose whether or not to deal first. Deal eight cards each in batches of three, then two, then three. Turn up the next card – the seventeenth – and lay it to

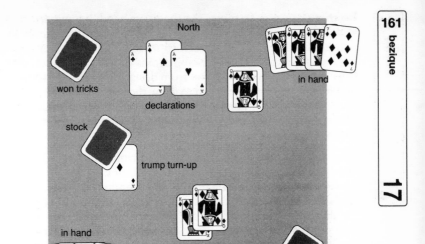

figure 17.2 Bezique

A game in progress. North has evidently scored '100 Aces' earlier on and since
played one to a trick rules of play forbid the same combination to be re-
formed and scored again by the addition of another Ace. Similarly, North's
♠Q on the table is left over from either a marriage for 20 or a bezique for 40
drawing another Queen would enable the addition of three Queens from hand
to that on the table to score 'sixty Queens'. If North has just won a trick, the
♦7 may now be exchanged for the turned Jack, enabling it to be added to the
♠Q for bezique. South, who has scored 20 for a diamond marriage, would
also very much like to get the turned Jack. It could be combined with the
marriage and the Ace–Ten in hand to yield 250 for the trump sequence and
then, on a later trick, the other three Jacks in hand could be added to it for
'forty jacks'

Restrictions on re-forming. On the other hand, having declared a marriage in spades, you may not remarry either partner by adding another King or Queen to it, since you will then have used a single card in two combinations of the same class. (But there is nothing to prevent you from declaring a second marriage in the same suit if you happen to draw the other King and Queen of the same suit.) Similarly, having declared a quartet (four Aces, Kings, Queens or Jacks), you cannot use any of them to form another quartet.

Most importantly, you cannot declare a trump sequence for 250 and subsequently claim the royal marriage it contains. You may, however, score the marriage first and then add the other three cards to score the sequence later. Similarly, you cannot score 500 for double bezique and subsequently count each constituent bezique for 40, but you are allowed to declare first a single bezique, then another single bezique, and finally the double bezique, for a total of 580, provided that you win a trick before making each declaration, and that all the relevant Queens and Jacks remain on the table throughout.

Some maintain that a combination is scorable only if at least one of its cards is played directly from the hand; but this is untrue. For example, it is perfectly proper to declare Kings for 80, Queens for 60 at the next opportunity, and then, as long as the appropriate cards remain on the table, to declare a marriage upon winning each of the next four tricks. Or, suppose Kings have been declared for 80, and two have been played out, leaving ♠K ♥K on the table. At a later turn, you can legally play ♠Q ♦J from the hand and announce 'bezique for 40, and a marriage to score', subsequently counting the spade marriage when you win another trick.

Seven of trumps. If you hold or draw the trump Seven, you may declare it at any time – usually upon winning a trick – and score 10 points for it. Alternatively, you may, upon winning a trick, declare it for 10 and exchange it for the turn-up. This, however, counts as a declaration, and prevents you from declaring any other combination at the same time. (There are conflicting rules about using the trump Seven. This one is a recommended compromise.)

End-game. When the loser of the twenty-fourth trick has taken the turn-up into hand, and no more cards remain in stock, the rules of play change. Both players take up all eight cards into hand and the last trick-winner leads to the first of the last eight tricks. The second to a trick must follow suit if possible and must win the trick if possible, by trumping if unable to follow suit. No combinations may be declared after the last card has been drawn.

The winner of the eighth trick scores '10 for last'.

Score. The game ends at the end of the deal in which one or both players reach the target of 1000 points. Unlike Sixty-Six, Cribbage, and many other games, it does not end in mid-play as soon as the first player reaches the target.

If neither player has reached 1000 after playing the last eight tricks, both players sort through their won cards and count 10 points for each Ace and Ten captured. If this still does not bring either player to 1000, the previous non-dealer deals to the next hand.

The play

When to win tricks. It is generally not worth winning a trick unless it contains a couple of brisque or you have something to declare. Otherwise it is usually best to lose a trick and play second to the next one, as this gives you more latitude. For example, a brisque is a good card to win a trick with if you are playing second, but not a desirable one to lead. On the other hand, situations often arise in which you suspect that your opponent has a valuable declaration to make, in which case you may attempt to keep winning tricks until the stock is exhausted in order to prevent them from being made. Bearing in mind that the same will be done against you, try to keep back trumps, especially high ones, to ensure that you will be able to declare a combination when you get one.

combination	definition	score
Sequence	A K Q J 10 of trumps	250
Royal marriage	K–Q of trumps	40
Common marriage	K–Q of plain suit	20
Hundred Aces	any four Aces	100
Eighty Kings	any four Kings	80
Sixty Queens	any four Queens	60
Forty Jacks	any four Jacks	40
Bezique	♠Q–♦J	40
Double bezique	♠Q–♦J ♠Q–♦J	500

bezique scores

The best cards to throw to worthless tricks, or to lead when you have nothing to declare, are obviously Sevens, Eights and Nines. Often, however, you find yourself with none in your hand, which seems to consist of part-combinations and valuable cards. In this case don't hesitate to treat Jacks as dispensable (other than the bezique Jack), as forty Jacks is not a very high scoring combination and not worth spoiling the hand for. Keep hold of a diamond Jack, however, as long as there is the possibility of making bezique. Also be prepared to play a Ten if it wins the trick, as Tens cannot form part of scoring combinations except in trumps, and are therefore not worth keeping from this point of view.

Making combinations. When it comes to breaking up part-combinations you must weigh the value of each against the probability of making it. Here you will be guided by what you can see among your opponent's declarations and what has already been played to tricks. For example, if they have declared a marriage in spades and you hold both Jacks of diamonds, it is impossible to make double bezique, and so one more Jack becomes available for discarding – unless, of course, you have seen so few of the eight Jacks to date that there seems a fair chance of forming a Jack quartet.

Cards still lying on the table after being declared are suitable candidates for playing to tricks, on the principle that you give your opponent less information about the state of your hand by playing a card they know you have rather than one they haven't seen. Marriage partners and quartetted Jacks are particularly good candidates for this purpose. At the same time, however, it is important to retain those which stand a fair chance of being re-used in other combinations, and those which belong to the trump suit and may therefore be needed for trick-winning. In particular, never break up (by playing a card from) a single bezique as long as the possibility remains of forming a second and scoring the double, as double bezique is the most valuable combination in the pack and will nearly always win the game.

Scoring double combinations. Given a choice of combinations, it is naturally better to score the more valuable ones first. But note the following profitable exception to this rule. Given a sequence, you may score 40 for the royal marriage first, and then, after winning another trick, complete the sequence for 250, making 290 in all. If, however, you put all five cards down at once and count 250 for the sequence, you cannot subsequently score its constituent marriage separately.

The same applies to beziques. You may declare, on three successive turns, a single, a single and a double, for a total of 580, but you cannot score for a single after counting the double. In these cases you score more for starting with the lower combination and working upwards. If, however, it seems unlikely that you will have time to make these scores the long way, in view of the number of tricks left to play and the state of your own hand, it may be better to score the higher combination first and be prepared to skip the lower.

The last eight. In the last eight tricks, the ideal is to lead into your opponent's void suit in order to weaken their trumps. Experienced players will know what cards their opponent holds and play accordingly. Experience, in fact, is essential to success at Bezique, as it is a game of judgement rather than analysis. The practised player soon develops an instinctive feel for the state of their opponent's hand, and will know when they can safely lose tricks and when they must keep winning in order to prevent a high combination to be scored against them.

Pinochle for two

Two-handed Pinochle is virtually identical, but is played with a double 24-card pack made by suppressing the Sevens and Eights used in Bezique. Some of the terminology is different, and it is (of course) the trump Nine that can be exchanged for the turn-up.

See also

Bezique is not well represented on the Internet. For variants and further details see:

Parlett, D. (2000) *The Penguin Encyclopedia of Card Games*, Penguin Books

Parlett, D. (2004) *The Oxford A–Z of Card Games*, Oxford University Press

18

klaberjass

- for two players
- tricky to learn
- a game of great skill

This classic two-hander originated in the Low Countries
towards the end of the 18th century and is now played played
throughout the western world, especially but not solely in urban
Jewish communities. It is a truly international game, and Mike
Block's description of it on the Pagat website includes this
eminently quotable paragraph:

> *The game of Bela – also more widely known as
> Clobyosh – is played by an unusual collection of
> people. I learnt it as Clobyosh in my childhood,
> thinking of it then as a peculiarly Jewish game. But I
> was amazed to discover it being played – nearly
> fifteen years ago – in a pub in Central Scotland (The
> Quarry Inn in Twechar to be precise). I subsequently
> found out that Bela (as it is called in that part of the
> world) is well known in mining communities in
> Scotland and also in the prisons (there is a unique
> four-handed variation called 'Barlinnie Rules'!).*

The name Jass (pronounced Yass) denotes a whole family of
games in which the highest trump is the Jack of its suit, counting
20 card-points, and the second highest its Nine, counting 14. If
you haven't played a card-point game before, such as Sixty-Six,
Pinochle or Skat, you may find Klaberjass a bit daunting at first
sight, but it well repays the effort of learning.

The game

Cards. Thirty-two, consisting of A K Q J 10 9 8 7 in each suit.

Deal. Whoever cuts the lower card deals first, and the deal then
alternates. Deal six cards each in two batches of three. Place the
remainder face down to form a stock. Turn the top card face up
and place it beside the stock. The suit of this card is the preferred
suit for trumps, unless and until both players reject it.

Object. After the bidding each player will receive three more cards and play nine tricks. Whoever accepts or nominates the trump suit (the 'maker') thereby undertakes to win the greater number of points for tricks and melds. Trick-points are scored by capturing certain counting-cards, as shown below. A meld is a sequence of three of more cards in the same suit, or the King and Queen of trumps, known as *bela*.

Rank and value of cards. In non-trump suits cards rank A 10 K Q J 9 8 7. Note the high position of the Ten. In trumps, the highest card is the Jack, called *Jass* (with J pronounced Y); second-highest is the Nine, called *Menel* (accent on the second syllable); and these are followed downwards by Ace, Ten, King, Queen, Nine, Eight, Seven. Certain cards have point-values, credited to the player winning them in tricks, as follows:

Jass (trump Jack)	20
Menel (trump Nine)	14
Ace	11 each
Ten	10 each
King	4 each
Queen	3 each
Jack	2 each (except in trumps)
Nine	0 each (except in trumps)
Eight, Seven	0 each
Total	152 + '10 for last' = 162

The rank and value of cards and melds are described first because you can only bid on your assessment of winning more points than your opponent. Note that the total value of all the counters in the pack is 152 (though they may not all be in play), and that an extra 10 points go to the winner of the last trick, bringing the trick-points to 162.

Melds. A sequence of three cards in the same suit counts 20, a sequence of four or more counts 50. For this purpose the sequential order of cards is A K Q J 10 9 8 7 in every suit including trumps. (Thus Q–J–10 is a sequence of three even though the ranks are not adjacent in trick-taking power.)

A player holding both the King and Queen of trumps scores 20 for 'bela'. Melds are not counted until both players have nine cards, and only the player with the best sequence may score for sequences.

Scoring features at Klaberjass	
Jass (trump Jack)	20
Menel (trump Nine)	14
Ace	11 each
Ten	10 each
King	4 each
Queen	3 each
Jack	2 each (except in trumps)
Nine	0 each (except in trumps)
Eight, Seven	0 each
Suit-sequence of 4+	50 order is A K Q J 10 9 8 7
Suit-sequence of 3	20 order is A K Q J 10 9 8 7
Bela	20 K–Q of trumps
Last trick	10

Bidding. In this game, as in many others, the non-dealer is known as Elder (or elder hand), and bids first and leads to the first trick. Dealer is known as Younger.

Elder has the first choice of accepting the turned suit as trump, thereby becoming the 'maker', and undertaking to win more points for tricks and melds than his opponent. If he passes, younger may either accept the preferred suit or turn it down (literally).

If both turn it down, elder may nominate another suit as trump, thereby becoming the maker, or pass this opportunity to younger.

If both pass again, the hands are abandoned and elder becomes younger by making a new deal.

Play. When a player becomes the maker, younger deals another batch of three cards to each player from the top of the stock, so that each has nine, then takes the bottom card of the stock and places it face up on top. This card is for information only and has no part in the play. (Its only function is to ensure that neither has had the unfair advantage of being the only one to know what the bottom card is in case it was observed during the deal.)

Dix. Pronounced *deece*, this denotes the Seven of trumps if the preferred trump was accepted. If either player has this card they may exchange it for the turned trump card at any time before the first trick is led. If the preferred suit was turned down, there is no *dix*, and the Seven of the nominated suit cannot be so exchanged.

Scoring for melds. Upon leading to the first trick, elder announces 'Fifty' if he holds a run of four or more cards or 'Twenty' if a run of three. If younger doesn't contest the announcement, elder scores for any and all sequences that he shows (though the scores will be annulled if he fails to win a trick). He is not obliged to declare any or all such sequences, but can only score for what he does show.

Upon playing to elder's lead, younger makes any of the following announcements, depending on whether or not elder made any claim:

If elder made a claim that younger cannot match or beat, she acknowledges the claim as good, and elder shows and scores whatever he can and wishes.

If elder made no claim, or claimed only 'Twenty' when younger holds a Fifty, younger may show and score for any or all sequences she can and wishes.

If elder made a claim that younger can equal, whether Twenty or Fifty, elder must declare as much detail of his claim as may be necessary to determine which of them has the better claim. For this purpose, the best sequence is:

- the longest; or, if younger can match the length quoted by elder
- the one with the highest top card; or, if younger can match the top card quoted by elder
- the one in the trump suit; or, if neither is in trumps
- that of elder hand.

Note. *You can exchange the dix for the turn-up either before or after declaring your melds, depending on which of them you want for a possible sequence. What you cannot do is to score a sequence with the dix, make the exchange, and then score another one with the turn-up. In short, you can't have two bites of the cherry. (Or have your cake and eat it.)*

Tricks. Elder leads to the first trick and the winner of each trick leads to the next. You must follow suit if you can. Furthermore:

- If you can follow suit to a trump lead, you must beat it if you can.
- If you can't follow suit to the card led, you must trump it if you can.

The trick is taken by the highest card of the suit led, or by the highest trump if any are played.

Bela. If you hold both King and Queen of trumps you may count 20 by announcing 'bela' upon playing the second of them to a trick.

Last trick. Whoever wins the last trick counts 10 for it.

Score. Each player, starting with the declarer's opponent, announces the total they have counted for cards, melds, bela and the last trick (as appropriate). If either player failed to win any trick, any melds they claimed are invalid, and they count nothing.

If the maker counts more than their opponent, each of them scores towards game exactly the amount they have made.

If not, the maker scores nothing, and the opponent scores towards game the combined total made by both players in that deal, unless they tied, in which case they score just the tied figure.

Game. The game ends when either player, at the end of a deal, has reached or exceeded a previously agreed total, usually 500.

The play

Nearly all points are scored for cards won in tricks plus 10 for last. A whole game may pass without the appearance of a bela or of more than two or three small sequences, so it's hardly worth taking them into account in the bidding unless you are dealt one to start with.

Although the theoretical maximum number of trick-points is 162, it's impossible for all 20 counters to be in play in one deal. In practice, the average number of points in play per deal lies between 100 and 120, of which the maker, if successful, should expect to score 80–90 against the loser's 20–30. If the game were played with a compulsory trump and no opportunity to pass, each player would expect to take an average of 50–60 points per deal. Since you are called upon to bid on only two-thirds of your final hand, you ought to hold 30–40 points in high prospective trumps and supporting Ace–Tens before accepting the preferred suit or choosing another.

Scoring features at Klaberjass	
Jass (trump Jack)	20
Menel (trump Nine)	14
Ace	11 each
Ten	10 each
King	4 each
Queen	3 each
Jack	2 each (except in trumps)
Nine	0 each (except in trumps)
Eight, Seven	0 each
Suit-sequence of 4+	50 order is A K Q J 10 9 8 7
Suit-sequence of 3	20 order is A K Q J 10 9 8 7
Bela	20 K–Q of trumps
Last trick	10

It is possible to bid successfully on a hand containing as little as a singleton Jass and two Aces or an Ace–Ten. But this doesn't mean that all hands are playable. The more expert players become, the more hands they tend to throw in. It doesn't take more than a few rounds of the game to discover how easily some weak-looking hands win while others, apparently quite promising, fall at the first fence. It's easy enough to recognize a strong hand when you see one, but it takes practice to know whether or not to pass or play on something less clear cut. Beginners, I think, should play boldly. You will learn much more from bidding and losing than from passing and never knowing.

In assessing the hand look first for the *dix* (Seven) of the turned card (unless the turn-up is an Eight, which isn't worth having, except for a possible sequence). In any prospective trump suit it is imperative to hold either the Jack or an accompanied Nine, preferably with an Ace or Ten for company. Don't play a trump suit containing the Ace or Ace–Ten as highest cards, unless they are accompanied by at least two others of the suit, as there is too great a chance of losing one or more big ones to Jass or Menel in your opponent's hand. Nor be tempted into entrumping a suit just because you have been dealt the King and Queen of it, worth 20 for the bela. If you have a mediocre hand including bela, or a sequence in any suit, the extra value may be just enough to make up either for weaknesses in the hand, or a stout opposition. But never bank on being dealt the marriage partner to a King or Queen already in hand, or a specific card required for a sequence. The odds are more than 7 to 1 against.

A two-card prospective trump including Jass or Menel is sufficient if adequately supported in plain suits, as the odds favour the appearance of a third trump in the last part of the deal.

In non-trumps the best holding is an unaccompanied Ace or Ace–Ten, and there is even a goodish chance (4 to 3 in favour) of winning a trick with an Ace-less Ten provided that the suit is not held so long as to risk being trumped. A long plain suit, say four or more, is not good for tricks unless it contains low cards which can be used to weaken the opposing trumps – bearing in mind the obligation to trump a suit in which one is void. A void suit in the prospective bidder's hand is a mixed blessing for the same reason. It must, for safety, be accompanied by long trumps, otherwise it will be used to weaken the trump holding.

Younger hand may always bid with greater boldness than elder, since elder's pass suggests some weakness.

If you have the lead as maker, your normal strategy on a reasonable hand will be to draw trumps first, partly to test the situation and partly to clear the way for Aces and Tens in plain suits. With a short trump suit, or one headed by a Ten–Ace (Jack–Ace or Nine–Ten) it is preferable to lead a short plain suit with solid top cards. If you feel that your opponent might hold too many trumps, force them out by leading worthless cards from a long plain suit.

When leading trumps, it is worth starting with the Jack if there is a chance of seizing the Ace or Ten thereby, but (of course) it is dangerous to lead the Nine, Ace or Ten if you lack anything higher. Much of the interest of the game derives from the peculiar positions – third and fourth highest – of the high-scoring Ace and Ten of trumps. With an average holding of two cards in each suit, it is desirable to win with Aces and Tens as soon as the opportunity arises. If (say) an Eight is led into your Ace–King, it is best to bring the Ace home while you safely can, rather than hold it back with a view to catching the Ten.

Example of play

Benny deals to Annie and himself the hands shown below and turns the ♥A for the preferred trump:

Annie ♠ K ♥ 9 7 ♣ 10 J ♦ A
Benny ♠ 7 ♥ 10 J 8 ♣ Q 7

As elder, Annie holds the Menel of the turned suit and can swap the dix for the Ace. Her hand is worth 38 in card-points (assuming hearts trump), and she accepts the turned suit. After three more cards are dealt, and ♠8 turned for information, the hands are:

Annie   ♠ A K ♥ 9 A ♣ A 10 J ♦ A 9
Benny   ♠ 7 ♥ J 10 8 ♣ K Q 8 7 ♦ 10

Neither player has improved their trump holding, and it is interesting to note that Benny was dealt three trumps including the Jass. With a short trump suit headed only by the second highest, Annie leads clubs in the hope of retrieving her Ace and Ten before drawing trumps. She takes 21 points on the first two tricks, but then loses her Jack to Benny's King (worth a point more than taking it with the Queen). Given the initiative, Benny now aims to make the most of his relatively long trumps. He starts aggressively with the Jass, drawing ♥A for 31 points and the certain knowledge that Annie has only the Menel in hand, which he next forces out by leading ♥8. Now lacking trumps, Annie plays her Aces, gaining 32 card-points in the process, and continues with ♦9. This Benny trumps with his Ten, and concludes with ♣Q, drawing ♠K plus 10 for last. Annie has just made her contract, taking 67 to Benny's 64. Benny was lucky to hold not only more trumps than his opponent, but also more cards in the same long suit.

Variations

Here are some of the variations and additional rules followed in different countries and localities.

- Schmeiss (rhymes with mice). Instead of turning it down or passing, elder hand may bid *schmeiss*. This is an offer either to accept the turned suit and become the maker, or to annul the deal, as younger chooses. If elder passes instead of accepting the trump or passing, younger also has the option of declaring *schmeiss*. In effect, it is a way of preventing the other player from choosing a different trump.
- In making trumps, first preference is always on clubs and second on the turned suit, if different. This variant increases demands on good judgement and is in keeping with the name of the game – which, as we have seen, means 'Jack of clubs'.
- If both players reject the turned suit, either of them may bid no trump (*sans atout*), which takes precedence over a bid in

suit and may be used to overcall it. In this case there is no Jass or Menel, cards rank A 10 K Q J 9 8 7 in every suit, and each player's final score for the deal is doubled. This makes it attractive to bid no trump on a safe hand, but expensive to fail on a bad one. If one player bids no trump, the other can overcall by bidding 'grand' (*tout atout*). In this case there is a Jass and Menel in every suit – in other words, cards rank J 9 A 10 K Q 8 7 in each suit, and all Jacks are worth 20 and all Nines 14. Otherwise it is played as no trump, and also scores double. Grand may only be bid to overcall a previous bid of no trump.

- If both tie for best sequence, the result is a stand-off. Elder's does not have priority.
- A sequence of five or more may be valued at 100 points instead of 50.
- In Belote, the French game, additional melds may be scored. Sequences of three count 20, of four 50, and of five or more 100. Also, whoever has the best four of a kind (a *carré* or quartet) may score for any and all quartets they may show, valued thus: four Jacks 200, Nines 150, Aces, Tens, Kings or Queens 100, lower ranks not valid. Game is usually at least 1000 points.
- If, during the course of play, you think you have reached the target score by counting melds or card-points so far captured in tricks, you may claim 'out' and end the game immediately – provided that you have already won at least one trick (Belote rule). If you are mistaken, you lose the game; otherwise you win, even if your opponent has a higher total.

See also

http://www.pagat.com/jass/klabberjass.html
Description of three- and four-player Klabberjass (with two Bs) by Günter Senst.

http://www.pagat.com/jass/bela.html
Description by Mike Block of the game as played in Scotland under the (Hungarian) name Bela.

19

skat

- for three players (or four at a table)
- not easy to learn, but worth it
- a game of great skill

> **The name of the game**
>
> Skat derives from the Italian word scarto, meaning the discard. In the earliest known form of the German game the player in prior position was dealt 12 cards to the other players' ten each, made two discards (constituting the 'skat'), and then announced a contract.

The popularity of Germany's national card game is not restricted to Germany, for there are a dozen or so countries affiliated to the International Skat Players Association and a world tournament is held every year. The number of British players has been increasing since Skat was introduced as a tournament event in the first Mind Sports Olympiad held in London in 1997, and tournaments are now organized from time to time by the British Skat Association founded at Oxford in 2001.

Skat is, admittedly, hard to get into without prior experience of card-point games; but it remains one of the deepest, most varied and most exciting games ever devised, and well repays the effort of mastering its intricate scoring system. A good approach, if you don't already play card-point games of this type, is through the two-handed game of Sixty-Six. Also helpful is some experience of Jacks as trumps, as in Euchre and Five Hundred. The following description incorporates rule changes representing an amalgamation of those of the ISPA and the Deutscher Skatverband, effective from 1999, in which year the DSkV celebrated its centenary.

Note. *Most English-language descriptions of Skat are of the American game, which differs substantially from the German and international game described here.*

The game

Players. There are three active players, but usually four at a table, with each player in turn sitting out the hand to which they deal. The turn to deal and play passes to the left. The player at Dealer's left, who will lead to the first trick, is called Forehand; the next one round is Middlehand; and the last (Dealer themself if only three play) is Rearhand.

Cards. Thirty-two, omitting numerals Two through Six.

Rank and value of cards. Cards rank and count as follows, from highest to lowest:

In trumps	♣J	♠J	♥J	♦J	A	10	K	Q	9	8	7
Card-points	2	2	2	2	11	10	4	3	0	0	0
Non-trumps					A	10	K	Q	9	8	7

When there is a trump suit, it consists of 11 cards, of which the four Jacks are always the four highest in the order shown (clubs, spades, hearts, diamonds) (see Figure 19.1). The Ace and Ten, therefore, though worth most points, are only the fifth and sixth highest of the 11 trumps.

Each non-trump suit contains seven cards, headed by its Ace, but lacking a Jack, as this is automatically co-opted to serve duty as a trump.

The total number of card-points is 120, there being 30 in each suit.

Object. In each deal there is an auction to decide who will play a solo contract against the other two players. The basic contracts are of three trump types:

- **Suit.** Cards rank and count as shown above, and the soloist's aim is (usually) to capture at least 61 card-points in tricks.
- **Grand.** Same object, but the four Jacks are the only trumps, forming a fifth suit of their own. The other four are non-trump suits, containing seven each.
- **Null.** The soloist's aim is to lose every single trick. There are no trumps or card-points, and in each suit the cards rank in their 'natural' order A K Q J 10 9 8 7.

Each of these games may be played either with or without seeking to improve the hand by taking the skat.

- **With the skat.** The soloist takes the skat, adds it to their hand, makes any two discards face down in its place, and then announces grand, suit or null before play begins. This enables them to improve the shape of their hand and to delay choosing a contract until they have seen all 12 cards.
- **From the hand.** The soloist leaves the skat untouched and announces grand, suit or null immediately. Not surprisingly, this carries a higher potential score.

In either case, any card-points contained in the skat will count to the soloist at end of play as if they had won them in tricks (except at null, where they are irrelevant).

The winner is the player with the highest cumulative score at the end of a previously agreed number of deals. There may be any number of deals, as long as everyone deals the same number of times. In tournament conditions, a game is 48 deals with four at a table or 36 with three.

Deal. Deal ten cards each in batches of 3–(2)–4–3, with two face down to the table after the first round of three. These two form the skat, which eventually goes to the highest bidder.

Contracts and game values. Bidding is done by game valuation – that is, the soloist is the player offering to undertake the *highest-scoring contract*. This is not the same thing as offering to win most tricks or take most card-points. Players must therefore calculate the scoring value of their proposed game before entering the auction. This is complicated by the fact that most game values are not fixed but are affected by a number of factors.

figure 19.1 Skat

the top four trumps on German cards (B = Bube = Jack)

Null contracts have fixed game values as follows: null with skat 23, from the hand 35, ouvert with skat 46, ouvert from the hand 59. 'Ouvert' means that the soloist spreads their hand of cards face up on the table before play begins.

All other game values are found by taking the base value of the proposed trump contract, namely:

diamonds 9, hearts 10, spades 11, clubs 12, grand 24

and *multiplying* this by a number of playing factors as follows:

- Consecutive top trumps ('tops') held or not held (as explained below). *Plus*
- 1 for 'game'. *Plus*
- 1 for *schneider* (if you think you can take at least 90 card-points in tricks). *Plus*
- 1 for *schwarz* (if you think you can win all ten tricks).

The following additional multipliers may be applied if, and only if, you intend to play without skat exchange:

- 1 for 'hand'
- 1 for announcing that you will *schneider* your opponents (take 90+ card-points)
- 1 for announcing that you will make them *schwarz* (by winning every trick)
- 1 for playing *ouvert* – that is, that you will win every trick even though playing with your hand of cards exposed on the table before the opening lead.

Tops (consecutive top trumps, sometimes called matadors) are explained as follows:

If you hold ♣J, then you are playing 'with' as many tops as you hold. For example, holding ♣J but not ♥J, you are 'with one'. Holding ♣J–♠J but not ♥J you are 'with two'. Holding all four Jacks and the trump Ace but not the Ten, you are 'with five', and so on.

If you don't hold ♣J, then you are 'without' (or 'against') as many top consecutive trumps as you lack – in other words, as many as outrank the highest trump you do hold. Thus, if your highest trump is ♥J, you are 'without two' (lacking ♣J–♠J). If your highest trump is the Ten, you are 'without five', and so on.

Note the following consequences:

- *In a suit contract, the most you can be with or without is 11, as the two cards of the skat belong to the soloist.*
- *In a grand contract, the most you can be with or without is four, as only Jacks are trumps.*
- *The fact that the skat belongs to the soloist means that, if you play from the hand, any Jacks found in the skat at end of play may change the number of tops you thought you held, and so increase or decrease the value of your game.*

To summarize, here is a table showing how the various trump game values are reached:

Base value: ♦ = 9, ♥ = 10, ♠ = 11, ♣ = 12, grand = 24 multiplied by	
if with the skat:	**if from the hand:**
'tops', plus 1 for game	'tops', plus 1 for game 1 for hand
1 for schneider	1 for schneider 1 for schneider announced
1 for schwarz	1 for schwarz 1 for schwarz announced 1 for ouvert, schwarz announced

The lowest possible contract is 18. (Diamonds, with or without 1 top trump, game 2, times 9 for diamonds = 18.)

The highest possible suit contract is 216. (Clubs, with 11, game 12, hand 13, schneider 14, schneider announced 15, schwarz 16, schwarz announced 17, open 18, times clubs 12).

The highest possible game is 264. (Grand with 4, game 5, hand 6, schneider 7, schneider announced 8, schwarz 9, schwarz announced 10, open 11, times grand 24).

The table on page 196 shows all possible game values (and therefore all possible legal bids) up to and including 100.

Examples of game valuation

♣ J ♠ J ♦ 10 K 8 7 ♣ A K ♠ K ♥ Q

The obvious contract is diamonds for a bid up to 27 (with 2, game 3, times diamonds 9). It can't be played from the hand because the skat is needed to protect or get rid of the two singletons, on which the opponents could make 49 in two tricks and require only the trump Ace to win. If the hand is played and takes in 90 or more card-points, it will gain an extra multiplier for schneider and so score 36. On these cards Forehand, having the lead, might bid up to 72 with a view to playing grand (3 × 24).

♥ J ♦ J ♣ A 10 Q 8 ♠ A K 9 ♥ 7

A safe 'Clubs, hand' worth 48 (without 2, game 3, hand 4, times clubs 12). If the Jacks were black instead of red, it would be a 'Grand, hand' worth 96 (with 2, game 3, hand 4, times grand 24).

♠ J ♥ J ♦ J ♥ A 10 9 ♠ A 7 ♣ 10 ♦ 7

	♦	♥	♠	♣	grand	null
18	2					
20		2				
22			2			
23						with skat
24				2		
27	3					
30		3				
33			3			
35						from hand
36	4			3		
40		4				
44			4			
45	5					
46					2	ouvert
48				4		
50		5				
54	6					
55			5			
59						ouvert, hand
60		6		5		
63	7					
66			6			
70		7				
72	8			6	3	
77			7			
80		8				
81	9					
84				7		
88			8			
90	10	9				
96				8	4	
99	11		9			
100		10				

Hearts for 20 (without 1, game 2, times hearts 10). If pushed, you might go to 30 in hope of taking the skat and either making schneider (without 1, game 2, schneider 3 × 10 = 30) or, with a good draw, playing grand (without 1, game 2 × 24 = 48). Despite the long suit, 'Hearts, hand' fails because of the two singletons and lack of the top Jack.

♦ J ♠ A 10 Q 9 8 7 ♦ A K 7

'Spades, hand' for 55 (without 3, game 4, hand 5 times spades 11). If forced, you might bid up to 66 in hope of making schneider. With schneider announced (risky), it would be 77. But a black Jack in the skat could reduce the game value to 33 (with or without 1, game 2, hand 3).

♣ K 10 8 7 ♠ 8 ♥ A J 9 7 ♦ Q

A probable null for 23 – note that Jacks and Tens rank in their so-called natural order. If pushed by the bidding, you would reject null from the hand for 35 because of the singleton Queen, but might risk taking the skat, burying the Queen and playing open for 46.

The auction. Bids are made only by stating genuine game valuations, and without any further details, for example, '18', '20', etc.

Theoretically, Forehand has a prior right to announce a contract. The purpose of the auction is to see if either of the others wishes to take it off Forehand by making successively higher bids. Middlehand starts by either passing or making a bid. If they pass, Rearhand does likewise. If they also pass, Forehand wins the auction and becomes the soloist – unless they also pass, when the hands are thrown in and the deal passes round to the next dealer.

Assuming Middlehand does not pass, they bid by stating successively higher game values, such as '18, 20, 22, 23 . . .', and so on. They may go up value by value, or in irregular jumps, or may jump immediately to their maximum bid, as long as every figure they quote is a genuine game value (see table).

To each of these Forehand replies 'Yes' if they are willing to play a contract worth at least that amount, or 'Pass' if not. This continues until one of them passes – either Forehand because they cannot accept the value proposed by Middlehand, or Middlehand because their last bid was accepted by Forehand and they will not go higher. Rearhand may then continue the auction by bidding the next higher game value against the survivor, or may pass.

This continues as before, until one of them passes. The survivor becomes the soloist, and is obliged to play a contract worth not less than the amount of the last bid.

Declaring the contract. If playing from the hand, the soloist immediately announces the trump suit, or grand or null if applicable, and adding, in this order, whichever of the following may apply: hand, schneider announced, schwarz announced, open. If playing open, they simultaneously spread their hand face up on the table.

If not playing from the hand, the soloist picks up the skat, adds it to their hand without showing it, makes any two discards in its place, and then announces the trump suit, or grand, null, or null open as appropriate. No other announcement is required or permitted.

Conceding. The soloist may throw their hand in before playing to the first trick. This usually happens when they take the skat and find it useless. They must, however, name a contract, however unsuited to their hand, in order to determine what game value is to be deducted from their score.

Play. Forehand always leads to the first trick. Suit must be followed if possible, otherwise any card may be played. The trick is taken by the highest card of the suit led, or by the highest trump if any are played. The winner of each trick leads to the next. The two partners pile all their won cards together in a single heap: there is no need to separate them into tricks.

Note. *It is important to remember that Jacks belong to the trump suit and not necessarily to the suits depicted on them.*

- At grand, the lead of a Jack calls for Jacks to be played if possible, and the highest Jack wins the trick. If a plain suit is led, a player unable to follow may trump by playing a Jack if able and willing.
- In a suit game, the lead of any trump calls for the play of any other trump, regardless of whether or not either is a Jack.
- At null, there are no trumps, and cards rank A–K–Q–J–10–9–8–7 in every suit.

All ten tricks must be played, unless the soloist concedes before playing to the first trick, or takes a trick in a null contract.

Score. At end of play, the skat is turned up (except at null) and counted as part of the soloist's won tricks.

Base value: ♦ = 9, ♥ = 10, ♠ = 11, ♣ = 12, grand = 24 multiplied by	
if with the skat:	**if from the hand:**
'tops', plus	'tops', plus
1 for game	1 for game
	1 for hand
1 for schneider	1 for schneider
	1 for schneider announced
1 for schwarz	1 for schwarz
	1 for schwarz announced
	1 for ouvert, schwarz announced

To fulfil their contract, the soloist must have taken at least 61 card-points in tricks, or 90 if they announced schneider, or ten tricks if they announced schwarz, or no trick if they bid null. If so, the game value of their contract is recalculated in retrospect by the base value of the trump times the number of applicable game factors, including those for schneider and schwarz if made but not announced. If this game value is not less than the amount they bid, they score it in full. If less, they lose.

If the soloist fails to make their contract, they take the full game value as recalculated above, and loses it doubled. If they announced schneider and failed to make it, their (lost) game value is increased by one multiplier for the failed schneider as well as for the declaration. The same applies to schwarz announced. However, if they themself is schneidered (taking in fewer than 31 card-points), there is no additional penalty: their (lost) game value is not increased by an extra multiplier.

If the game value of the contract played is less than their bid, it must be increased by as many more multipliers as are necessary to make it equal or exceed their bid. For example, if they bid up to 45 but found their spade game contract worth only 33, the latter must be increased to 55. Any lost game is lost doubled after being calculated in full. (Prior to the 1999 revision, games played from the hand were lost singly under the rules of the Deutscher Skatverband.) The doubling is not taken into account as a way of bringing their game value up to the level of the amount bid.

If the soloist takes the skat and concedes without play, they must nevertheless announce a contract in order to calculate the amount of their penalty score, which is calculated in the normal way as if they had played it, and then doubled.

The play

Pick out any Jacks and put them together in high–low order. Sort the other cards by suit and place your likeliest trump suit next to the Jacks in the same high–low order.

If you haven't any Jacks, you are unlikely to have a game on unless you have one of the following three types of hand:

♣ A K Q 9 8 7 ♥ A K Q ♦ A

With six or more trumps and safety in side suits you can try for a game 'without four', or even five, in the long suit. With a fair break, the opposition should not make more than about 40 on this example of 'without four, game five, hand six, times clubs 12 = 72'. But change the diamond Ace to a lower diamond or spade, and you will need a favourable skat to make the game safe.

♣ A 10 7 ♠ A 10 7 ♥ A K 7 ♦ A

This could be a 'grand hand without four', worth 144, if you are prepared to chance a balanced distribution of Jacks and suits in the partners' hands. One or more Jacks could be in the skat.

♣ A 10 9 7 ♠ 10 8 7 ♥ 9 7 ♦ 8

Given the lead (the low diamond), this is a pretty safe 'null ouvert, hand' for 59. Even without the lead the opponents would need a freakish distribution and clever play to beat it.

If you are holding one or more Jacks, consider whether your hand looks best for a suit bid, grand, null, or no bid. Most hands are either a suit bid or nothing; relatively few are right for grand or null. As a very rough guide:

- If about half your cards are Nines, Kings and Queens, pass.
- If about half your cards consist of Jacks and a good suit, consider a game in that suit. With six or more trumps and a void suit, consider playing it from the hand. With both black Jacks and a long suit headed Ace–Ten, consider grand.
- If about half are Jacks and Aces, especially Ace–Tens, consider grand.
- If about half are Sevens, Eights and Nines, and you have no more than one Ace, King or Queen, consider null. Null bids have fixed game values. If you can lose every trick with the hand as dealt, you can bid up to 35, or 59 if you can play it ouvert.
- If you need to take the skat in order to get rid of a dangerous card, you can play five trumps including Ace or Ten, at least two side suits which are either void or headed by an Ace, and not more than five losing cards.

Suit bids

For a safe game in suit the normal requirement is at least five trumps including Ace or Ten, at least two side suits which are either void or headed by an Ace, and not more than five losing cards. If dealt such a hand, you can reckon on playing it from the hand – for example:

♣ J ♥ J ♣ A K 9 ♥ A 10 8 ♦ Q 9

This is a game at clubs, hand. The opposition will probably make up to 20 in clubs and 28 in diamonds, giving you a safety margin of 12 card-points to compensate for an Ace or Ten dropped on the other's winning trump. As Forehand, having the opening lead, you could play 'grand, hand'.

Given a void suit, look first for a hand game rather than reaching directly for the skat, as the latter all too often produces nothing but two useless cards of your void suit – and in this game 'useless' means King–Queen rather than anything lower, as the latter can be discarded to worthless tricks without giving anything away. Playing from hand also entitles you to announce schneider in advance. To do this, you must be sure of winning preferably nine tricks, possibly eight. It is the equivalent of a small slam at Bridge. The normal requirement for a hand game is six trumps, or five including the black Jacks, a void suit, and a suit headed Ace–Ten, or at least Ace alone.

The time to think of a skat game is when you need the draw and discard in order to produce the sort of hand on which you would have bid 'hand' if originally dealt it. For example:

♣ J ♥ J ♣ A K 9 ♠ K ♥ A 10 8 ♦ Q

In a hand game, the opposition could make 49 straight off in spades and diamonds, and finish you off with the trump Ten. Here, you need the skat to enable you to ditch the two dangerous singletons, or one of them if the skat offers support to the other.

Two points to watch in bidding suit games are Jacks and non-trump Tens.

The risk a Ten runs is being caught by the Ace, giving the opposition, in a single trick, one third of the points needed to beat you. A Ten in hand is obviously safest when covered by the Ace, and most dangerous when held singleton. With a singleton Ten, therefore, you should only consider playing from hand if you can be sure of winning most of the other tricks. It is not unknown for the soloist, playing third to the first trick, to win it with a singleton Ten; but you wouldn't want to bank on it. A Ten once guarded (e.g. 10–9) is a natural risk. On a low lead from your right, you may play the Ten and find it captured by the Ace on your left; or you throw the Nine, and then lose the Ten to the Ace on a subsequent trick. A Ten twice guarded (e. g. 10–Q–7) is safer, as the suits rarely go three times round and you can hold up the Ten until you have drawn trumps.

Note: *If you are dealt one suit consisting of the Ten and a low card, and take the skat, it is often right to keep the guarded Ten. With two such suits, however, it is usually best to bury both Tens in the skat in order to secure 20 towards your 61 card-points.*

The point to watch about Jacks is the danger of bidding 'without' too many of them. Suppose you have only the diamond Jack and take the game at 36, bidding on the basis of 'without 3, game 4, times spades' = 44. You turn the skat and find it contains, say, the heart Jack. Now your game is devalued: you are 'without 2, game 3, times spades' = 33. Having bid 36, you are 'bust', and threatened with loss. The best thing to do is to play on, hoping to make schneider. This will give you the extra multiplier you need to justify your bid. If you turned a black Jack, you would be 'with (or without) 1, game 2, times spades' = 22 – worse still. In this case you must look for other ways of justifying your bid. Can you make clubs trump and win schneider? If so, you will score 'with 1, game 2, schneider 3, times clubs' = 36. If not, can you make a brave attempt at a grand (48), or a clever discard for null open (46)? Generally, it is not wise to bid too high when playing 'without' Jacks, unless you can tell from the auction that the higher trumps are in one player's hand rather than lurking in the skat. Being double-crossed by Jacks in the skat tends to disconcert inexperienced players. Experts take this danger into account intuitively and are very rarely caught out by it.

Grand bids

American Skat expert Joe Wergin has shown that, for a 'grand hand', what you must have is at least five of the nine power factors represented by the four Jacks, the four Aces, and the lead, and what you must *not* have is more than four sure losers. You therefore bid grand hand on:

♣ J ♦ J ♣ 10 K Q ♠ A 10 ♥ A 9 8 and the lead

♣ J ♠ J ♣ A 10 K 9 ♠ 7 ♥ 9 8 and the lead

♠ J ♥ J ♦ J ♠ 10 Q 9 ♥ A 10 regardless of the lead

If just short of these values, you may consider playing grand with the skat. For example:

♣ J ♥ J ♣ A K 9 ♥ A 10 8 ♦ Q 9

This is the same as the hand which we saw earlier was good for a bid of clubs, hand. Given the lead, you have five of the nine power factors, but five probable losers – one Jack, and two each in clubs and diamonds. If the auction forces you beyond 36 for your hand game in clubs, you may make the mental switch to grand and go up to 48.

Null bids

Starting at the top, for a bid of 'null open hand', worth 59, it goes without saying that any void suit is an unbeatable advantage. Any other suit must be bottomed on a Seven (though a singleton Eight is not bad, especially if you are Forehand and can lead it straight off), and no card above Seven should be separated by more than one gap from the one below it. Thus a holding of J–9–7 is unbeatable, and even A–J–9–7 would lose only if one opponent held the other four of that suit and was able to lead them from the bottom up. A singleton Eight is not bad, especially if you have the lead and get rid of it immediately. With only one dangerous card you can play hand, but not open, for 35. For example:

♣ K J 9 7 ♠ Q 8 7 ♥ 8 ♦ 9 7

The Queen is the danger card, and you could be forced to take that spade trick if you played open. An alternative approach would be to take the skat, dump the Queen, and then play open for 46. But if the skat yielded, for example, two high hearts, you could be lost. A simple null for 23, in which you take the skat and do not play open, is a very chancy business, and one you should only call as a substitute for drawing a bad skat on a lower bid.

Trick-play

Skat is full of opportunities for clever and subtle play, but there is only space here for one or two particular points of interest.

In a suit game, the soloist should generally lead trumps at every opportunity. With five or six trumps, a good procedure is to lead high, then low, then high again, attempting to win the third trick in order to prevent the opponent who has no trump left from throwing a high counter to a trump trick won by their partner.

From a side suit headed 10–K, it is often best – sometimes even vital – to play the Ten at the earliest opportunity. This forces the Ace out, leaving your King in command of the suit, at a time when the other opponent is still able to follow suit and hence unable to fatten the 21-point trick by discarding another Ace or Ten. If you play the King, and the Ace-holder ducks, you could lose 31 or more card-points ('half the rent', as they say) on the next round.

Always keep track of the number of card-points currently won by yourself and your opponents. This takes practice, but soon becomes second nature, and is well worthwhile. For example, when a suit is led which you cannot follow, don't automatically trump. It may be worth throwing useless Kings and Queens to dud tricks in order to void your side suits without giving too many away, and you can only do this with safety as long as you know the score.

At grand, don't hesitate to use a long suit to force Jacks out if your own Jacks are either vulnerable or needed for a later purpose. For example:

♥ J ♦ J ♠ A 10 K 8 7 ♥ A 10 7

Given the lead, this is a 'grand, hand, without 2'. Don't lead a Jack – it could lose you the contract. Instead, play spades from the top down. If the Ace is trumped, re-enter with a top heart or a red Jack, and lead the spade Ten. If this also is trumped, you are left with the only Jack in play and certainly five, probably six remaining tricks. (You will try to get rid of the heart loser cheaply, rather than rely on clearing the suit with your Ace–Ten.)

The main thing for the partners to do is to take advantage of every opportunity for larding tricks being won by each other with high-counting cards – especially vulnerable Tens. A typical suit-game opening sees the soloist leading a red Jack and the second dropping a black Jack in case their partner can lard it with the Ace or Ten of trumps, which might otherwise be lost. Alternatively, the second to play, having no black Jack, will themselves drop the Ace or Ten, hoping their partner can play a high Jack. If not, they are both in the soloist's hand (or hand and skat, same thing), and the fat trump would probably have been lost anyway, so there was no harm in trying.

Note: *One of the most important principles of play for the partners is to keep the soloist in the middle, i.e. playing second to a trick, whenever possible. Therefore, when you are leading to a trick to which they will be playing third, and have nothing positive to contribute, lead low in a suit which your partner either heads or can trump, in order to get them into the lead.*

Sample deal

Rearhand deals as follows:

Forehand	♣ J ♠ J ♣ 10 K 9 8 7 ♥ 10 Q 7 ♦ *none*
Middlehand	♥ J ♣ A Q ♠ 10 K Q 8 7 ♥ *none* ♦ A 8
Rearhand	♦ J ♣ *none* ♠ A ♥ A K 9 8 ♦ 10 K 9 7
skat	♠ 9 ♦ Q

Middlehand, to open, is looking at a prospective spades from the hand, having six trumps, a void suit, and two side Aces. He starts bidding '18', '20', '22', etc., and continues up to 44 (without 2, game 3, hand 4, times 11). Forehand accepts all these because she has a prospective hand game in clubs worth 48 (with 2, game 3, hand 4, times 12). So when Forehand accepts '44', Middlehand passes, as there is little chance of making schneider and so increasing his game value to 55. Rearhand now takes over the bidding against Forehand, and tries '45', looking at a possible 'diamonds, hand, without three' (game 4, hand 5, times diamonds 9).

Forehand accepts '45'; Rearhand passes; Forehand announces 'Clubs, hand', and leads. The play runs as follows:

	FH	MH	RH	soloist	partners
1	♠J	♣Q	♦J	7	
2	♣J	♥J	♦7	+4 = 11	
3	♣7	♣A	♠A		22
4	♥7	♦8	♦K		+4 = 26
5	♥Q	♦A	♦9		+14 = 40
6	?	♠10	♥9		

At trick 4, Middlehand avoids leading ♦A in case the soloist trumps it, but leads a low diamond in an attempt (successful) to put his partner in the position of leading though the soloist. Forehand's ♥7 is the typical throw of a worthless card to cheap (4-point) trick. Middlehand's next lead, ♠10, which he knows to be best now the Ace has gone, ruins Forehand's solo. It is true that he has the four remaining trumps, but his ♥10 is now unguarded and cannot fail to be lost to the Ace, giving the partners a win by at least 61 to 59. Forehand will in fact play on, just in case the ♥A is in the skat; but loss is inevitable. The actual loss is 96 points – the value of the bid, doubled.

If Forehand had passed earlier, and either opponent had played their hand game, it is still likely to have been lost. Middlehand or Rearhand could, however, have played a successful skat bid. Middlehand would have gained an extra trump (♠9) and probably have discarded the two non-trump Queens, laying 6 points aside and nursing a nice singleton Ace. Rearhand would have gained an extra trump (♦Q) and probably discarded the two non-trump Nines.

See also

Skat is well covered on the Internet and there are many opportunities for on-line play, although, naturally enough, most emanate from Germany and are in German. Several English-language sites emanate from America, where a different form of the game is played.

http://www.weddslist.com/skat
The home page of the British Skat Association gives notices of meetings and fixtures, publishes my English translation of the Laws of the game from those of the Deutsche SkatVerband, and includes a discussion forum. The BSkA holds playing sessions and tournaments in London approximately every two months.

http://www.pagat.com/schafk/skat.html
John McLeod's page gives rules, variants and links to other sites.

http://www.davidparlett.co.uk/skat

My page covers background and history and links to other pages. You can also email me from here if you would like your name to be added to the mailing list. Beginners welcome.

http://www.playingcardsales.co.uk
German Skat cards are available over the counter from specialist games shops in Britain, but if you aren't near one you can order them on-line from here.

http://www.ispaworld.org
The home page of the International Skat-Players Association is available in English. The ISPA promotes Skat and organizes tournaments in many countries, as well as running a world championship.

http://www.skat.com
The home page of the Deutsche Skat-Verband (German Skat Federation) is in German only.

part three

matching games

20

the bum game

- for three to five players, four best
- easy to learn
- fast and fun, but rewards skill

The name of the game

Its Chinese title carries the sense of climbing up to a higher position – social climbing perhaps. The Japanese call it Dai Hai Mm, 'Very Poor Man', or possibly 'Drop-out'. In the West it is widely known as Arsehole, of which the French equivalent is Trouduc and the American is Asshole, though in American books it bears the alternative title President – whether from prudery or irony is anyone's guess. Some call it 'Pits', and my group plays a localized version which we call the 'The Bum Game'.

This amusing but skill-rewarding game is basically the Chinese game of Zheng Shangyou, or 'Climbing Up', that started spreading to the West in the 1970s. Its many but fundamentally similar titles (see above) should give you an idea of the general sociological flavour of the game, and may even put you off by its unsavouriness. But persevere! It is not only great fun to play, and unlike anything you've played before, but also, when you once get into it, turns out to call for unusual elements of skill.

The most novel, and indeed defining, feature of the game is that it is the only one in which players physically change positions from deal to deal. If you want to play it properly, you should even provide four different types of chair for them to sit on. The basic idea is that players race to play out all their cards. For the first deal it doesn't matter who sits where. The first to get rid of all their cards is designated 'the Boss', and takes their position on a dignified but comfortable chair at the head of the table. The second to go out becomes 'the Foreman', and moves to a more functional office chair placed to the left of the Boss. Third out becomes 'the Worker', and occupies a hard wooden chair to the left of the Foreman and opposite the Boss. The last player left with cards in hand is the Bum, or Dogsbody, referred to in the title. They sit on a broken stool or creaky packing-case at the fourth side of the table. Subsequent deals may produce different results, causing players to occupy higher or lower positions in the hierarchy. But, as you will see, the game is so designed as to favour the current Boss and Foreman at the expense of the Worker and Bum, so that it is not so easy to make your way up the ladder if you have the misfortune to find yourself at the bottom at the end of the first deal.

The following member of the 'social climbing' family of games is the one that has evolved in my group of players, but different schools have different rules and it is easy to ring changes on the basic scheme.

The game

Cards and positions. Use a 52-card pack plus two Jokers. Draw for initial positions, the lowest taking the Bum's place, the highest sitting at their left in the Boss's chair, and the others following the same principle.

Deal. The cards are always shuffled and dealt by the current Bum, or, in the first deal, by the player occupying that seat. Deal all the cards out as far as they will go, so that two players receive 14 to the others' 13 each.

Rank of cards. The two Jokers are the highest cards. They are followed by the Deuces (Twos), Aces, Kings, Queens, and so on down to the Threes, which are lowest of all. Suits are irrelevant. Jokers and Deuces are wild in certain circumstances, as explained below.

Object. To get rid of all your cards as soon as possible by playing them out to rounds of play that may as well be called 'tricks' for convenience.

Play. The opening lead is made by the player at Dealer's left (the Boss), and the winner of each trick leads to the next. Won tricks are worthless in themselves and are thrown face down to a common waste pile. The advantage of winning a trick is the quite powerful one of being able to lead to the next.

The leader may lead:

- a single card, *or*
- two or more cards of the same rank, such as K–K, 4–4–4, etc., *or*
- a run of three or more cards, such as 3–4–5 (the lowest possible), 9–10–J–Q–K, K–A–2–Joker, etc.

Each player in turn thereafter is free to pass or play, but in the latter case must play the *same* number and combination of cards as the previous player, but *higher* in rank.

In other words:

- If a single card is led, each must play a higher card, and a Joker is unbeatable.
- If a pair is led, each subsequent pair must be higher, and a pair of Jokers is unbeatable.
- If a triplet or quartet is led, such as 7–7–7(–7), each must play the same number of a higher rank, for which purpose 2–2–2(–2) is unbeatable. You can't beat three of a kind by

playing four of a kind, or a pair by playing three of a kind, as it is always necessary to play the same number of cards as the leader.

- Similarly, a three-card sequence, such as 8–9–10, can only be beaten by a higher three-card sequence, such as 10–J–Q. It can't be beaten by, and indeed may not be followed by, a four-card sequence.

Wild cards. Jokers and Deuces may be used as wild cards in sets of matched cards. For example, 7–7–7–7 is beaten by 8–2–2–Joker, representing four Eights, and A–2–2 (three Aces) by 2–Joker–Joker (three Deuces). With the aid of wild cards it is possible, and permissible, to lead five or more of a kind. Jokers and Deuces may be used in runs, but only in their normal positions (e.g. K–A–2–Joker), not as wild cards.

Winning a trick. Play continues with each in turn either passing or playing higher than the previous player. The turn may go round several times, and a player who has passed once is not debarred from playing again if able to do so. However, the same player may not play twice in succession. Three consecutive passes end the trick, and whoever played last must then turn it down and lead to the next. If they ran out of cards on their last play, the lead passes to their left.

End of deal. A player who runs out of cards ceases play. The first out of cards scores 3 points and becomes the next Boss, changing places if not already in that position. The second scores 2 and becomes the Foreman, the third 1 point and becomes the Worker. The last player, or Bum, scores nothing, but bunches and shuffles the cards and deals to the next round, starting with the Boss and ending with the Foreman.

Card exchanges. Before play, the Boss must remove the two lowest-ranking cards from their hand and pass them face down to the Bum, receiving in return the Bum's two highest-ranking cards. Similarly, the Foreman passes the Worker their lowest card – one only – in exchange for the Worker's highest. The purpose of this rule is to give the Boss and the Foreman an unfair advantage. The only consolation for the Bum and the Worker is that if either is dealt a Joker they are not obliged to give it away in the exchange, but may hang on to it.

When cards have been exchanged, the Boss leads to the first trick.

End of game. The game ends when one player wins by reaching a target score, say 20 for about three-quarters of an hour's play. One's final position in the hierarchy, whether Boss or Bum, is of no particular significance but may be used to break a tie.

Variants. Many variations are recorded in respect of scores and allowable combinations. As a matter of particular interest, the Chinese game also includes multiple sequences so that, for example, 6–6–7–7–8–8 is beaten by 7–7–8–8–9–9 or higher. In the Japanese game, if both Jokers are dealt to the Worker or the Bum, they may declare a revolution. The Boss then changes places with the Bum, and the Worker with the Foreman, with all the advantages of the exchange appertaining thereto.

The game may be played with varying numbers of Jokers. If they are distinguishable from one other, for example by colour, it may be agreed that they beat one another in a particular order when played as singletons. In some versions of the game, Jokers may be used to represent Deuces but not to beat them in their own right.

It may be agreed that, in runs, Jokers may be used as wild cards, and Deuces as natural low cards, so that 2–3–4 . . . etc. is a valid run.

Note: *If you are too lazy (or too old) to keep changing places, you can instead prepare four place-cards labelled with the four titles, and simply shift them about at the end of each deal. In this case, however, you should ensure that when a player goes out, the next lead is made by the player occupying the highest hierarchical position from the previous deal.*

The game for five players. The third to run out of cards occupies a position between the Foreman and the Worker, and does not exchange any cards.

The game for three players. The positions are Boss, Middleman, Bum. The Boss passes their lowest card to the Bum and second lowest to the Middleman. The Bum passes their highest to the Boss and second highest to the Middleman. The Middleman passes to the Boss the highest card, and to the Bum the lowest card, from the hand originally dealt to them (before receiving a card from each other player).

The play

It is best not to arrange your cards in suits, which are irrelevant, but in ranking order:

Jo–2–A–K–J–9–9–9–7–6–5–5–3 (Jo = Joker)

The first thing you must do is to plan how to make the best of your combinations and how to get rid of your lowest-ranking cards, which are always the most difficult. In this hand, for example, you must decide whether to play the two Fives as a pair at the earliest opportunity, leaving you with two middling and one low singleton to dispose of (7–6–3), or to play 7–6–5 as a run, leaving you with two low stragglers (5–3). An advantage of the run 7–6–5 is that if the turn comes round again you can play your unbeatable Jo–2–A, or, with slight element of risk, your 2–A–K, enabling you to lead your Three upon winning the trick.

Having made a decision, it is usually best to stay with it. If your right-hand neighbour plays a pair of Threes or Fours, you should resist the temptation to play your Fives. If a single Five precedes you, the best response is the straggler Jack, which belongs to no set or sequence, rather than break into your three-card sequence or trio of Nines. Following a Three or Four, however, you would promptly throw a Five, as your decision to retain the sequence has turned it into a straggler.

You will aim to get rid of low cards as soon as possible and at every opportunity. For example, it's nearly always better to lead one Three than three Fives. If you lead four Threes early in the game you may well find opponents unable to follow to quadruplets, thus putting you well ahead; but if you get stuck with only Threes in hand, whether one or all four, and haven't got the lead, you'll certainly finish bottom. A minor exception is when you hold one very low rank and a lot of high ones, when you can sometimes bank on winning a round with a bunch of high cards and then going out by leading the low one – or pair, or however many you have.

If your highest card is, say, an Ace, you should, unless you can see a quick way of going out by playing it, hang on to it until you have counted out all the Deuces and Jokers, so that you can be sure of winning a trick on a singleton lead. If you play it early and have it overtaken, you may never come in at all. If you have nothing higher than, say, Jacks, don't panic: just wait, and play carefully. You can hardly expect to win on such a hand, but it is by no means a foregone conclusion that you will come bottom. The all-important skill factor is a sense of timing.

Example of play

After several rounds, Bum deals the following hands (Jo = Joker):

Boss	Jo 2 A Q J J 10 9 8 8 7 4 3 3
Foreman	2 2 A J 10 10 9 9 8 7 7 5 5 3
Worker	A K K K Q J 10 6 6 6 5 4 4
Bum	Jo 2 A K Q Q 9 8 7 6 5 4 3

After the exchange of high and low cards, these become:

Boss	Jo 2 2 A A Q J J 10 9 8 8 7 4
Foreman	2 2 A A J 10 10 9 9 8 7 7 5 5
Worker	K K K Q J 10 6 6 6 5 4 4 3
Bum	Jo K Q Q 9 8 7 6 5 4 3 3 3

The Boss kicks off with his long sequence of Seven to Queen, which no one can follow, and leads his singleton Four to the next trick. Foreman plays an Ace, Worker passes, Bum wins with her Joker, and leads her long sequence from Three to Nine. After three tricks the hands are:

Boss	Jo 2 2 A A J 8
Foreman	2 2 A J 10 10 9 9 8 7 7 5 5
Worker	K K K Q J 10 6 6 6 5 4 4 3
Bum	K Q Q 3 3

Bum now leads her pair of Threes, which are followed by Eights from the Boss (the natural Eight and a wild Deuce), Tens, Kings, pass, Aces, and finally Deuces from the Foreman.

This leaves:

Boss	Jo 2 J
Foreman	A J 9 9 8 7 7 5 5
Worker	K Q J 10 6 6 6 5 4 4 3
Bum	K Q Q

The Foreman, after much thought, leads his pair of Fives rather than 7–8–9 which would leave four straggly cards. These are followed by Sixes, Queens, and the Boss's unbeatable Deuce–Joker. The Boss now exits with his Jack, to which Foreman plays an unbeatable Ace to find himself on lead again from this position:

Foreman	J 9 9 8 7 7
Worker	K Q J 10 6 5 4 4 3
Bum	K 3 3

This time he opts for the three-card sequence, 7–8–9. The Worker overtakes with 10–J–Q, wins, leads 3–4–5–6, which no one can follow. Neither can they follow her King, and she goes out second with the Four. Bum thereupon goes out with her King, leaving Foreman with J–9–7 and changing places with him in the hierarchy. Had Foreman led his pair of Sevens from the above position, he would have held the trick, led Nines, held it again, and led the Eight, leaving himself with an odd Jack. He would then only have lost if Worker had been concentrating enough to realize that her King was now unbeatable and should be played. Otherwise she would have played the Ten (keeping J–Q–K intact), and Foreman would have dropped by only one position instead of two.

The more you play this unusual game, the more fascinating it becomes.

See also

http://www.pagat.com/climbing/shangyou.html

21

crazy eights

- for three to seven players
- easy to learn
- fun to play, good for children

Crazy Eights is one of several names for one or more of a family of games where you aim to get rid of all your cards by discarding them one by one to a wastepile. The catch is that you may only discard by matching the previous player's discard by rank or suit. If you can't, you have to draw more cards, thereby enlarging your hand and taking longer to go out. Games of this type have increased in popularity since the 1960s, mainly through the introduction of ever more elaborate and tricky rules about how cards are required to match one another. These rules get shunted around from game to game, as do the various names they go under, making it very difficult to keep track of exactly what is meant by which. So we will start with a basic version, and then add some of the extras.

Crazy Eights

Preliminaries. From two to seven play. Use a single 52-card pack for up to five players, doubled to 104 if there are more than five. Deal five cards each, or seven if only two play, and stack the rest face down. Turn its top card face up and place it next to the stock to start a wastepile. If it's an Eight, bury it in the stock and turn the next instead.

Object. To be the first to play off all your cards.

Play. The player at Dealer's left goes first. On your turn to play, you may discard one card to the wastepile provided that it matches the previous discard by either rank or suit. For example, if the previous upcard is the Jack of spades, you can play a spade or a Jack.

Eights are wild: you can play one whenever you like, and nominate a suit for the next player to follow, which needn't be that of the Eight itself. If you are unable (or unwilling) to match, you must draw cards from the top of the stock and add them to your hand until you do make a discard, or the stock runs out. If you can't play when the stock has run out, you can only pass.

Ending. Play ends as soon as someone plays their last card, or when no one can match the last card. The player who went out collects from each opponent a payment equivalent to the total face value of cards remaining in the latter's hand, counting each Eight 50, courts 10 each, others face value. If the game blocks, the player with the lowest combined face value of cards remaining in hand scores from each opponent the difference between their two hand values. In the four-hand partnership game both partners must go out to end the game.

Note. *Some play with Aces wild instead of Eights. This was the case in Rockaway, the earliest recorded version of the game.*

Two-Four-Jack

This game, also called Switch, or Black Jack, became popular in the 1960s, and gave rise to a successful proprietary version called Uno™. Play like Crazy Eights, except that a player unable to follow draws only one card from stock, and with the following special rules.

Aces are wild.

Twos. Playing a Two forces the next in turn either to play a Two, or, if unable, to draw two cards from stock and miss a turn. If they draw, the next in turn may play in the usual way; but if they do play a Two, the next after them must either do likewise or draw four cards and miss a turn. Each successive playing of a Two increases by two the number of cards that must be drawn by the next player if they cannot play a Two themselves, up to a maximum of eight.

Fours have the same powers, except that the number of cards to be drawn is four, eight, twelve, or sixteen, depending on how many are played in succession.

Jacks. Playing a Jack reverses ('switches') the direction of play and forces the preceding player to miss a turn, unless they, too, can play a Jack, thus turning the tables.

Twos, Fours, and Jacks operate independently of one another. You cannot escape the demands of a Two by playing a Four instead, or of a Jack by playing a Two, and so on.

The game ends when a player wins by playing their last card. A player with two cards in hand must announce 'One left' or 'Last card' upon playing one of them.

The penalty for any infraction of the rules (including playing too slowly) is to draw two cards from stock.

The winner scores the face value of all cards left in other players' hands, with special values of 20 per Ace, 15 per Two, Four or Jack, and 10 per King and Queen.

Go Boom

This is a simpler relative of Crazy Eights, suitable for children.

Deal seven cards each (but some prefer ten) from a full pack – or, if more than six play, a doubled pack of 104 cards – and stack the rest face down. The player at Dealer's left plays any card face up. Each in turn thereafter must play a card of the same suit or rank if possible. A player unable to do so must draw cards from stock until able, or, when no cards remain in stock, must simply pass. When everyone has either played or passed, the person who played the highest card of the suit led turns the played cards down and leads to the next 'trick'.

Play stops as soon as someone plays their last card. That player scores the total values of all cards remaining in other players hands, with Ace to Ten at face value and face cards 10 each.

See also

http://www.pagat.com/eights/crazy8s.html

22

adding-up games

- for two to seven players
- easy to learn
- fun if you like mental arithmetic

A group of simple games suitable for younger players or lighter moments is based on the idea of adding up the face value of cards played as you go along, and trying to make or avoid certain totals. Games of this sort have only recently made their way to western Europe from eastern Europe. It is an odd fact that the only Western card game with anything like this feature is the peculiarly English game of Crib.

One Hundred

One Hundred is the simplest of several games. You can easily make up others of your own.

Divide a 32-card pack between from two to seven players so that all have the same number of cards. If any are left over, deal them face up to the table and announce their combined face values, counting as follows:

Rank	A	K	Q	J	10	9	8	7
Value	11	4	3	2	10	9	8	7

Each in turn plays a card to the table and announces the total of all cards so far played. For example, if five play and the two undealt cards were a Jack and a Nine, the dealer would announce 'Eleven', and if the first to play added an Ace, they would announce 'Twenty-two'.

Keep adding cards one by one, in turn, and announcing the new total. If you make the total exactly 100, you win. If you bring it to more than 100 from a figure below 100, you lose.

Obstacle Race

Divide a 32-card pack evenly between from two to seven players and play as above (One Hundred), except that cards now have these face values:

Rank	A	K	Q	J	10	9	8	7
Value	1	4	±3	2	10	9	8	7

If you play a Queen, note that you can either add or deduct 3 from the current total, whichever you prefer.

The 'obstacles' in this race are 55, 66, 77, 88, 99 and 111. You score a point if you bring the total exactly to an obstacle number, but lose a point for causing the total to jump an obstacle number without making it exactly. Because the Queen either adds or subtracts, it is possible for an obstacle to be hit or jumped either upwards or downwards, and more than once.

When the total reaches or exceeds 120 it is re-set to zero, and play continues as before. The winner is either the player with the highest score after one or more deals, or the first to reach an agreed target.

Ninety-Nine

This is said to be a Romany game.

From two to seven players receive three each from a 52-card pack and the rest are stacked face down.

The order of play runs to the left around the table to start with, but may change (as in the game of Switch).

Each in turn, starting with the player at dealer's left, plays a card face up to the table, announces the total face value of all cards so far played, and draws a replacement from stock.

Whoever brings the total over 99 ends the round and loses a life. Another deal follows, and the first player to lose three lives is the overall loser.

The cards have the following face values:

Black Ace	any	Seven	7
Red Ace	1	Eight	8
Two	2	Nine makes	99
Three	0	Ten minus	10
Four	0	Jack	10 and switches
Five	5	Queen	10
Six	6	King	10

Playing a black Ace entitles you to make the total anything you like, from 0 to 99.

A Nine automatically brings the total to 99, and can therefore only be followed by a Three, a Four, a Ten, or a black Ace. Playing a Jack adds 10 and reverses the order of play. For example, when the first Jack is played, the next card is played by the person to the right of the one who played the Jack, and play continues to the right until another Jack is played.

See also

http://www.pagat.com/adders

23

scopa and scopone

- for two to four players
- easy to learn
- a game of skill

The name of the game

Scopa is Italian for broom or brush and is related to the English word scoop. The game is so called because catching all the table cards in one turn is called making a sweep.

Scopa and its partnership equivalent Scopone are basically the same game. It is very old, being first described in an 18th-century treatise by a one 'Chitarrella' (thought to be a monk or a clergyman), and can rightly lay claim to being Italy's most distinctive national card game. Deceptively simple to learn, but cunningly wrought to play well, it belongs to a category generically known as 'fishing' games. This is partly because such games may be of Chinese origin, in which country the most characteristic member is itself called Fishing, and largely because the term is so descriptive of what actually goes on in the play. At each turn there are a number of cards on the table – like fish in a pool, so to speak – and your aim is to play a card from your hand – like casting a fly – in such a way as to 'catch' one or more of them. If the card you play fails catch anything, you have to leave it on the table, where it becomes a fish itself awaiting capture on some future turn.

Fishing games are not well known in the English-speaking world. The only one you're likely to meet in the average card-games compendium is Cassino, or Casino, which flourished briefly in the early 19th century. It remained popular in America, however, where it subsequently developed a lot of additional features that in my view make it too elaborate for its own good. (I have never actually been able to understand it, though it is said to be a game for children.) The earliest known western game of this family goes back to the early 16th century and is called – believe it or not – 'Laugh and lie down'. This really is a fun and simple game, and if you want to play it you will find a full description on the Historic Card Games page of my website (see http://www.davidparlett.co.uk/histocs/laughand.html).

Scopa

Players. Best for two. If three or four play, the turn to deal and play passes to the right, as customary in all Italian games. If four play, players sitting opposite each other are partners, and whichever of two partners first wins any cards subsequently stacks all the cards won by both of them in front of him- or herself. Four-player Scopa is neither as interesting nor as skill-rewarding as its more advanced equivalent Scopone.

Cards. Scopa is played with a 40-card Italian pack, which you can emulate by removing all the Eights, Nines and Tens from a standard 52-card pack. The ten cards of each suit do not go in any particular order, but for capturing purposes they have face values as follows:

A	2	3	4	5	6	7	J	Q	K
1	2	3	4	5	6	7	8	9	10

Deal. Deal three cards to each player, face down, then four face up to the table, and stack the rest face down to one side. (Be careful not to get this stock of cards mixed up with the pile of cards you will win during the course of the game!) When everyone has played out all three cards from their hand, deal three more each, and keep doing this throughout the game so long as any remain. The game ends when all have played out their last three and none remain in stock. (There will be five redeals when two play, three when three play, and two when four play.)

Note: *If the table cards include three or four Kings, it is usual – but not obligatory – to deal again, as more than two of them make it impossible to score for sweeps.*

Object. To capture as many cards as possible, especially Sixes, Sevens, diamonds, and, above all, the ♦7, known as *sette bello* (the beautiful Seven).

Play. Each in turn, starting with the player at dealer's right, plays a card face up to the table. Their aim is to capture one or more table cards by either pairing or summing.

- Pairing means catching a table card by playing from hand a card of exactly the same rank. For example, a Two captures a Two, a Jack a Jack, and so on.
- Summing means catching two or more table cards by playing from hand a card whose face value equals the sum of the cards so captured. For example, since a Queen counts 9, playing a Queen would enable you to capture 4–5, or 2–3–4, etc.

You can only make one capture in one turn, and if you can use a given card to capture by either pairing or summing you may only do it by pairing. For example, if the table cards are 2–4–6–J, and you want to play a Jack (or have only a Jack left to play) you can only catch the Jack, not the 2–6. Having made a catch, you place all the captured and capturing cards involved face down on the table before you in a pile of winnings.

A card that cannot capture must be left in place as a new table card. This is called trailing. You may not trail a card that can make a capture. If it can make a capture, it must.

Scopa. A sweep (*scopa*) is made when you play a card that captures all the table cards in one turn by summing, or the only remaining table card by pairing. Since you will score a point for each sweep at the end of the game, you mark your sweep by placing the capturing card face up instead of face down in your pile of won cards. Another advantage of making a sweep is that it leaves no table cards, so your opponent cannot capture but can only trail by playing a single card to the table.

Ending. Play continues until everyone has played all their cards out and none remain in stock. Any cards remaining untaken on the table are added to those of the player who made the last capture.

Note: *This does not count as a sweep, even if it would otherwise technically be one.*

Score. Players sort through their won cards and score, where applicable, points for the following features:

    1 for winning a majority of cards (no score if tied)
    1 for winning a majority of diamonds (no score if tied)
    1 for winning the *sette bello* (♦7)
    1 for having the best prime (or *primiera*), as explained below
    1 for each sweep

It doesn't matter in what order these points are counted.

Counting the prime. *Primiera*, or 'prime', is a feature borrowed from an old (but still current) Italian ancestor of Poker. The prime is a combination consisting of the highest-valued prime card you hold in each of the four suits. If you fail to take at least one card in every suit then you cannot have a prime. The prime value of individual cards differs from their arithmetical value for summing purposes during the play. To contest the prime, you display the highest card you have in each suit according to the following table of values:

each Seven counts	21	each Six counts	18
each Ace counts	16	each Five counts	15

| each Four counts | 14 | each Three counts | 13 |
| each Two counts | 12 | each K, Q, J counts | 10 |

For example, if your four highest cards are ♠A ♥7 ♣3 ♦6 then your prime counts 68 (16 + 21 + 13 + 18). Whoever has the highest such count scores the point for prime. In case of a tie for highest, no one scores that point.

This may look needlessly tiresome to work out, but in the two-player game it is usually easy to see at a glance who has the best prime, as it is generally won by whoever has the most Sevens and Sixes. If you have four Sevens you are bound to win, and in the two-player game you will nearly always win with three of them. If both have two Sevens, the player with most Sixes usually wins. In the three-player game it is usually obvious who has won on Sixes and Sevens, but will sometimes be necessary to do the calculations to clear up any doubt.

Some prime values

Here are the best primes with their values and potential for winning in the two- or four-player game. Four Sevens always wins, as do three Sevens accompanied by a Three or better. (C = court card = Jack, Queen or King.)

prime	value	result
7777	84	wins
7776	81	wins
777A	79	wins
7775	78	wins
7774	77	wins
7773	76	wins
7772	75	could tie (with 7666)
777C	73	could lose (to 7666 = 75)
7766	78	could tie (with 7666)
776A	76	could lose (to 7766 = 78)
7765	75	could lose (to 776 + 6 or better)
7764	74	could lose (to 776 + 5 or better)
7763	73	could lose (to 776 + 4 or better)
7666	75	could lose (to 777 + 3 or better)

Game. The game ends when either player reaches a target score. This is normally 11 points, but may be 15 or 21 or any other agreed number. Unless otherwise agreed, score-points are not counted until the deal has been completely played out (unlike in

Cribbage, where you stop in mid-hand as soon as you reach 121). In case of a tie, play as many more deals as necessary to establish a winner.

Variations. Scopa lends itself to many variations and is hardly anywhere played in the simplest and purest form described above. Two of the most popular are as follows:

1   Playing an Ace from your hand entitles you to capture all the table cards (or just itself, if no table cards remain), thus forcing the next player to trail. However, this doesn't count as a sweep, so you don't leave it face up and you won't score a point for it.

2   Captures are made by 'fifteening' – that is, you can capture by playing from your hand a card that makes up 15 with those you capture from the table. For example, with only 3–J on the table and 4 in your hand, you can make a sweep, since the total value of all won cards is 15.

The play

Scopa is one of those games which, like Cribbage, consists of many small combinations, making it difficult to outline an overall winning strategy. The best thing to do in any given situation depends so much on individual circumstances that advantage will always lie with the more experienced player. Look at this example play:

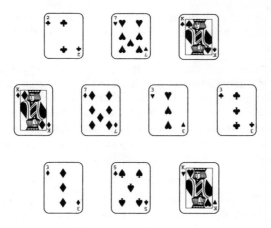

figure 23.1

Both players would like to play their King (= 10) and take the *sette bello* (♦7) and one of the Threes. Unfortunately, there is a King on the table, so the play of a King would necessarily have to pair with it, leaving the other's King to capture the 7 + 3. South, to lead, might take a Three with his Three. North would then take Seven with Seven, South King with King, leaving North to play the Two to the table and South to capture it and the Three with his Five.

Unlike Cribbage, the play of Scopa relies very much on a good memory and accurate card-counting. When it comes to the last deal of three cards, an expert player will know exactly what his opponent holds.

In general, you should aim to win more cards rather than fewer, as the player with more cards not only scores a point for most but also is more likely to win most diamonds for another point, and to end up with the best prime for yet another. So, for instance, if the table cards include A–3–5 and you hold a Four and a Queen, it is better to win them all with the Queen, giving you four cards, than to play the Four for the 1–3, giving you only three.

This aim may be modified, however, if diamonds are involved. For example, if your Four is of diamonds, and none of the other cards are, then it might be better to play the Four and capture the A–3. You will only have won three cards instead of four, but 33% of them will be diamonds as opposed to 0% if you play the Queen, or to the average 25% of all won cards. This becomes less important, however, once you have already captured six diamonds and so assured yourself of the point for diamonds (or five of them, and assured your opponent of *not* winning that point).

Another obvious feature of diamond management occurs when you hold a diamond and another card of the same rank. Here you must remember to play the other rank first with a view to catching it on your next turn with its diamond partner. Of course, your opponent might take it first, but at least you will have saved your diamond, and there is then less chance of its being paired if and when you eventually have to trail it.

Keeping track of how many diamonds you have won is just one of many instances of how important a good memory is to the play of this game.

No less important than diamonds are Sevens and Sixes, as these contribute to the point for prime. The *sette bello* (♦7) is, of course, the most important card of all. For one thing, winning it scores a point in itself and contributes to the points for cards, diamonds and *primiera*; for another, it is the only point that is bound to be scored and cannot possibly be tied.

Sweeps are valuable because they are capable of scoring an indefinitely high number of points towards game, and also because a tie for sweeps does not annul the points they score. There's not a lot you can do to set up sweeps for yourself, but you can play so as to reduce your opponent's chances of making them. The most common and often easiest tactic is to ensure that you always leave cards totalling at least 11 on the table. So, if the only card on the table is a Five, and those in your hand are A–3–6, your best play is the Six. Or again: suppose on the table are 2–4–J and you hold 6–Q. You could take the 2–4 with your 6, but leaving only a Jack on the table invites a possible sweep. So play the Queen first, and hope the 2–4 remain available after your opponent has played the next card.

When unable to make any capture, you should try to avoid trailing Sevens, Sixes or Aces because of their value towards the prime. Not only is the prime value of an Ace (16) the third highest after Sevens and Sixes, but also it more dangerously lends itself to captures by summing. The same applies to Twos (bearing in mind that K = 2 + J) so, all in all, from this point of view, the best trailers are Fours, Fives and face cards.

Unless you keep careful track of what has been played, so that you know the approximate chances of your opponent's holding any given rank, it does not usually pay to trail a card with a view to catching it as part of a summation on your next turn. For example, if the table cards are 3–6–Q and you hold 4–7–K, it would be dangerous to play the Four with a view to capturing with the Seven, unless you have counted the Sevens and know that your opponent cannot have one to make the capture before you. Best also not to play the Seven, for the same reason; so King it is.

One way in which experts keep track of what's going on is to make a mental note of which ranks remain paired or unpaired. At start of play there are two pairs of cards of each of the ten ranks. If every capture made throughout the game were made by pairing, the last card played by the dealer would match the last card left on the table. But captures made during the play by summing rather than pairing leave some ranks temporarily 'unpaired'. Keeping mental track of paired and unpaired cards enables experts to know exactly what cards remain in their opponent's hand when the last three are dealt. Here's how it's done.

Suppose the first summing capture is a 7 from hand taking 3 + 4 from the table. Then you memorize the values 7–3–4. These are unpaired values, as there remain three of each in the pack.

The next summing capture is, let's say, a King from hand taking 3 + 7 from the table. You can now forget the remembered 3 and 7, as they have been 'paired' again, there being only two of each left in the pack. But you continue to hold the unpaired 4 in mind, together with the King, as it has now just become unpaired.

Suppose now only one more summing capture is made before you are dealt your last three cards, and that it is a King from hand capturing A + 3 + 6 from the table. Now the unpaired King has been evened out, but the 4 remains unpaired, as do the 3 and 6 that have just been played.

When the last three cards are dealt, you find yourself holding A–3–J and facing 4–J–Q on the table. What are your opponent's cards? Well, consider the unpaired ranks A–3–6. Of these, you can only see one Ace, so the other one must be in your opponent's hand. The 3 in your hand pairs off with the one you have been carrying in memory, and the Jack in your hand pairs off with the one on the table. The 4 on the table is unpaired, as you know from memory. The Queen on the table and the 6 in your mind don't match anything you can see, so they can only pair off with cards in your opponent's hand. So your opponent must be holding A–6–Q. If you are the dealer, you will win the most possible of these nine cards provided you remember to hold back your Ace until your opponent trails the other one. If not, you will just have to hold back your Ace for as long as possible and hope that the dealer's inadvertently comes out first.

If after making these calculations you find yourself inexplicably short of a value, it may be that your opponent has ended up with two of a kind in hand. Suppose, following the example given above, you know that 3–4–6 are the unpaired values, and you are holding 3–6–J to 4–J–Q on the table. The 3–4–6 carried in your memory pair up with the 3–6 in your hand and the 4 on the table, and the Queen on the table must pair with a Queen in the opposing hand. This leaves no rank unpaired, which means, in turn, that your opponent's other two cards are themselves a pair.

An interesting aspect of the game is the difference between the positions of the dealer and the non-dealer. As non-dealer, and playing first after each deal of three, you have the advantage of first bite at the cards on the table. If few cards remain after the previous round, you are well placed for a sweep; if many, you will often have a useful choice of captures. On the other hand, if you've nothing to capture and have to trail, you have the disadvantage of offering more choice of capture to the dealer. As dealer, you will often find yourself better placed to make the last capture in the last round, thereby adding the unmatched table cards to your winnings.

Scopone

This more advanced partnership version of Scopa is played exactly like the parent game after the following differences in the opening set-up.

Players. Four play in two partnerships of two, with the members of each partnership sitting opposite each other and playing in rotation (to the right). One member of each partnership keeps all their won cards together.

The deal. There are two ways of starting off:

1 Deal nine cards to each player and four face up to the table.
2 Deal ten cards to each player and none to the table. This means that the dealer's right-hand opponent, having to play first, has no choice but to trail, as there is nothing to capture from the table.

Each of these methods has its own dedicated following, and the followers of each method refer to their own game as *Scopone Scientifico* – that is, 'scientific' or 'intelligent' Scopone.

The nine-carders maintain that their game is more scientific because you cannot be truly scientific unless you have something on which to exercise your powers of observation and deduction, namely the existence of four open table cards.

The ten-carders maintain that their game is more scientific because the opening player has only the content of his or her own hand on which to make an intelligent assessment of what to play first, unadulterated by the chance element of four random table cards.

Both sides are right, of course, and science has nothing to do with it. When, around 1750, Chitarrella described Scopone as *scientifico* he was describing the nine-card game and declaring it to be more intelligent than partnership Scopa, in which only three cards are dealt at a time. The ten-card game is a relatively modern development. Try both and play whichever you prefer.

The play

Scopone is one of the most fascinating partnership games, and one requiring great partnership skill. The basic principles of Scopa remain valid, but must now be shared between two partnered players.

If at the start of the hand each player were to capture exactly one card, the dealer would score a sweep, eldest hand (his right-hand opponent) would be forced to trail, and there would be a strong tendency for the dealer's side to be continually sweeping while the opponents continually trail. The elder partnership must therefore seek to break up this potential pattern. Suppose the table cards dealt are A–3–4–J. Eldest plays a Five and captures A–4. Dealer's partner is now awkwardly facing 3–J, a combination worth 11 and so unsweepable. If he pairs either card he leaves his next opponent one card and the chance of a sweep, though his own holding may enable him to assess this risk. For example, holding two Jacks and a Three he could capture the Three, arguing that it is two to one against the next player's holding the other Jack. Otherwise, his safest play is to trail, which scores nothing, but costs nothing either.

The first move ($5 = 1 + 4$) leaves Aces, Fours and Fives unpaired, as in Scopa. Generally, it favours the non-dealer's side to maintain as many ranks as possible unpaired. To redress the balance, dealer's side should seek to trail the lower cards of three or more unpaired ranks so that they may capture by summing – an attempt which the opponents will try to frustrate by trailing the highest unpaired rank before the others can get both of the lower ranks into play. In the above example, dealer's side will now seek to trail a Four and an Ace so as to capture both with a Five of their own. But if the non-dealers can themselves trail a Five before a Four and an Ace gets into play then the dealer's side will not be able to catch them, since, by the rules of the game, capture by pairing has priority over capture by summing.

Another common sequence of play is the *mulinello* ('whirlwind'). Suppose the table cards are A–3–4–5 and eldest has two Threes. Trusting that his next opponent does not have the fourth, he plays K = A + 4 + 5, leaving the Three in situ. Dealer's partner does not have the Three and must trail a court to prevent a possible sweep. Suppose he trails a Jack. Now third-hand, who does have the fourth Three, pairs the Jack, thus leaving dealer in exactly the same fix as his partner. As the fourth Three is a constant threat this painful situation can be dragged out for some time.

When forced to trail it is natural to choose a rank of which you are holding two or three, a fact which can give useful information to one's partner and possibly enable him to reap a whirlwind as described above. For example, suppose the first move is 6 = 2 + 4. Second-hand trails a Four from a pair. If now his partner, dealer, has the other Four, the two of them can set up a whirlwind based upon that rank – rather like a squeeze at Bridge.

As in Scopa, much of the play is directed towards catching ♦7, the *sette bello*, or at least preventing the opponents from catching it too easily. The other three Sevens come next in importance, as the prime point can be won on three Sevens if the fourth card is a Three or better. A side that has already lost a majority of Sevens must chase after the Sixes, then the Aces, and so on down the scale.

See also

http://www.pagat.com/fishing/scopone.html

24

cribbage

- for two to four players, ideal for two
- easy to learn
- a fast game of skill

Cribbage, mostly called Crib, has been the English national card game some 400 years – perhaps even 500, if you count its immediate ancestor, Noddy – and is widely played throughout the English-speaking world. Originally favoured by royals and aristocrats, it sank down the social scale in the 19th century, and for most of the 20th century remained the archetypal pub game. It remains, in fact, the only game legally playable in public houses without special licence from the local magistrates, and is played on a league and championship basis in many parts of the country. However, the recent advent of computerized games has led to a resurgence in popularity, and it is now taken seriously enough to rate inclusion in various Mind Sports Olympiads.

Crib is a game of adding up and scoring for making card combinations. It is easy to learn and fast to play. The skill involved is largely that born of experience rather than of brain-busting strategic calculation, and the most experienced player will usually win consistently. It is an excellent way of introducing children to card games.

Cribbage is played in various forms. The most widespread, globally speaking, is Six-card Cribbage for two players. British pub and club leagues recognise two older forms: the original five-card game for two players, and its partnership equivalent for four.

For *Teach Yourself* purposes my approach will be to start with the older and simpler five-card game and then proceed to the modern six-card game for two. You may prefer to skip to the six-card game immediately, but before doing that you should look first at (a) the use of that ingenious and age-old scoring device, the cribbage board (Figure 24.1), and (b) the table of card combinations, and their scores, that are common to all varieties of the game.

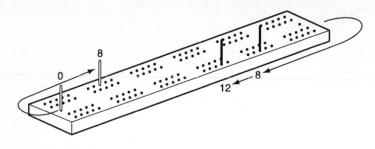

figure 24.1 Cribbage board

Each player starts from zero at each short edge of the 61-hole Crib board and records scores by moving two pegs alternately 'up the outside' (from 1 to 30) and 'down the inside' from 31 to 60. Two such circuits are made in the standard game to 121 points. As illustrated here, White has evidently pegged nothing in play and 8 in hand, while Red must have made 8 in play and hand followed by 4 in the box. The players' pairs of pegs traditionally move in opposite directions, but some prefer both players to move theirs in parallel – that is, starting from the same end – for greater ease of comparison, especially when playing two or three times round the board (up to 121 or 181 respectively).

Five-card Crib (for two players)

Cards. Use a standard 52-card pack.

The running order of cards is A 2 3 4 5 6 7 8 9 10 J Q K. (Ace is always low.)

For the purpose of adding up card values the numeral cards count at face value (with A = 1) and face cards count 10 each.

Object. To be the first to reach 61 (or any other agreed target), over as many deals as it takes, by (a) making card combinations and (b) playing up to 31.

Deal. Each in turn cuts the pack and shows the bottom card of the top half. Whoever cuts the lower card deals first, Ace being lowest of all. The dealer is said to be 'in the box', and has several scoring advantages. The deal therefore alternates to even this advantage out.

Before the first deal, non-dealer pegs 3 points to compensate for the disadvantage of not being first in the box.

Deal five cards each, face down, one at a time, starting with non-dealer, and stack the rest face down.

Laying away. Both players examine their hands and make any two discards face down. These four discards form the crib, which is put on the dealer's side of the table. Once they have been laid away, neither player may examine them before the end of the hand. Each player's aim is to retain three cards that will be of most use in the play and will score best for the standard Cribbage combinations as shown in the table.

Scoring features at Five-card Cribbage		
in hand, crib, or play		
fifteen	2	two or more cards totalling 15
pair	2	two of the same rank
prial (pair royal)	6	three of the same rank
double pair royal	12	four of the same rank
run	3–6	three or more in sequence
in hand or crib only		
flush	3–4	three or four of a suit*
his nob	1	Jack of the turned suit
in play only		
go	1	last card played if not 31
thirty-one	2	last card makes 31 exactly

*Pegs 3 for a 3-card flush in the hand, or 4 if this also matches the starter. A 3-card flush in the crib is not valid – all four, including the starter, must be of the same suit.

Note. Any individual card may be counted as many times as it forms part of a distinct combination. For example, 7–7–7 scores 6 because the prial consists of three distinct pairs of two cards, scoring 2 each. Similarly, the combination 8–7–7–7 would score 12, counting 6 for the prial of Sevens, plus another 6 for the three different fifteens that can be made by attaching the Eight to each of the three Sevens in turn.

As to the crib, the dealer will naturally seek to lay aside cards that promise to combine well, such as a pair, a fifteen, or a two-card run, while the non-dealer will try to contribute cards bearing no such relation to each other.

The starter. When both have discarded to the crib, non-dealer cuts the pack (without revealing the bottom card of the top half), and Dealer takes the top card of the bottom half and places it face up on top. This is called the starter, or turn-up. If it's a Jack, Dealer scores 2 'for his heels'.

The play. Non-dealer leads to the play by placing any card face up on the table and announcing its value, e.g. 'One' if an Ace, 'Ten' if a court, and so on. Dealer responds by playing a card face up and announcing the combined value of the first two cards. If these form a pair, or total 15, dealer announces that fact and pegs two points immediately.

Note. *Play your cards face up in front of yourself, taking care not to muddle them up with those played by your opponent.*

This continues, with each in turn playing another card, announcing the new total made by all cards so far played, and pegging for any combination they may make when considered in conjunction with those immediately preceding it in unbroken succession (other than a flush, which doesn't count in this part of the game).

Note. *A run is valid regardless of what order the cards were played in, as long as they were played in unbroken succession. For example, if North plays Four, South Seven, North Six, South Three, and North Five, then North pegs 5 for completing the five-card run. South could then play a Two and peg for a run of 6. But if the cards played in order had been 4–7–6–3–3–5, the last card would not have made a run because it was interrupted by the pair of Threes (which pegged 2).*

The 'go'. Neither player may bring the count beyond 31, but each must play if able to do so without breaking that rule. If you can't play without exceeding 31, or have played your last card, you say 'Go', and your opponent then continues the series alone by playing as many more cards as possible and scoring for any combinations they make with one another.

Whoever plays the last card pegs 1 point, or 2 points if the final total is 31 exactly.

If either player reaches 121 in course of play, the game ends. If not, continue as follows.

The show. Both players now pick up the cards they played, add them to any cards they didn't get to play, and score for whatever combinations they contain. For this purpose, however, each player includes the starter as if it were a fourth card in their own hand.

Non-dealer shows and scores first, counting for each and every combination that can be made from the four cards concerned. A run may therefore consist of three or four cards for a score of 3 or 4. A three-card flush in hand pegs 3, or 4 if it matches the suit of the starter. Finally, if the original three-card hand includes the Jack of the same suit as the starter, it pegs an extra '1 for his nob'.

Note. *If the starter is a Jack, neither player can claim 'one for his nob', as this is precluded by the dealer's original score of 'two for his heels'.*

The dealer then scores in exactly the same way for their own hand when non-dealer has finished, unless non-dealer reached 61 and thereby won. If this doesn't bring the dealer to 61, they then turn the crib face up and scores for that in almost the same way. The only difference is that a flush of four cards doesn't count. To score for a flush, all five cards, including the starter, must be of the same suit.

End-game. The game ends as soon as one player has pegged out by reaching or exceeding a score of 61. From that point on, no further cards may be played or combinations counted by either player. If the loser fails to reach 31, they are lurched, or in the lurch (or, in America, skunked), and the winner counts a double game or stake.

Example of play

South deals as follows:

North   ♦A ♥6 ♥7 ♠7 ♥9
South   ♣3 ♠5 ♣6 ♦6 ♠J

North decides to keep the Six and Nine for a fifteen and the ♥7 for a three-card flush. He therefore discards ♠7 and ♦A to South's crib. He is sorry to lose the Ace, which often scores 1 for the go in the play up to 31, but doesn't mind splitting the pair of Sevens, and is glad that his two discards bear no useful relation to each other.

South, discarding to her own crib, throws the Jack and Five for a fifteen, keeping in hand another fifteen for 2 and a pair for 2.

North cuts the cards and South turns ♠8 as the starter, much to North's delight.

North	♥9 'Nine'
South	♣6 'Fifteen for 2'
North	♥6 'Twenty-one and a pair 2'
South	♦6 'Twenty-seven and a prial 6'
North	'Go'
South	♣3 'Thirty for 1'

(North led the Nine, thinking that the fact that he held a Six reduced South's chances of making a fifteen. He did consider leading the Seven, then if South had made fifteen with an Eight, he could have played the Six or Nine for a run of three.)

North, having pegged 2 points in the play, now reveals his hand and pegs as follows: 'Fifteen 2, fifteen 4, run of four 8, flush 11'.

South, having pegged 9 in play, retrieves her cards and declares 'Fifteen 2 and a pair's 4'. She then turns the crib and counts: 'Fifteen 2, fifteen 4, and one (for his nob) 5'. She naturally regrets that her Ace is not of spades, otherwise she would have pegged 5 for the flush.

The net result, at the end of the first deal, is that North has pegged a total of 16 (including 3 to compensate for not dealing first), to South's 18.

Partnership Cribbage (for four players)

Partners sit opposite each other and play alternately.

Everyone receives five cards and discards one to the crib, which belongs to the dealer.

A starter is turned and the player at Dealer's left begins the play up to 31, which proceeds as at two-handed Crib.

Each in turn, starting with the player at Dealer's left, then counts their hand, and the dealer, finally, counts the crib.

Each side scores the total made by its two members, but it is usual for individual players to receive from everyone else side-payments for special occurrences, such as dozens (a hand scoring 12 or 24), or 'nineteens in the box'. A 'nineteen in the box' is a crib that pegs no points at all – so called in allusion to the fact that no possible combination of five cards can ever score exactly nineteen.

Scoring features at Five-card Cribbage		
in hand, crib, or play		
fifteen	2	two or more cards totalling 15
pair	2	two of the same rank
prial (pair royal)	6	three of the same rank
double pair royal	12	four of the same rank
run	3–6	three or more in sequence
in hand or crib only		
flush	3–5	three to five of a suit*
his nob	1	Jack of the turned suit
in play only		
go	1	last card played if not 31
thirty-one	2	last card makes 31 exactly

*Pegs 3 for a 3-card flush in the hand, or 4 if this also matches the starter. A 4-card flush in the crib is not valid – all five, including the starter, must be of the same suit.

Note. Any individual card may be counted as many times as it forms part of a distinct combination. For example, 7–7–7 scores 6 because the prial consists of three distinct pairs of two cards, scoring 2 each. Similarly, the combination 8–7–7–7 would score 12, counting 6 for the prial of Sevens, plus another 6 for the three different fifteens that can be made by attaching the Eight to each of the three Sevens in turn.

The game is played up to 121 or 181 – that is, twice or three times round the standard cribbage board, though it is possible to obtain boards of 121 or 181 holes.

Cribbage (for three players)

Deal five cards each and one face down to the crib, which belongs to the dealer, and to which everybody then contributes one card, leaving a playing hand of four. The player at the dealer's right cuts the pack, the dealer turns a starter, and the third player leads to the first round of play. After play, the player at the dealer's left counts first, then the player at the dealer's right, and finally the dealer, who counts for hand and crib.

Six-card Cribbage (for two players)

Cards. Use a standard 52-card pack.

The running order of cards is A 2 3 4 5 6 7 8 9 10 J Q K. (Ace is always low.)

For the purpose of adding up card values the numeral cards count at face value (with A = 1) and face cards count 10 each.

Object. To be the first to reach 121 (or any other agreed target), over as many deals as it takes, by (a) making card combinations and (b) playing up to 31.

Deal six cards each, face down, one at a time, starting with non-dealer, and stack the rest face down.

Scoring features at Six-card Cribbage		
in hand, crib, or play		
fifteen	2	two or more cards totalling 15
pair	2	two of the same rank
prial (pair royal)	6	three of the same rank
double pair royal	12	four of the same rank
run	3–7	three or more in sequence
in hand or crib only		
flush	4–5	four or five of a suit*
his nob	1	Jack of the turned suit
in play only		
go	1	last card played if not 31
thirty-one	2	last card makes 31 exactly

*Pegs 4 for a 4-card flush in the hand, or 5 if this also matches the starter. A 4-card flush in the crib is not valid – all five, including the starter, must be of the same suit.

Note. Any individual card may be counted as many times as it forms part of a distinct combination. For example, 7-7-7 scores 6 because the prial consists of three distinct pairs of two cards, scoring 2 each. Similarly, the combination 8-7-7-7 would score 12, counting 6 for the prial of Sevens, plus another 6 for the three different fifteens that can be made by attaching the Eight to each of the three Sevens in turn.

Laying away. Both players examine their hands and make any two discards face down. These four discards form the crib, which is put on the dealer's side of the table. Once they have been laid away, neither player may examine them before the end of the hand. Each player's aim is to retain four cards that will be of most use in the play and will score best for the standard Cribbage combinations as shown in the table (p. 233).

As to the crib, the dealer will naturally seek to lay aside cards that promise to combine well, such as a pair, a fifteen, or a two-card run, while the non-dealer will try to contribute cards bearing no such relation to each other.

The starter. When both have discarded to the crib, non-dealer cuts the pack (without revealing the bottom card of the top half), and Dealer takes the top card of the bottom half and places it face up on top. This is called the starter, or turn-up. If it's a Jack, Dealer scores 2 'for his heels'.

The play. Non-dealer leads to the play by placing any card face up on the table and announcing its value, e.g. 'One' if an Ace, 'Ten' if a court, and so on. Dealer responds by playing a card face up and announcing the combined value of the first two cards. If these form a pair, or total 15, Dealer announces that fact and pegs 2 points immediately.

Note. *Play your cards face up in front of yourself, taking care not to muddle them up with those played by your opponent.*

This continues, with each in turn playing another card, announcing the new total made by all cards so far played, and pegging for any combination they may make when considered in conjunction with those immediately preceding it in unbroken succession (other than a flush, which doesn't count in this part of the game).

Note. *A run scores regardless of what order the cards were played in, as long as they were played in unbroken succession. For example, if North plays Four, South Seven, North Six, South Three, and North Five, then North pegs 5 for completing the five-card run. South could then play a Two and peg for a run of 6. But if the cards played in order had been 4–7–6–3–3–5, the last card would not have made a run because it was interrupted by the pair of Threes (which pegged 2).*

The 'go'. Neither player may bring the count beyond 31, but each must play if able to do so without breaking that rule. If you can't play without exceeding 31, or have played your last card, you say 'Go', and your opponent then continues the series alone by playing as many more cards as possible and scoring for any combinations they make with one another.

Whoever plays the last card pegs 1 point, or 2 points if the final total is 31 exactly.

If any cards remain in hand after the Go, those so far played are turned face down and another bout of play is begun by whichever player did not play the previous card. (And they play alone, if the other has no cards left.) If this also does not exhaust the cards, there is a third round of play up to 31, but this rarely happens.

If either player reaches 121 in course of play, the game ends. If not, continue as follows.

The show. Both players now pick up the cards they played, add them to any cards they didn't get to play, and score for whatever combinations they contain. For this purpose, however, each player includes the starter as if it were a fifth card in their own hand.

Non-dealer shows and scores first, counting for each and every combination that can be made from the five cards concerned. A run may therefore consist of four or five cards for a score of 4 or 5. A four-card flush in hand pegs 4, or 5 if it matches the suit of the starter. Finally, if the original three-card hand includes the Jack of the same suit as the starter, it pegs an extra '1 for his nob'.

Note. *If the starter is a Jack, neither player can claim 'one for his nob', as this is precluded by the dealer's original score of 'two for his heels'. (Sadly, one must report that the traditional phrase 'one for his nob' is unknown to many modern players.)*

The dealer then scores in exactly the same way for their own hand when non-dealer has finished, unless non-dealer reached 121 and thereby won. If this doesn't bring the dealer to 121, they then turns the crib face up and scores for that in almost the same way. The only difference is that a four-card flush doesn't count. To score for a flush, all five cards, including the starter, must be of the same suit.

End-game. The game ends as soon as one player has pegged out by reaching or exceeding a score of 121. From that point on, no further cards may be played or combinations counted by either player. If the loser fails to reach 91, they are lurched, or in the lurch (or, in America, skunked), and the winner counts a double game or stake.

Example of play

South deals as follows:

North   ♦A ♣3 ♦4 ♦6 ♥9 ♣9

South   ♣A ♠2 ♠6 ♥7 ♣8 ♣J

North likes the look of his potential runs (A–3–4–6, requiring a 2 or 5 to fill), and would prefer to keep low cards for the play. However, he doesn't want to throw a pair (of Nines) to South's crib for the sake of nothing for a might-have-been, and instead parts with A–3. This gives him a hand worth 6 for the fifteens.

South has no hesitation about keeping the run of three and the Ace, and discards the Two and the Jack to her crib.

The play proceeds:

North   ♦4 'Four'
South   ♥7 'Eleven'
North   ♥9 'Twenty'
South   ♣8 'Twenty-eight for 3'
North   'Go'
South   ♣A 'Twenty-Nine for 1'

The cards are turned down and North leads to the next round:

North   ♣9 'Nine'
South   ♠6 'Fifteen for 2'
North   ♦6 'Twenty-one, pair 2 and one's 3'

North counts his hand as follows: 'Fifteens 2, 4, 6, and a pair's 8, nine-ten-eleven'. Note that the Six counts with each of the Nines to make two separate fifteens, and that a third is formed by summing the run of 4–5–6, which also counts 3 as a run.

South's hand is: 'Fifteen 2, fifteen 4, five-six-seven-eight-nine' (for the run of four). Note that the Eight makes a fifteen with the Six–Ace as well as with the Seven.

Turning her crib, South counts: 'Fifteen 2, fifteen 4, five–six–seven (for the run), and one for his nob, eight'.

Net result: North pegged 3 in play and 11 in hand, total 14. South pegged 6 in play, 9 in hand, and 8 in the crib, total 23.

Points of order. The correct procedure for making the starter is as follows. Non-dealer lifts off the top of the pack a packet of cards numbering at least six, and leaving at least six on the bottom half. To prevent the bottom card of the top half from

figure 24.2 Cribbage

'One for his nob' and 'two for his heels' are phrases dating back to the days when court figures were depicted at full length. Both his 'nob' (= head) and his heels are clearly visible on this 17th-century Knave (Jack) of spades.

being seen, they should not be tilted or lifted any higher than necessary to enable Dealer to extract the next card down. Non-dealer then places the top half squarely atop the bottom half, and Dealer places the starter face up on top of that.

Disputes sometimes occur about the validity of combinations pegged in play. The main thing to notice is that the cards of a run need not have been played in numerical order, as illustrated in the playing example given above. A run is, however, broken by a pair. For example, if the cards played in order are 3–4–6–5, the Five makes a run of four, but if they are 3–4–6–6–5, then it does not. However, they could be followed by a Four or Seven, making a three-card run with the last-played Six and Five.

The following is true even if apparently illogical. Suppose the cards played are 7–2–7. The last Seven does not make a pair, as it is separated from the first by the intervening Two. But if the cards played are 7–7–7, the third Seven is not regarded as being separated from the first, so all three of them peg 6 for the prial.

For the sake of discipline, and to ensure that players keep track to their own and the other's rightful score, combinations should be reckoned in this order: fifteens, pairs, runs, flushes and his nob. Scores are announced cumulatively as you go along.

The play

There are 15 different ways of discarding two cards from a hand of six cards, and the knack of Crib lies in choosing the best two. To add to the interest, the best two discards from any given hand usually depends on whether it's you or your opponent in the box. A perennial problem is that many hands are easier to split 3–3 or 5–1 than 4–2, and it's in the handling of these that you'll need all your wits about you.

In throwing to your opponent's crib, you will naturally avoid discarding Fives, Tens, courts, pairs, and two sequential cards, though you needn't worry about offering two of a suit, as the chances of making a five-card flush are remote. There are, however, two circumstances in which you can ignore these dangers. One is if the four cards left in hand give you higher-scoring combinations than the dealer is likely to get, bearing in mind that they may not be laying aside cards that fit in with yours. The other is when you're close enough to 121 to stand a chance of getting there first, either in the play, or by virtue of being first to score for the show. In either of these cases it hardly matters which two cards you lay aside.

Throwing to your own crib is not so nerve-racking. Given a hand rich in combinations, just work out which of the possible 4–2 splits give you the most points for certain, and go for that. Given the opposite, just keep the cards that are likely to be most useful in the play to 31. Obviously, these will include low cards like Aces and Twos, and adjacent or nearby ranks that may enable you to score for runs.

In leading to the play, you'll want to avoid a Five, Ten or court, which runs the immediate danger of offering a fifteen. Any card lower than Five is a good lead, as it makes an immediate fifteen impossible. Having passed fifteen, the worst thing you can do is to let the other player go out with a pair to 31. For example, avoid playing a Ten or court to a count of 2l, Nine to 22, and so on.

Variations

Losing Crib

This is played exactly like the parent game, but the first to reach 121 is the loser. This may sound trivial, but a little practice will prove there's more to think about than meets the eye at first. At least one Cribbage software program offers the Losing game as an option, and it is an interesting challenge to see how low you can get your final score. The lowest I have ever managed is 36 – can you beat it?

Auction Crib

Deal six cards each as in the standard game, and discard two to the crib. In this case, however, neither player knows for certain which of them will be in the box. Whoever it is will have the advantage not only of counting the crib, but also of counting for hand and crib before the other counts their hand. This privilege goes to whichever of them bids higher in the auction. A bid is a number of points that the bidder is prepared to deduct from their current score before starting play. Non-dealer may pass or make an opening bid of 'One (or more). Dealer may pass or bid higher, and bidding continues alternately until one of them passes. The other then deducts the amount of their bid by moving their forward peg backwards by the stated number of holes, and the dealer cuts the pack for the starter, scoring 2 for his heels if it is a Jack. The final bidder plays first, and, after play, counts hand and crib before the other counts the hand. The deal alternates, regardless of who took the box in the previous deal.

See also

http://www.pagat.com/adders/crib6.html

http://www.pagat.com/adders/crib5.html
John McLeod's Pagat website has separate pages for the five- and six-card games, with links to many other sites.

Cribbage is one of the most popular and widespread games available for on-line play.

part four

rummy games

25

rummy

- for two to five players
- easy to learn
- good balance of chance and skill

Rummy is an old and simple card game (the only one my parents ever played, and then only at Christmas) that forms the basis of a whole family of more advanced and elaborate games such as Gin, Kalookie, Contract Rummy and Canasta. First recorded in the USA towards the end of the 19th century, it has since spread throughout the western world and even reconquered the Orient, where many believe it originated in the form of that Chinese tile game, Mah Jong.

The simplest form of the game is basic Seven-Card Rummy, played with a single pack, which reached its heyday in the 1920s and 1930s. It makes a solid introduction to further members of the Rummy family described in subsequent pages.

Before we begin, here are some essential Rummy terms common to all varieties.

Features common to all Rummy games

The general idea is to collect groups of three or more matched cards. Such a group is called a meld, and the verb 'to meld' means either to accumulate such a collection or to declare it by laying it face up on the table. (The latter is more accurate, since the word comes from German *melden*, meaning to announce or declare.)

A meld is either a set or a sequence.

A set, also called a group, is three or more cards of the same rank, regardless of suit, such as A–A–A, 7–7–7–7, etc.

A sequence is a series of three or more cards of the same suit and in numerical sequence, such as ♠2–3–4, ♥J–Q–K, etc. Whether Ace counts low (A–2–3) or high (Q–K–A) varies from game to game.

Many Rummy games include Jokers as 'wild' cards – that is, you can use one to stand for any 'natural' card missing from a meld. For example, you can meld ♣3–♣4–Joker, counting the Joker as ♣5.

In most Rummy games a meld, once it has been laid face up on the table, may be extended by the addition of extra cards one or more at a time. This is called 'laying off'. For example, with ♦5–6–7 on the table you could lay off ♦8 to one end of it, or ♦4 to the other, or both. Some games only allow you to lay off cards to your own melds, not to other players'.

Note that since all Rummy games by nature put the cards very much in order, it is essential to shuffle thoroughly between deals.

Seven-card Rummy

Players and cards. From two to five players use a single 52-card pack without Jokers. Ace counts low in a sequence: A–2–3 is valid, but Q–K–A is not. (Unless otherwise agreed – see Scoring.)

Deal. Deal seven cards each in ones. Stack the rest face down to form the stockpile or stock. Turn the top card of the stock and lay it face up to start the waste pile. Throughout play, the current top card of the wastepile is called the upcard.

Object. The aim is to be the first to go out by getting rid of the last card from your hand, whether by melding, laying off or discarding.

Start. The player at Dealer's left either passes or takes the upcard in exchange for any unwanted card from their hand. If they pass, the next in turn has the same option. This continues until someone starts the game by taking the upcard. If no one takes it, the player at Dealer's left starts the game by drawing the top card of stock, adding it to their hand, melding if possible, and discarding one card face up to the waste pile.

Play. Thereafter, each in turn from the left of whoever started plays as follows:

1 Draws either the upcard or the top card of the stockpile and adds it to their hand.
2 Lays a meld face up on the table in front of themselves (if able and willing), and/or (provided they have already made a meld of their own) lays a card off to a meld made by themselves or anybody else.
3 Ends their turn by discarding one card face up to the waste pile. If they drew from the waste pile, they may not discard the card they drew in the same turn.

End of stock. If a player draws the last card of the stockpile and does not go out in the same turn then, after they have discarded, Dealer gathers up the waste pile, shuffles it thoroughly, lays it face down as a new stock, and turns the top card face up beside it to start a new waste pile.

Going out and scoring. Play ceases the moment one player goes out, whether by melding, laying off or discarding the last card from their hand. They score or are paid by each player, according to the total value of cards left in their hands, counting Ace to Ten at face value and courts 10 each. (If it is agreed to allow runs ending in –Q–K–A, so that Ace counts high or low, then unmelded Aces left in hand count 11 against instead of 1 point.) This amount is doubled if the winner went 'rummy', that is, disposed of all their cards in one turn without having previously made any meld.

See also

http://www.pagat.com/rummy/index.html

26

gin rummy

- for two plays
- easy to learn
- a fast game of skill

The name of the game

Nobody knows for sure who first called this version Gin, but it would certainly have been with the same alcoholic idea in mind. The nomenclature of Rummy games is nowadays completely muddled, and you may find this game played under many other names.

Gin is a member of the Rummy family of card games, all of which are based on a single, simple theme – that of changing the cards in your hand one by one until they can be 'melded' into sets and sequences.

Although Gin first appeared in the early 1900s, it wasn't until the 1930s that it struck gold in the annals of popular culture by revealing itself to be the game of the great movie stars, as you may readily see if you set your video to record the films of this period. There's a simple explanation for this. Gin is easy to learn and fast to play, requires no fiddly in-deal scoring, can be performed on mental auto-pilot, and can be picked up and dropped out of at a moment's notice in between takes or walking-on parts. It has been said that the characters written about by American humorist Damon Runyon are mostly to be found playing Klob or Klaberjass, but I have now read his entire *oeuvre* and discovered that, while Klaberjass is often mentioned, they do in fact play mostly Gin.

So what is it, exactly? Well, it is not greatly different from the earliest known form of Rummy, the mid-19th century Mexican game of Conquián. Conquián was a simple win-or-lose game for a fixed stake, and if Elwood T. Baker, the supposed inventor of Gin, can be credited with anything, it is most probably with the refined scoring system, which made it more interesting to play for money, and gave an edge to players who could think and calculate just that little bit faster than their opponents. The great thing about Gin is that everyone thinks they can play it well, so, if they lose, they can blame it on card distribution. Those who really can play it well keep quiet about it, and just pocket their winnings.

Gin Rummy is very easy to learn and the rules are clear, simple and fairly well standardized.

The game

Cards. A standard 52-card pack is used. For the purpose of making sequences they run A2345678910JQK, the Ace always being low. For scoring purposes they are worth their face value, with Ace = 1 and court cards 10 each.

Deal. Whoever cuts the higher card chooses whether to deal first. Thereafter the winner of one hand deals to the next, and the winner of a game deals first to the next. It is important that the cards be thoroughly shuffled before play, Dealer having the right to shuffle last. Deal ten cards each, one at a time. Place the remainder face down to form a stock. Take the top card of the stock and lay it face up beside it to form the first 'upcard'. This will form the base of a gradually constituted waste pile of faced cards, the topmost of which is always known as the upcard.

Object. To be the first player to score 100 points over as many deals as it takes. In each deal, the aim is to be the first to go out by melding enough cards from your hand for the total value of your unmelded cards ('deadwood') not to exceed 10 points – or, better still, to 'go gin' by melding them all.

Melds. A meld is either:

- three or four cards of the same rank, or
- a sequence of three or more cards in the same suit.

Aces and Kings are not consecutive. The lowest possible sequence therefore starts A–2–3, and the highest ends J–Q–K.

To start. Non-dealer starts by either exchanging the upcard for any unwanted card from hand, or passing. If they pass, the dealer has the same option. If either player takes the upcard, that constitutes the first turn and the game continues from there. If both refuse it, non-dealer must start the game by drawing the top card of the stock and discarding any card face up on the original upcard to continue the waste pile.

Play. Thereafter, each player in turn must draw either the top card of the stock, or the faced upcard at the top of the waste pile, and finish by making one discard face up to the waste pile. It is not permissible to draw the upcard and discard it on the same turn. This continues until one player ends the game by spreading all or most of their cards face up on the table in valid melds of at least three cards each, which they cannot do until the value of any unmelded cards (deadwood) does not exceed 10.

Knocking. When satisfied with the low value of your deadwood, you can end the game by (theoretically) knocking on the table after drawing an eleventh card and before making a final discard. Actually, it is now usual to close the game by laying your final discard face down on the waste pile, an action still referred to as knocking.

Having knocked, you spread your hand of cards face up on the table, arranged in melds and with any deadwood clearly separated from them. Your opponent then does the same, but also has the privilege of 'laying off' any cards of their own deadwood which may be matched with any of your own melds, in order to reduce the penalty value of their deadwood. They cannot do this, however, if you went gin, having all melds and no deadwood.

The stock may not be reduced to fewer than two cards. If neither of you knocks by the time only two remain, the result is a no-score draw, and the same dealer deals again.

Score. If the knocker has the lower count for deadwood, they score the difference between the two deadwood values, plus 20 if they went gin.

If the opponent has an equal or lower value of deadwood, they score the difference (if any) plus a bonus of 10 for the 'undercut'. But they cannot undercut a gin hand, for which the knocker always counts 20, nor may the knocker's opponent score for gin, whether they had it already (in which case they should have knocked) or laid off all their deadwood.

The two players each keep a running total of their scores, so that it will be clear when one of them has reached or exceeded the game target of 100.

Game score. As soon as either player reaches or exceeds 100 points, the game ends and a line is drawn beneath both totals, beneath which various bonuses are recorded. The winner first records a bonus of 100 for game, then a 20-point 'box' bonus for each hand that they won. Finally, if they won every hand they add a bonus for 'shut-out'. The shut-out bonus is equivalent to twice the basic amount they scored, plus another 100 for game. (In some circles, the box bonuses are also doubled. Other bonus systems may be encountered.) The difference between the two final totals is the margin of victory.

Hollywood scoring system. For those who can't get enough of it, this is a method of playing three or more games simultaneously. Three sets of double columns are drawn up, each double column headed by the initials of the players. When you win your first hand, you record your score in the first set only. The score for your second won game is recorded in the first and second sets, and that for your third in all three, unless and until any of them has been ruled off with a win. As soon as a player reaches 100 in any of the three (or more) sets of columns, that set is ruled off and bonuses noted in the usual way. Play continues until all games have been completed and scored.

Oklahoma variant. In this version the most deadwood you are allowed to hold after knocking is not necessarily ten but is equivalent to the face value of the initial upcard. For instance, if the initial upcard was a Six you must have six or less to knock; if a King, ten. If the first upcard was an Ace, you must have a gin hand to go out. This adds some much-needed variety to the game and may now be regarded as standard.

The play

Managing your hand can be a somewhat mechanical affair, in the sense that for any given situation there is a fairly calculable best move. It is because there is a 'best' move that observation is the foremost aspect of skill required. What you do is:

- observe what your opponent is discarding and which of your discards they are drawing
- infer what sort of cards they have, assuming that they are either making the best moves or following a habit of play that you are used to
- remember all the key cards that have gone, and the changing contents of your opponent's hand as the play proceeds.

As to the play of your own hand, the first thing to note is the inadvisability of going all out for gin. The bonus of 20 isn't usually enough to compensate for the times when you should have knocked instead of waiting around for glory, and thereby found yourself more knocked against than knocking. And, worse still, being undercut for your pains. A typical game ends about half way through the pack, so if you get a knocking hand much earlier than that do not hesitate to go down for all you can get.

The draw. It is generally better to draw the stock card than the upcard. The more upcards you draw, the more transparent your hand becomes. Drawing upcards also means you are taking cards your opponent doesn't want (except when they are bluffing), while drawing the next card of stock may well prevent them from going gin. The best exception to the rule is when you need to take the upcard to convert two matching cards into a meld of three, thus eliminating three pieces of deadwood (including the discard) – or, of course, when it enables you to knock immediately. It may also be useful to expand a meld, especially if you thereby eliminate a high unmatched card; but this should be done with caution rather than as a matter of course, as it can do more harm than good. If, for example, you hold:

♠K–♥K–♣K, ♦7–8–9, ♠5 ♦5 ♥2 ♣2

it isn't worth taking ♦10 as the upcard, as you must then throw one of a pair and so halve the number of draws that will enable you to knock. One other conceivable reason for taking the upcard might be to reduce your deadwood when you suspect an imminent knocking from the other side of the table. The lower the rank discarded, the worse the danger would appear to be.

Because it is desirable to throw high cards instead of low ones, in order to keep your deadwood down, it is also reasonable to keep hold of pairs and two-card sequences acquired early in the game, in the hope that your opponent will discard a matching third in exchange for a lower-valued draw. But you shouldn't keep this up too long. When to give up such expectations and start reducing deadwood is a matter for fine judgement.

Keeping track of discards is fundamental to the play. Suppose your opponent throws ♠J. The easy assumption is that he is 'not collecting Jacks', so you discard ♥J at the next opportunity and are surprised to see him pounce on it. Too late you spot the ruse. He probably held something like ♥9 ♥10 ♣J and threw the Jack to draw one of the proper suit for the sequence. Even more cunningly, and perhaps at greater risk (depending on how well he knew the contents of your hand) he might have discarded from ♠J ♦J ♣J. Why, then, should he run a risk to bluff the fourth out of you? Because he thereby not only reforms his meld, but also prevents you from laying off a Jack when he goes out on the next turn, and perhaps undercutting him.

Of course, what's sauce for the gander is sauce for the goose, and you are at liberty to practise such stratagems yourself. And here's another. Suppose your opponent throws a Jack and you have two Jacks. You are tempted to take it immediately and complete a meld. But resist! She might have been playing from a pair. If so, leave it. She will be bound to throw the other Jack, and then you can take it and be certain she cannot lay off against that meld of yours and be in a position to undercut. For this to work, you must be pretty sure that she was playing from a pair to start with, and that she is not retaining the other Jack as part of a sequence. If all the Tens and Queens have gone, there is no danger of this; and if you've held your Jacks for some time, there's a fair chance that her discard was made from two. If it does go wrong, there is still the chance that either you will draw the other Jack or she will draw and discard it before too great damage is done. Unless she knows every card in your hand, she would be unlikely to draw it and keep it.

So much depends upon observation and remembrance of the contents of the waste pile that you must clearly be very careful in your choice of discard. The first card not to throw out is the one you have just drawn from stock and are still holding in your hand: if it really is useless don't let them know. Hang on to it for a turn or two before getting rid of it. On general principles, as already noted, it is desirable to throw out a high unmatched card in order to reduce deadwood. The time not to do so is when you suspect that it may be of use to your opponent. In particular, they may be deliberately forcing a card out of you by one of the bluffing stratagems described above, in which case you must hold it back for a turn or two. Check this by matching your proposed discard against the current upcard. The less relation it bears to it, by rank and suit, the better. One player of my acquaintance insists that the ideal discard is different in suit from, but adjacent in rank to, the current upcard.

It's possible to select a discard in such a way as to elicit useful information. Suppose you have to split up ♠K ♥K ♠Q ♣Q. In this case throw ♠K. If it is picked up, it can only be to go with another King (in which case you keep yours to lay off if necessary), since your own holding of the Queen shows that it can hardly be wanted for the sequence.

In arranging your melds after knocking, use a card in a set of four rather than in a sequence if you have the choice and it could go with either. In this way you certainly prevent your opponent from laying off against it, whereas with a sequence there is the danger that they may hold (and therefore lay off) an odd card attaching to one end of it.

In brief, play your own hand with methodical accuracy, and devote all your thinking to the constitution of the waste pile and the probable structure of your opponent's hand. Above all, remain flexible. Don't pick on a likely-looking meld at start of play and concentrate upon it for the rest of the game. Gin is a game of constantly shifting circumstances and you must be ready to change your plan of campaign at any moment.

See also

http://www.pagat.com/rummy/ginrummy.html

27

kalookie

- for two to five players, best for four
- easy to learn
- more skill than chance

Kalookie is a game spelt in various ways (also Kaluki, Caloochie, etc.) and played in even more varying ways in different parts of the (largely the English-speaking) world. Basically, it is ordinary Rummy played with two packs.

The version described here is derived from material collected by John McLeod from various Internet sources, referring to the game played in English sporting clubs as well as in private circles. Here it is usually played for stakes, but for ease of description and comprehension I have left the staking system till last. Even with stakes, it still requires a written score sheet.

The game

Cards. One hundred and six, consisting of two 52-card packs and two Jokers.

Object. To be the first to get rid of all your cards by gradually laying them out, face up, in melds (valid combinations). If you lay out all 13 at once it is a 'kalookie', which wins double if played for stakes.

Deal. Decide first dealer by any agreed means. The turn to deal and play passes to the left. Each player receives 13 cards dealt one at a time. The next card is dealt face up to the centre of the table to start a discard pile and the remaining undealt cards are stacked face down beside it as a stock. The top card of the discard pile, whatever it may be at any point in the game, is called the upcard.

Melds. A meld is either –

- three or four cards of the same rank and different suits, such as ♠K–♥K–♣K (but not ♠K–♠K–♦K–♣K), or
- three or more cards in suit and sequence, such as ♥4–5–6–7. Aces are always high, so ♣A–K–Q . . . is valid but not ♣A–2–3 . . .

The value of a meld is the sum of the point-values of its individual cards, as follows:

Ace	11
K, Q, J	10 each
2 to 10	face value
Joker	+(2 to 11) or −15

A Joker can stand for any desired card in a meld. In this case it assumes the point-value of the natural card that it represents, from 2 to 11 as the case may be. It counts 15 only as a penalty, when not forming part of a meld.

Play. The dealer's left-hand neighbour plays first. They must take either the upcard or the top card of the stock and add it to their hand, may then lay out an initial meld if able and willing, and finally must end their turn by discarding one card face up to the discard pile.

An initial meld – that is, the first meld that each player makes – must be worth at least 40 points. For example, ♠6–7–8–9–10 is a valid initial meld, but not ♠9–10–J–Q.

Thereafter, each in turn from the first player's left plays in the same way, except that they are not allowed (unlike the first player) to take the upcard unless they have already made an initial meld, or can use the upcard to make one.

Once you have made an initial meld, you are thereafter (or in the same turn) free to make new melds of any value, and to extend any meld on the table by adding one or more valid cards to it. This is called building and is subject to the following rules.

Building. You can add an individual card to a meld of your own or to anyone else's.

To a set of three, you can add a fourth, provided that it is of the fourth suit. For example, you can build only ♠3 to a set of ♥3–♣3–♦3. (And you cannot add a Joker to a set of four and claim that it represents an imaginary fifth suit.)

To a sequence of three or more cards, you can add one card to either or both ends, but not more than one to either end. For example, to a run of ♣7–8–9–10 you can build ♣6 or ♣J, or both, but not ♣5–6 or ♣J–Q.

You cannot count the value of a card you build towards the minimum of 40 needed to make an initial meld.

Jokers in melds. A meld may contain one or more Jokers. For example, a Joker in a set of three or four cards represents the same rank and whatever suit or suits are necessary to ensure that they are all different.

If you meld both Jokers and a natural card, you must say whether they form a set or a sequence, and, if a sequence, which of the several that are possible. For example, ♥6–Jo–Jo could be three Sixes, or ♥6–7–8, or ♥5–6–7, or ♥4–5–6.

If a suit-sequence contains a Joker, whether made as part of it or built to it later, the cards of the sequence must be arranged in order and with the Joker in the position that would be occupied by the natural card it represents.

Taking Jokers. If a meld contains a Joker and you hold the natural card it represents, you may, on your turn to play, take the Joker in exchange for your natural card. (This is why it is important to show by its position what card a Joker represents in a sequence.) However, you may do this only if:

- You have already made a valid initial meld, and
- You can immediately use the Joker in a new meld or build it on another one. You're not allowed to take it into hand for use on a subsequent turn.

Note. *There is an oddity about taking Jokers from sets. If a set of three contains a Joker, and you hold two natural cards that would complete the set to four, you may build them both in exchange for the Joker. Similarly, if it consists of a natural card and two Jokers, you can use one of the Jokers elsewhere and replace it with any two natural cards that would turn it into a valid set of four.*

No changing melds. Once a meld has been made, it cannot be changed or rearranged but only extended by building. If, therefore, you meld (say) ♥3–4–5 on one occasion and ♥7–8–9 on another, and then draw a ♥6, you can attach it to the appropriate end of either meld, but cannot coalesce all seven cards into a single sequence. (If you did, it would prevent anyone from building the other ♥6.) On the other hand, if you can meld a run of six or more cards at once, it is better to do so than to make two separate melds.

End of stock. If a player draws the last card of the stockpile and doesn't call up in the same turn, they withhold their discard while the dealer shuffles the discard pile and turns it face down as a new stock, then makes their discard to start a new pile. If this happens a second time, the game is declared null and void.

Calling up (Going out). If you are left with three or fewer cards in hand after ending your turn with a discard, you must announce how many cards you hold, otherwise you will not be allowed to call up on your next turn.

Play ceases the moment one player makes a final discard and is left with no cards in hand. Note that it is obligatory to make a final discard when calling up – you can't do it by melding and building all your remaining cards.

For a kalookie – melding 13 cards in one turn – you must first make a valid initial meld worth at least 40, then make any additional melds and builds you can, and finish with a final discard.

Once a player has called up, no one else may make any further melds or builds. (There is no laying off as in other Rummy games.)

Score. Everyone else totals the value of cards left in their own hand and records these as penalty points. The game ends when all but one player have reached or exceeded a previously agreed maximum, typically 150, and the overall winner is the one player who has not done so.

Ace	11
K, Q, J	10 each
2 to 10	face value
Joker	+(2 to 11) or –15

Some players count penalty points double if the winner goes kalookie. This is appropriate when not playing for stakes, as the staking game rewards it instead by doubling the payment.

Stakes. The game is often played for fixed stakes which must be agreed in advance, specifically for the following features:

- **call up** – the amount received by the winner of each hand from each other player
- **kalookie** – the amount received if they win by melding all 13 cards at once
- **initial stake** – the amount paid into the pool by every player at the start of the game
- **buy-in stake** – the amount that a player must add to the pool in order to re-enter the game when they have reached a maximum of penalty points.

A typical schedule is 1 unit for a call-up, 2 for a kalookie, and 5 each for the initial and buy-in stakes (where 1 unit represents any agreed amount, such as 10p or 10 cents).

Buying in. In the staking game, a player who runs over 150 points can buy in by paying the appropriate amount into the pool. Their penalty score is then reduced to equal that of the player who, having not yet reached 150, has the highest number of penalties. Nobody can buy in more than twice in the same game, nor can anyone buy in if all but one player have reached the maximum, leaving a winner.

See also

http://www.pagat.com/rummy/kaluki.html
Describes different forms of the game as played in Britain, Sweden and North America, and links to pages for the substantially different games played under similar names in Jamaica and South Africa.

28

contract rummy

- for three to eight players
- elaborate but easy to learn
- fun but skill-rewarding

Name of the game

Contract Rummy was so named in the 1930s when the deliberately hyped-up novelty of Contract Bridge was sweeping America and consigning Auction Bridge to the dustbin. It remains the best of all available names, though 'Progressive Rummy' is equally appropriate.

Every so often somebody posts a message on the card games mailing group (rec.games.playing-cards) outlining some basic rules for a domestic game and either asking what it is called, or calling it by some domestic name and asking whether it has any official rules. The commonest candidate for this treatment was originally and is best called Contract Rummy. In fact, it is less a single game than a variety of games based on a single idea – namely, that a game consists of several deals, typically seven, each imposing a specific pattern of melds (the contract) that a player must make before being entitled to go out. The earliest (Zioncheck) dates from the 1930s. Other names, each denoting a more or less trivial variant, include Hollywood Rummy, Joker R., Liverpool R., May I?, Seven-deal R. and Shanghai R. Enthusiasts continue to invent variations on the underlying pattern, often giving them names either knowingly or unwittingly used for obsolete forerunners, making it impossible to keep track of who means what by which.

Here follows a typical version.

The game

Preliminaries. Three or four players use two packs shuffled together, with one Joker. Five to eight use three such packs and two Jokers.

Deal. A game is seven deals. Choose the first dealer by any agreed method. Thereafter the turn to deal and play passes always to the left. Deal ten cards each in the first four deals and 12 each in the last three. Stack the rest face down, turn its top card face up, and place beside the stock to start a discard pile. The top card of the discard pile is called the upcard.

Object. To be the first to go out by getting rid of all your cards. Do so by combining them into melds and laying off individual cards to extend existing melds.

Melds. A meld is either:

- a set (also called a group or book) of three or more cards of the same rank, regardless of suit, such as ♣J–♠J–♥J etc., or
- a run of three or more cards in suit and sequence, such as ♠3–4–5–6 . . . etc. For this purpose the ordering is A2345678910JQKA. Ace counts high or low but not both at once. (Thus A–2–3 . . . and A–K–Q . . . are valid, but not K–A–2).

The Joker is wild – it may be used in a meld to represent any desired card.

Note. *Some circles play 'Deuces wild', meaning that all four Twos can be used as Jokers.*

Contracts. The point of the game is that no one may start melding until they can exactly match the pattern of melds required for that deal, which becomes progressively harder over the course of the game, as follows:

deal	dealt	required meld	sets	runs
1	10	6 cards as:	2 of 3	–
2	10	7 cards as:	1 of 3	1 of 4
3	10	8 cards as:	–	2 of 4
4	10	9 cards as:	3 of 3	–
5	12	10 cards as:	2 of 3	1 of 4
6	12	11 cards as:	1 of 3	2 of 4
7	12	13* as at least:	–	3 of 4

*including the card drawn, and without discarding

Where two or more runs are required they may be of the same suit, and may overlap, but they must not be consecutive. For example, ♠ 2 3 4 5 ♥ 6 7 8 9 or ♠ 2 3 4 5 ♠ 4 5 6 7 are valid, but not ♠ 2 3 4 5 ♠ 6 7 8 9 melded by the same player at the same time. (But they may later become consecutive by the addition of cards laid off.)

Play. The basic procedure is that common to all Rummy games, but with one significant difference. At each turn, you:

1 Draw the top (face down) card of the stock, or the top (face up) card of the discard pile, and add it to your hand.
2 Lay out face up on the table the minimum melds required to fulfil the relevant contract, or, having done so in a previous turn, lay off one or more cards to existing melds.

3 End your turn by making one discard face up to the discard pile (except in the last deal, as explained later).

So much is common. The difference is this. If, on your turn to play, you do not want the current upcard, you may not draw from stock without first asking if any other player wants the upcard. (Which the polite ones do by asking 'May I?', thereby giving the game one of its many alternative names.) In this case the right to take it passes to each player in rotation until someones takes it or everyone passes. If anyone does take it, they must also draw the top card of stock, but may not discard. This increases their hand as a penalty for gaining a wanted card out of turn.

If a player does take the upcard, this will leave another upcard exposed (except after the first turn, in which case it is replaced by turning the next card from stock). Once again, as the person in turn to play, you have first choice of the new upcard, and if you don't want it must offer it around as before. This process may be repeated again, but no player is allowed to take more than one such upcard in the course of a single turn.

When everyone has had a chance to take the upcard, you continue your turn by taking either it or the top card of stock and continuing your play.

Whether or not you meld or lay off, you complete your turn by making a final discard, which must differ from the upcard if that is what you took.

Melding. You don't meld anything until you can meld the required pattern of melds for the deal, and you may not meld more than the basic requirement on that turn.

Laying off. Having once melded, you may, on subsequent turns (but not in the same turn as fulfilling your contract), lay off one or more cards to your own or other players' melds, but may not open any new ones. Sequences may be extended to a maximum of 14 cards, with an Ace counting low at one end and another counting high at the other.

Wild cards. No initial meld may contain more than one wild card. The only wild card you may take in exchange for a natural card is a Joker forming part of a sequence, and you may only do so if you can immediately lay it off to an existing meld: you cannot take it into hand for future use. When you hold a natural card that is being represented by a wild card in a sequence, you may add it to the sequence and move the wild card to either end.

For example, holding ♥7, you can lay it off to ♥ 6 W 8 9, making the W either ♥5 or ♥10. (W = wild card.)

Note. *You can never take a Joker from a set of cards of the same rank.*

End of stock. If the stock runs out before anyone goes out, shuffle all the discards except the final upcard, and stack them face down to make a new stock. The previous upcard remains in place to start a new discard pile.

If there have been many instances of players exercising the privilege of drawing an upcard out of turn, and thus also drawing two cards from stock, it is just possible for all the cards of the stock and discard pile to run out before there is a winner. In this case no one wins that deal, and everybody scores penalty points for deadwood, as described below.

Going out. In order to go out, you must, after drawing a card from the stock or discard pile, lay out all 13 cards in the form of two runs of four and one of five, leaving no cards in hand and making no discard.

Play then ceases immediately, and everyone else scores penalties for deadwood (unmelded cards remaining in their hands) at the rate of 15 each for Aces and wild cards, 10 each for courts, and numerals at face value.

The winner is the player with fewest penalty points at the end of seven deals.

See also

Most references to Contract Rummy (under that name) do no more than describe a set of rules or express some enthusiasm for the game. There may be others under different names.

http://www.pagat.com/rummy/ctrummy.html
http://www.pagat.com/rummy/carioca.html
http://www.pagat.com/rummy/push.html
McLeod's Pagat website has several pages devoted to related games, with links where appropriate. The Contract Rummy page lists a variety of names and rules. Another page is devoted to Carioca and Loba, two South American versions of the game, and a third to the closely related Push Rummy.

29

canasta

- for four players in partnerships
- complicated but worth the effort
- a game of skill

Canasta, the Bridge of the Rummy family, is a partnership game developed in Uruguay and Argentina some time around 1940. In 1949 it swept its way across the USA and became for a while the most preferred second-fiddle game of previously dedicated Bridge addicts. Just as it reached craze proportions in 1950s' Britain, the American version started developing even more complex varieties such as Samba and Bolivia. These games are now rarely played under their original names, but many of their features have been incorporated into the modern American variety of Canasta, with which the rest of the world has yet to catch up.

The following description is of what might now be called the classic game as played in Britain and almost everywhere else.

The game

Cards. One hundred and eight, consisting of two standard 52 packs plus Jokers. They needn't all be of the same back design and colour, but must be of the same size.

Game. Partners sit opposite each other, North-South versus East-West. A game may consist of one or more deals and is won by the first side to reach or exceed 5000 points. If both sides reach it on the same deal the one with the higher total wins. Scores are recorded at the end of each deal.

Deal. Decide first dealer by any agreed means; thereafter the turn to deal passes to the left. Deal 11 cards each, in ones. Place the undealt cards face down and squared up in the middle of the table to form the stock. Turn up the top card of the stock and lay it face up beside the stock. This starts the discard pile – best referred to as the pack – which must also be kept squared up throughout the game. The card on top of the pack is known as the upcard. If the first upcard is a Joker, a Two or a red Three, it must immediately be covered by the next card of the stock, and so on, until the upcard is of some other rank or a black Three.

With the stock and the first upcard settled, any player who has been dealt a red Three must place it face up on the table before them and is then dealt the top card of the stock to bring their hand back to 11 cards.

You are now ready to start play, but should first note the following basic facts about the game, which will give you an initial sense of direction.

Object. The object of the game is to collect and display on the table 'melds' of three or more cards of the same rank. A meld of seven or more cards is a canasta. No one can end the game until their side has made at least one canasta.

Jokers and Twos are 'wild' cards. They cannot be melded, but can form part of melds of non-wild or 'natural' cards (i.e. ranks from Four up to Ace).

Threes also cannot be melded (except black Threes in certain circumstances), but have special powers in play as outlined below.

All meldable cards have a melding value, which at the end of the game counts to your credit if they are lying in melds, but against you if still left in hand. The individual card values are shown in the accompanying table of Canasta scores.

In addition to individual card values, each completed canasta carries a bonus of 500 if it consists entirely of natural cards, or 300 if it contains one or more wild cards. (These are known respectively as a 'natural' and a 'mixed' canasta.)

Black Threes may only be melded when you are going out, as explained later.

Red Threes are bonus cards. Every time you get one you must lay it face up on the table before you. They are worth 100 each (doubled if you get all four) and count in your favour if you have made any melds, but against you if you have not.

The game normally ends when one player goes out by melding in one turn all the cards left in their hand.

Canasta scores	
Card values (each)	
Jokers	50
Aces and Twos	20
High cards (K Q J 10 9 8)	10
Low cards (7 6 5 4, black 3s)	5
Minimum initial meld	
Current score under 0	any
0 to 1495	50
1500 to 2995	90
3000 or more	120
Going out	
For going out	100
or, for going out blind	200
For each red Three	100
or, for all four, a total of	800
for each natural canasta	500
for each mixed canasta	300

Finally, you must be aware that Canasta is essentially a partnership game. Partners keep melds made by both of them together in one place on the table, not separately in front of each other. It is usually inadvisable (and always impolite) to end the game by going out without first asking your partner's permission.

Play. Starting with the dealer's left-hand opponent, each player in turn does one or more of the following three things in the following order:

- draw (take the top card of the stock or the pack)
- meld (start or add to a meld, if able and willing)
- discard (unless having just melded all one's cards).

These actions are subject to certain rules and regulations as follows.

Draw. You may always take the top card of the stock and add it to your hand. If you draw a red Three, you place it face up before you and draw again.

Instead of drawing from stock, you may take the whole of the pack, provided that you immediately meld the upcard – either by laying it off to one of your existing melds on the table, or by using it to start a new meld in conjunction with two or more matching cards from your own hand (for which purpose a matching natural card plus one wild card is sufficient, though some insist that you must hold a natural pair to start a new meld with the upcard).

But you may not take the discard pile in this way if it is *frozen*, which it is in the following circumstances:

- it is frozen to you and your partner until your side has made its first meld
- it is frozen to everybody whenever it contains a wild card (or a red Three as the result of the initial turn-up).

In these cases you may only take the pack if you can immediately use the upcard to start a new meld in conjunction with at least two matching natural cards from your own hand. (If you have none on the table already, this may count as your initial meld provided it meets the initial meld scoring requirement described below under 'melds'.) Furthermore:

- The pack is frozen to you personally if the upcard is a black Three. In this case you may not take it at all but can only draw from stock. (The pack is said to be stopped, rather than frozen.)

Melds. All melds made by you and your partner are kept together in one place. Subject to rules governing composition and value of melds, you may in your turn start one or more new melds, and/or lay off one or more natural or wild cards to any of your partnership's existing melds. Cards once melded cannot be retrieved for further play.

A meld must contain three or more cards, of which at least two must be natural, and not more than three may be wild. All natural cards in a meld must be of the same rank.

A canasta is a meld of seven or more cards. It may be melded in one go or gradually built up by laying off additional cards to smaller melds. Once completed, the cards of a canasta are squared up in a pile, with a red card face up on top if it is a natural canasta (having no wild cards), or a black card if it is 'mixed' (having one or more wild cards).

A canasta must contain at least four natural cards, but there is no limit to the number of wild cards that may belong or be subsequently added to it. As soon as any wild card is laid off to a natural canasta, remember to replace the top red card by a black one.

Red Threes are not melded. Black Threes may only be melded if you go out on the same turn (see below).

Canasta scores	
Card values (each)	
Jokers	50
Aces and Twos	20
High cards (K Q J 10 9 8)	10
Low cards (7 6 5 4, black 3s)	5
Minimum initial meld	
Current score under 0	any
0 to 1495	50
1500 to 2995	90
3000 or more	120
Going out	
For going out	100
or, for going out blind	200
For each red Three	100
or, for all four, a total of	800
for each natural canasta	500
for each mixed canasta	300

Initial meld. The first melds or melds made by a partnership must total not less than a certain minimum value. This value depends on your partnership's cumulative score in the current game, as shown in the accompanying table of Canasta scores.

You may count the combined values of more than one meld towards this minimum requirement, but you may not count the 500 or 300 point canasta bonus towards it, nor any bonus deriving from red Threes.

Although the pack is frozen to you and your partner until one of you has made an initial meld of sufficient value, the initial meld does not have to be made entirely from the hand. Provided it meets the minimum requirement, you can make it by melding the upcard with at least two natural cards from your hand.

Discard. Having drawn a card or taken the pack, you complete your turn (whether you melded or not) by taking a card from your hand and placing it face up on the pack, unless in your turn you go out and have nothing left to discard. In discarding, note that:

- you may not discard a red Three
- if you discard a black Three, you thereby freeze the pack to your left-hand opponent for one turn only
- if you discard a wild card you thereby freeze the pack to everybody, and it remains frozen until taken.

To show that the pack is frozen, place the wild card crosswise on top of the pack, so that it will remain projecting from the pack in future turns, signalling the fact that it is frozen.

Ending by going out. The game normally ends when one player goes out by melding, laying off or discarding the last card from their hand. Going out is subject to certain rules and restrictions.

You may not go out unless your side has made at least one canasta. But you can meet this requirement by melding or completing a canasta on the turn in which you go out. It is only when you are going out that you may meld three or four black Threes.

If after drawing from stock you are in a position to go out, you are permitted (but not required) to ask your partner's permission. If you do ask, you must do so before melding any card at all. The correct wording is 'May I go out, partner?', to which they must reply either 'Yes' or 'No'. You are then bound by their reply. In fact, if they assent and you find that you cannot go out after all, you are penalized 100 points.

You get a bonus of 100 for going out 'blind' – that is, if you personally have not previously melded anything during the course of the current deal. But you only qualify for the bonus if all your cards are meldable in their own right – you don't get it if you lay off cards to your partner's melds.

Ending by exhausting stock. Somebody usually goes out before the stock is used up, but in case they don't, this is what happens. If you draw the last card from stock and it is a red Three, turn it face up, make whatever melds you can, but don't finish with a discard. That ends the deal.

If it isn't a red Three, play in the usual way and finish with a discard. The next in turn must then take the pack (by melding the upcard) if legally able to do so. If they can't, the deal ends.

If they can, they make his play and then discards. From now on the 'pack' will only ever consist of the previous player's discard. If on your turn the previous discard matches one of your melds, you are obliged to take it, lay it off, and then discard. If it doesn't match, but can still be melded with the aid of cards from your hand, you may either take no action, in which case the deal ends, or you may make your meld(s), in which case you must discard unless you go out.

This continues until any player in their turn either goes out or fails to take the previous player's discard because unable or unwilling to do so.

Canasta scores	
Card values (each)	
Jokers	50
Aces and Twos	20
High cards (K Q J 10 9 8)	10
Low cards (7 6 5 4, black 3s)	5
Minimum initial meld	
Current score under 0	any
0 to 1495	50
1500 to 2995	90
3000 or more	120
Going out	
For going out	100
or, for going out blind	200
For each red Three	100
or, for all four, a total of	800
for each natural canasta	500
for each mixed canasta	300

Scores. Each side reckons its score first for bonuses and then for cards. The bonuses for going out are shown in the third section of this table of Canasta scores.

To these bonuses, each side adds the total face value of all the cards they melded, counting for each card its face value as shown in the table.

From the combined total for bonuses and cards, each side now subtracts the total meld value of all cards remaining unmelded in the hand. The side that went out, of course, will have cards left only in one hand; the other side will have two handfuls to count against them.

Note the following about red Threes:

- if a player proves to have a red Three in hand, having failed to expose it on the table, it counts 500 against their side
- if a partnership has melded nothing at all then any red Threes they have drawn count not as bonuses but as further penalties (of 100 each, or 800 for all four).

The play

There are two sorts of Rummy game: those where the aim is to meld out as fast as possible for a quick bonus, and those where the main object is to build up a large score by making as many melds as possible. Canasta is of the second or big-melding type. The side that melds first gains an immediate advantage, having, as it were, hatched the goose that lays the golden eggs, and they should go on exploiting this advantage for all it is worth. As soon as the other side has caught up, the first side should be in or approaching a position where it has the minimum canasta requirement for going out – not for the sake of using it quickly, but for its power as a threat to the opponents. When you get a real chance of going out, you should wait till you have a good reason for doing so. For example:

- Despite your lead and initiative, your opponents are now beginning to catch up or even threatening to overtake you.
- Your opponents are so far ahead that going out is your best defence against a huge loss.
- You may have been dealt the sort of hand on which a 'quick out' will produce a small profit without your having to work too hard for it. But this does not happen very often, and you needn't go out of your way to look for it.

Otherwise, your main aim should be to break into a scoring vein as soon as possible, get as much out of it as you can while the going is good, and pull out when your advance begins to lessen – or, if you find yourself on the wrong side, to prevent your opponents from doing the same thing, even to the extent of pulling out prematurely if you consider the task hopeless.

How to set about this? Inevitably, this aspect of the game revolves around the taking of the pack (the discard pile). Even if it contains no more than three or four cards, it is nearly always advantageous to the player who takes it, and most of your play will be directed towards this end. Usually the first side to take the pack is then able to seize the initiative and dictate the course of the game. If your opponents get it first, you must be prepared to play defensively until you can afford to meet them on their own ground.

Initial meld. At start of play your immediate aim is to make the initial meld that will set you off on a scoring spree. So strive for it – but not at the expense of all other considerations. In particular, try to meld as economically as possible. The fewer cards you keep in hand, the less chance you have of taking the pack, so it can be self-defeating to use up too many in making an initial meld. For this reason you should also prefer not to make your initial meld entirely from the hand: wait until you can meld by taking the pack, so as not to deplete your hand unnecessarily.

In subsequent rounds of play, when your initial meld requirement advances to 90 or 120, you may have to accept the sacrifice of more cards in order to compensate for the extra difficulty of meeting the minimum value. Even so, you should try not to spend more than four cards for the 90, or six for the 120.

Further melding. Having started, make as many melds as you can, in order to keep the pressure up and increase your ability to take the pack. The more melds you can lay off to, the greater difficulty your opponents have in finding safe discards. Don't hesitate to devalue natural canastas by adding wild cards to them, and don't cripple yourself for the sake of working towards the bonus for going out blind. The bonus is fine if your hand happens to lend itself to that fortunate prospect; but if not, forget it.

There are times when you can usefully exercise restraint in making melds. The question of economy is one of them, as it was in the case of the initial meld: don't part with too many cards, and in particular don't part with any which may be of use in capturing the pack later. For the same reason it is also sensible to refrain from melding when the discard pile is large: the more cards you keep in hand the more chance you have of taking the pack. A good time to do your melding is when the pack has just been taken, even if not by yourself.

The importance of completing your first canasta is obvious, as it puts you in a position of constant threat (to go out). It is also important throughout the game not to fall behind in the completion of canastas, for which purpose mixed canastas, though less profitable than natural ones, are infinitely better than none at all.

Freezing the pack. It is a beginner's irritating habit to freeze the pack for no better reason than that they happen to be able to, and can't think of anything else to do. So when is it right and when is it wrong to freeze?

The most important time to freeze the pack is when your opponents have started melding and you have not, as it is your only effective defence against their ability to keep on recapturing it for continual rewards. Freezing is also a good defensive move when your opponents have too many cards in hand and melds on the table, as it enables you with relative safety to discard their players (cards which match their melds and would otherwise enable them to take the pack) and improve the overall meldability of your own hand.

When the pack is frozen it helps to have a hand containing many pairs, as they give you more chance of capturing it. But this doesn't mean that a hand full of pairs is a good excuse for freezing the pack. You obviously don't want to freeze it when it seems highly probable that the other side can easily take it. Finally, avoid freezing for no better reason than that you can't decide what to discard. In the long run this can do you more harm than good.

Black Threes. If you can find a better discard than a black Three, make it, and save the Three for the time when it's the only solution to an otherwise impossible position. Given a black Three early in the game, a good time to discard it is often when you have just made an initial meld. Since it freezes the pack to your left-hand opponent only, it prevents them from taking the pack before your partner has a chance to take advantage of the position.

Wild cards should be put to work, not hoarded. Each one added to a meld is a bird in the hand when it comes to the score. The same goes for Aces.

Discarding. Discard low in early rounds, as such cards are not suitable for initial melds. Watch the discards made by your left-hand opponent and try to match them for as long as you feel they are genuinely throwing away unwanted cards. Since your right opponent will be watching you with the same objective in view, don't make things easy for them by automatically throwing out singletons. There are times when you can quite happily discard from three or more, so that when they subsequently discard the same rank you can capture the pack and meld. The only time to concern yourself seriously with your partner's discards is when there is a real danger of your opponents going out. By matching your partner's discards in this situation you may save yourself a lot of penalties.

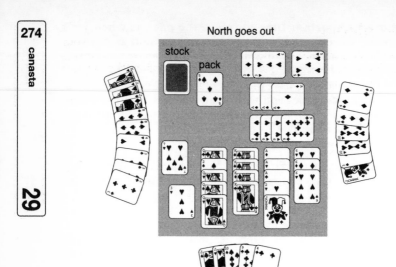

North goes out

stock

pack

left in South's hand

figure 29.1 canasta

You have just given your partner, North, leave to go out. Your side scores 100 for going out, 100 for the red Three, 300 for the mixed canasta (black Seven on top) and 90 for its component cards, 245 for melds on the table, total 835 less the 45 in your own hand, total 790. East-West score 200 for the red Threes, 500 for the natural canasta (red Five on top) and 35 for its component cards, 100 for melds on the table, total 835, less 160 for cards left in both hands = 675.

The time to throw out cards matching your opponents' melds is when the pack is frozen and they appear to have little chance of capturing it. Any cards that are of no use to you but possibly of use to them are best reserved for discarding until the pack is small.

Going out. We have already noted that going out is more of a defensive measure than anything else, either because you are too far behind and want to cut your losses, or because your opponents are beginning to catch up and you don't want to cut your profit margin. Watch the timing. A good time to go out is when your opponents have too many cards in hand.

See also

http://www.pagat.com/rummy/canasta.html
Description of many varieties of Canasta, including the modern American game, plus links to other sites.

part five

gambling games

30

newmarket

- for three to eight players, best for four
- easy to learn
- more fun than skill

This popular pastime of pubs, clubs and day centres has undergone many changes since first recorded under the name Newmarket. It can be traced back, in one form or another, to the 17th-century games of Hoc and Comet.

Differences of detail will be encountered from place to place. The following rules are ones I collected from my local day centre in South London in the early 1990s.

The game

Players. Three to eight; ideal for four.

Cards. Standard 52-card pack. Cards run from low to high as follows: A 2 3 4 5 6 7 8 9 10 J Q K.

Deal. Remove the four Kings and set them out face up on the table. Deal all the cards out one at a time, the last of each round going to a 'dead hand' which is left face down. It doesn't matter that some players have more cards than others.

Stake. Everybody stakes the same agreed amount to a pool or kitty, and another agreed amount on each of the four Kings.

Object. There are two aims.

- one is to be the first to play out all your cards, thereby winning the kitty
- the other is to win a King stake by playing the Queen of the same suit.

If no one goes out, the kitty is increased and carried forward to the next deal. The game ends when all four King stakes have been won. This may take several deals, and sometimes many more.

The buy. A player who doesn't fancy their cards can exchange hand for the dead one. Only one player may do this. Dealer has the first option, and, if they decline, it rotates to the left until someone else has exercised it or everyone has passed. Anyone who takes the dead hand, other than the dealer, must pay another stake to the kitty. The two hands may not then be changed back again.

Play. Each in turn plays a card face up to the table in front of themself. Whoever holds the lowest diamond starts by playing it. The holder of the next higher diamond plays next, then of the next up, and so on, in numerical order one at a time. If this sequence gets as far as the Queen, the player of that card wins the stake on the diamond King, turns the King down, and starts a new sequence as described below.

More usually, the sequence will peter out because the next diamond in sequence is lying in the dead hand so no one can play it. In this case the player of the last card starts a new sequence by playing the lowest card they hold of either black suit. If they have no black suit, the turn to start passes to the left until someone can go.

Play continues in the same way. Each sequence is continued by the player holding the other card of the same suit. Whoever plays a Queen wins the stake on the matching King (if it hasn't already been won in a previous deal), turns it down, and starts again. The starter of a sequence must play the lowest card they have of a suit opposite in colour from the one last played.

End of hand. There are two ways a hand can end:

- whoever plays the last card from their hand ends the play and wins the kitty
- if no one can start a new sequence because they can't change colour, play ceases and the kitty is carried forward.

In either case, the cards are gathered up, the deal passes to the left, and everyone adds another stake to the kitty.

Burying the Jack. When three King stakes have gone and only one remains, no one may buy the dead hand, and a new rule comes into play. The player holding the Queen matching the last King announces 'Bury the Jack' – or, if they also hold the Jack, the next card below the lowest card they hold of the sequence headed by the Queen. (Fox example, holding 9–10–J–Q they would say 'Bury the Eight'.) The holder of the card called for burial must then exchange their hand for the dead one, free of charge.

If no one holds the Queen, she being in the dead hand, play continues with the hands as dealt, and the King stake will be carried forward to the next deal.

End of game. The game ends when someone plays the Queen matching the last King. This wins both the King stake and the kitty.

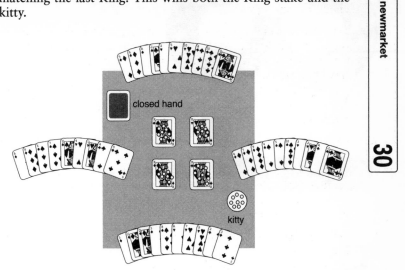

figure 30.1 Newmarket

West leads, holding the lowest diamond (Ace). No one has the Two, so West leads again, switching colour as required the play continues:

West	♣4–5, ♥4
North	♥5 ♣8 ♥2
East	♥3 ♠4–5
West	♠6–7
South	♠8 ♥A ♣2–3 ♦3
East	♦4
North	♦5–6
East	♦7
West	♦8
East	♦9 ♣A ♥J
West	♥Q ♠Q = out

West sweeps a King with each Queen and the kitty for going out. This looks like the first deal played with a new pack. It is rare for the suits to be evenly distributed and for everyone who completes a sequence to be able to switch colour for a new lead. The nature of the game is such that in subsequent deals players are more likely to be dealt hands containing a void suit or dominated by cards of one colour.

31

pontoon

- for two to eight players
- easy to learn
- good balance of chance and skill

The name of the game

Pontoon is probably a corruption of the French *Vingt-un* (nowadays *vingt-et-un*), meaning Twenty-One, the name by which it is universally known.

This gambling game is played all over the world. Its most general and accurate title is Twenty-One, but different versions of it appear in different countries and in various social contexts under a variety of characteristic names. Pontoon denotes the informal British game played at home, in school and (if permitted) in the pub. Its American equivalent is Blackjack, which in America denotes the home game (the casino game being known as Twenty-One), but in Britain and nearly everywhere denotes the version played in casinos and gaming clubs. As a casino game, it has the remarkable, if not unique, property of enabling an intelligent and assiduous player to consistently break even against the house, if not actually to stay ahead. This can be done by means of complex computer-aided analysis, but of course this makes the game less fun to play, especially as casino proprietors are quick to spot it and keen to stamp it out.

The following rules of the common or garden domestic British Pontoon are typical rather than definitive. As with all gambling games, details vary from school to school. It is important to note that this is not the game played in casinos under the name Blackjack. You will find the casino game described by Belinda Levez in *Teach Yourself How to Win at Card Games*, which deals only with casino games.

The game

Preliminaries. Informal Pontoon, as distinct from casino Blackjack, is played:

- by any number of players from two to about seven
- with a standard 52-card pack, and
- for chips, counters or other manageable objects.

Agree first on minimum and maximum permitted stakes – for example, one and five chips respectively. Each deal is a separate event and is settled individually. The game ends when one player goes broke, or after an agreed time-limit.

Choose the first banker by drawing a card from the pack: Ace counts high, and highest banks first. The bank subsequently passes to the first punter (non-banker) who makes a winning pontoon. A pontoon is a two-card combination consisting of an Ace and a tenner – that is, a card that counts ten (Ten, Jack, Queen or King).

Shuffling. The cards are shuffled before the game starts, and by each player upon taking over the bank. After each deal the banker returns all played cards to the bottom of the pack and cuts, but does not shuffle, before dealing. (Players may agree beforehand to dispense with the cutting rule.)

Value of cards. Cards are only of interest for their numerical values – their suits are irrelevant. Face cards count 10 each, others their face value, and Ace either 1 or 11 at the discretion of the holder (and they may change their mind about it as often as they like). Cards worth (10 J Q K) may be called tenners.

Object. In each deal your aim is to draw cards totalling more than the banker's cards, but not more than 21 or less than 15. The possible hands rank as follows:

Bust (over 21):	always loses to the banker
A count of 15–21:	wins if higher than the banker's total
Pontoon:	21 made with an Ace and a tenner (pays double)
Five-card trick:	five cards totalling not more than 21 (pays double)
Royal pontoon:	21 made with three Sevens (pays treble) (this hand is not universally recognized)

The deal and stake. The banker deals one card face down to each player, in clockwise rotation ending with themselves. Each punter (but not the banker) looks at their card and places a stake beside it, leaving the card face down on the table before them. This stake must not be less than the agreed minimum or more than the agreed maximum.

The banker then deals everyone a second card face down.

Pontoons? Having dealt two cards each, the banker now looks privately at his own cards to see if he has a pontoon. If so, he shows it, and each punter pays him twice their stake – except for a punter who also has a pontoon, in which case they show it and only lose their single stake.

If the banker does not have a pontoon he leaves his cards face down and indicates his readiness to play further. In this event, any player holding a pontoon must turn the Ace up to show that they cannot lose and will be taking over the bank.

Pairs? If you (not being the banker) have been dealt two cards of the same rank, you may split them and play them as two separate hands. They must be of exactly the same rank, not just different tenners, like a Queen and a Jack.

You indicate this by separating the two cards, placing the whole of your stake against one of them, and placing exactly the same amount as your stake against the other.

The banker will then deal you two more cards, one for each hand. Again, you look at your second cards, and may split again if you have another pair. In all subsequent play, you will count yourself as two (or more) separate people, and play each hand in turn as if you were several consecutive punters.

Stack, buy, twist or bust. The banker now addresses themself to each player in turn, dealing them as many more cards as requested, until the punter either sticks or declares themself bust.

- if your count is less than 15, you cannot stick, but must either buy or twist another card
- if it is 15 or more, you may buy or twist again, or stick if you're satisfied with your total
- if it is 22 or more you must declare yourself bust and return your cards to the banker, who places them face down at the bottom of the pack and wins your stake.

To buy a card, you add to your stake an amount not less than your initial stake and not more than twice that amount. The banker will then deal you a card face down, which you (alone) may look at.

When you twist a card, the banker deals it to you face up, free of charge. Once you have twisted a card, you cannot revert to buying but may thereafter only twist or stick.

Optional rule. Some play that if you have a total of four cards with a combined count of 11 or less, thus assuring yourself of a five-card trick, you cannot buy but may only twist a fifth.

When you have either bust or stuck, the turn passes to the player on your left, or to your next left hand if you are playing one or more split pairs. When everyone has done this, it is time for the banker's performance.

The banker's play. As banker, you play by the following advantageous rules.

- If everybody busts, you win all their stakes without further play. Otherwise, you now reveal your two cards and may either stick or continue to deal yourself more cards, face up, until you either stick or bust. (You may not split pairs.)
- If you bust, those left in the game turn their cards face up and you must pay each of them (provided their hand is valid) the total amount of their stake, doubled if they have a pontoon or a five-card trick, or trebled if they have a royal pontoon (three Sevens).
- If you stick at 21 you win the single stake of any punter with 21 or less, but pay a single stake to a punter's pontoon, or double stake to their five-card trick, or treble stake to their royal pontoon.
- If you stick at less than 21 you pay anyone who has a higher valid count. For example, with a count of 17 you say 'Pay 18', and anyone with 18 or more turns their cards face up to claim payment. As before, a pontoon or five-card trick is paid double and a royal pontoon treble.
- If you have a banker's five-card trick you beat anything except a pontoon or royal pontoon. (If you have a royal pontoon, however, you have no extra advantage. In the banker's hand it counts as an ordinary 21, and loses to pontoons and five-card tricks.)

Settlements at Pontoon:

Pontoon pay-offs		
hand below	is beaten by banker's	otherwise is paid
bust (over 21)	anything	–
count of 15–21	equal or higher	single stake
pontoon	pontoon (only)	double stake
five-card trick	five-card trick	double stake
royal pontoon	(unbeatable)	treble stake

Note. *A punter's five-card trick can't be beaten by a banker's pontoon, because if the banker had one then nobody could have drawn five cards. In some circles, incidentally, a banker's five-card trick beats a pontoon. This marginally increases the excitement on some hands, but there seems little point in increasing the banker's already generous advantage.*

Bank take-over. The bank is taken over by any punter who wins a pontoon (not a royal pontoon or a five-card trick), but not if they do so on a split hand. If more than one has a pontoon, it goes to the first of them to the present banker's left.

Alternatively, the banker may offer to sell the bank for any mutually agreeable price (but only between hands, of course).

The play

Skill at gambling consists in playing systematically, though not necessarily to a 'system'; adjusting the amount of your stake to the probability of winning; and resisting the temptation to stake wildly when low on resources. The recommended one-to-five minimum maximum stake enables you to (a) distinguish between a low, a middling and a high stake, in accordance with the probabilities, and (b) adjust this scale to your current resources. For example, when low on funds you should play cautiously and fix your stakes at, say, 1, 2 or 3; when well off you may fix them at 2, 3, 4 or 3, 4, 5; or at any other time work to a 1, 3, 5 series of gradations.

Don't underestimate the bank's advantage. Most of the banker's income derives from punters who bust, since they still pay even if the banker busts. Another large proportion comes from the fact that the banker wins from equals. And, in their own play, they have an advantage in knowing how many punters are standing against them. As a punter, your safest course is to stick when you can – even at 15, since the mean value of a card is seven, and the chances of your not busting are 2:1 against. The banker may conceivably stick at 15 if there is only one punter against them, but with three against them (or up to six, counting split hands) the draw of another card is more likely to win than an agreement to 'pay seventeens'.

The probability that the banker has a pontoon, or that you will be dealt one from scratch, is about 0.024, equivalent to less than 2.2 per cent, or one in every 41 hands. (Hence, in a four-player game expect to see a pontoon once in every ten deals.) The probability of being dealt a five-card trick from scratch, according to my calculations, is twice as high – amounting to about 0.045, or 4.4 per cent, or one every 22–23 hands. If fewer actually appear than this figure suggests, it is clearly because many potential five-card tricks are not filled out, but abandoned at the fourth or even third card. The probability that the banker will bust after you have stuck is about 0.3, or 3 in 10. This figure assumes that they follow the policy of always sticking when they can; if not, your chances improve.

The fact that an Ace may count 1 or 11 introduces some fascinating complications. In Blackjack terminology a hand containing an Ace and not exceeding 21 is described as 'soft'; if it exceeds 21 by counting the Ace as 11 it is 'hard'. It is pretty obvious that you should always stick at, say, 18 – but what about a 'soft' 18, which alternatively counts 8? Here the answer depends in part on how many cards you have – with four, for example, a count of 8 guarantees you a five-card trick; with three, you must consider the possibility of drawing an Eight or Nine, which gives you a lower stickable number, an Ace, Two or Three, which gives you a 21 or a five-card trick, a tenner, which leaves you back where you started (with 18), or one of the other four ranks, which complicate matters further.

Whether or not to split pairs is not a difficult question provided that you follow a policy in deciding which counts are good and which bad. If the individual count of each card is better than the total count of both, split them; otherwise, don't. All you need then is a good policy.

In view of the possibility of a five-card trick, the number of cards on which you reach a given count is of considerable significance. The following suggestions for strategy are therefore subdivided into the numbers of cards held.

First card. Stake high on an Ace, for obvious reasons. The probability of being dealt a tenner next is about 0.38, giving two chances in five of making a pontoon. On a tenner, stake high, but with reservations. The probability of a pontoon is less than 0.08 (12:1 against). You have a 3 in 10 chance of getting a second tenner, and must weigh that against the possibility that banker will make 20 or 21. In straitened circumstances, make it a middling stake. On anything else, prefer to stake low.

Second card (no pair). Stick on 15–20 (hard): your chances of not busting if you twist at 15 are barely 2 in 5, and naturally worse on higher numbers. The banker will certainly beat your 15 if they stick, but it is safer to bank on their busting than to try it yourself. On a soft 18–20, stick if you want to play it safe. Soft 16/17 is better counted as 6 or 7.

A hard count of 12–15 is the worst range of all and the safest procedure is to twist. The fact that the mean value of a card is seven doesn't mean that 14 is the most promising count: 12 is clearly better, as it gives you the smallest chance of busting. A soft count of 12–15 should, of course, be regarded as 2–5.

A count of 10 or 11 is highly favourable – see First card for the probabilities. Here it is better to buy than to twist.

On a count of less than 10, buy, for a modest amount. Don't start splashing out yet against the possibility of a five-card trick.

Second card (of a pair). Whether or not to split a pair depends on their rank, as follows:

- **Aces:** safer to split them than to keep them and go for a five-card trick.
- **Tenners:** the question here is whether a count of 20 in the hand is better than two chances of a pontoon in the bush. It surely is. Don't split.
- **Nines:** your choice is to stick at 18, or to try for two slightly-better-than-even chances of not doing worse. Don't split unless you can afford to indulge a delight in gambling for the sake of it.
- **Eights:** your choice is to stick at 16, twist to a 5 in 13 chance of improving, or split on two 9 in 13 chances of improving a count of eight. Splitting is best; sticking worst.
- **Sevens, Sixes:** neither rank allows you to stick, and both put you in the dreaded 12–15 range. Always split. (The odds against drawing a royal pontoon to a pair of Sevens are about 24:1.)
- **Fives:** don't split, as 10 is a good count to buy to.
- **Fours:** Split. It's true that they are of a favourable average value for a five-card trick, but the chances are not good, and 8 is a bad count to buy to.
- **Threes or Twos:** don't split. Both 6 and 4 are acceptable counts to buy to, and you may be permitted the thought of a five-card trick.

Third card. Stick on hard 15–21. If you must gamble on soft 20, twist, don't buy: you have one chance of improving, four of equalizing, eight of doing worse. Whether you count this as only a 5-in-13 chance of not doing worse, or an 8-in-13 chance of not doing better, the odds are still not in your favour. Soft 18 or 19 is best left alone, but you may twist (or even buy, if you can afford it) to soft 15 or 16, either of which is at least in the running for a five-card trick.

With 12–15 (hard), twist, as for the same total on two cards. Count soft 14–15 as 4–5 and buy with a view to a five-card trick. If you have soft 13, you have been playing it all wrong, as a soft 12 on three cards is only obtainable with a card counting zero, which Pontoon has not yet invented.

Buy gladly with 10 or 11, and with a view to a five-card trick on a count of 4–7. Buy cheaply or twist, on a count of 8–9.

Fourth card. If you have from 5 to 11, you must twist, as the five-card trick is beyond question. From 12 to 20, of course, your only concern is not to bust, and the probability of doing so gradually increases as follows:

Count of 12: 0.31 probability (3 in 10 chances of busting)
13: 0.38
14: 0.46
15: 0.54
15: 0.62
17: 0.69
18: 0.77
19: 0.85
20: 0.92

In general, then, you may consider buying as long as your chances of not busting are better than even, i.e. up to a count of 14. You can't stick at 15, so whether you buy or twist is a question that must be answered by balancing the slightly-worse-than-even chance of improving against how much you can afford to gamble.

From 15 upwards the probability of making a five-card trick is exactly the same as that of improving a similar count on a smaller number of cards. However, the difference is that you now stand to win twice your stake if successful as against losing only your single stake if you bust. At 15, then, you have 62 chances in 100 of losing one stake (total: minus 62), but 38 chances of gaining two stakes (total: plus 76). This produces a balance of +8 in your favour, so at 15 it is worth buying if you can afford it, or twisting if not. At a count of 17, a similar calculation of the balance turns out to be almost the same amount against you, so it would be slightly better to stick. At 18 or more, you should stick.

Banker's play

The same suggestions as those made above for punters apply also when you are the banker, only more so, since you have a natural advantage. If you always stick when you can, you are bound to win in the long run. But, since you don't know how long a run you are going to get, you may be influenced in some of your decisions by the number of punters standing against you. For example, with three against you it is hardly worth sticking at 15; with only one against you, you will already have gained two stakes and can well afford to take another card to a count of 15.

Illustration

The players are Annie, Benny, Connie and Denny. As banker, Denny deals the following:

First two cards:

Annie gets ♣3, stakes 3, then ♣2, counting 5.

Benny has ♥K, stakes 4, is dealt ♥2, counting 12.

Connie gets ♥8 then ♠8, and splits them, staking 2 on each.

Connie Right gets ♦6 for 14 and Connie Left ♠3 for 11.

Denny deals himself ♠A, ♦2, counting 3 or 13.

Further transactions:

Annie (staking 3 on 5) buys ♣10 for 2, making 5 or 15, twists ♥5, and sticks at 20.

Benny (staking 4 on 12) twists ♣9, sticks at 21.

Connie Right (staking 2 on 14) twists ♠K, busts.

Connie Left (staking 2 on 11) buys ♥A for 2, counts 13, twists ♦A, making 14, twists a fifth card and gets ♣4, giving her a five-card trick counting 18.

Dealer, with a count of 3 or 13, now confronts three hands with counts of 20, 21 and a five-card trick. He draws ♠Q for 13, then ♥7 for 20, and announces 'Pay twenty-ones'.

Result:

Annie on a count of 20 pays 5 to Denny.

Benny on 21 receives 4 from Denny.

Connie Right (bust) pays 2.

Connie Left, having a five-card trick, receives 8 (twice her stake of 4). This leaves Dealer 5 down on a somewhat exceptional deal. But he's sure to make it up soon.

Variations

The Royal Pontoon of three Sevens is not recognized by all schools.

In some circles, a pontoon is strictly defined as an Ace and a 'royal', Ace and Ten being only an ordinary 21. The objection to this is that it increases the banker's advantage by reducing a punter's chance to take over by 25 per cent.

Some permit the banker to look at their first card before dealing out anyone's second, and to call for double stakes if they like what they see. In this case all players must double the stake made on their first card before seconds are dealt. Again, it may be objected that this works to the banker's advantage.

There are various ways of changing the bank. The least satisfactory, though clearly the fairest, is for each player to deal in turn. Or the banker may offer to sell the bank, or entertain an offer to buy it, at any time, as long as the price is acceptable. This is usually followed when the banker has been playing so badly that they can't afford to lose too heavily on the following round.

A Joker may be conveniently put to use as a marker card. Place it at the bottom of the pack before the first deal. When it appears at the top, shuffle the cards, or allow the bank to pass to the left or be sold by auction.

See also

There is nothing useful on Pontoon under that name, apart from the Pagat website page. On the casino game of Blackjack, however, references and opportunities to play are ten a penny. Every casino game and card game site offers Blackjack and it is impossible to make a more meaningful selection than the following basic essentials:

http://www.pagat.com/banking/pontoon.html
http://www.pagat.com/banking/blkjack.html
Basic description, variations, and links to other sites.

32 brag

- for three to eight players
- fairly easy to learn
- a game of bluff and nerve

Brag is the traditional English vying game and has been so, under that name, for nigh on 300 years. 'Vying' denotes the sort of gambling game, like Poker, in which all the play consists in betting that you have been dealt, or think you have been dealt – or try to make everybody else think you have been dealt – a better hand of cards than anybody else at the table – and to do this by gradually raising the stakes until everyone else either throws their hand in or pays to see the one you're betting (or bluffing) on.

For many years, from the early 1800s to about the 1970s, Brag has been so much more a folk game than a book game that the sort of people who wrote books (and so tended not to belong to the Brag-playing social stratum) continued to perpetrate a garbled version, copied from other books, of a form of the game that had long since died out. It is only since the study of games became a respectable pursuit, towards the end of the 20th century, that more authentic descriptions have begun to appear.

As with most all folk games, the broad principles of Brag remain pretty constant while actual details of play vary from place to place, so that many alternative rules and peculiarities will be encountered.

All, however, are based on the same range of three-card combinations named and illustrated in Figure 32.1.

- **Prial** (= Pair Royal). Three cards of the same rank. A prial of Aces beats a prial of Kings, and so on, down to the lowest prial (Twos). A prial of Aces, however, is not the best hand but is beaten by a prial of Threes, although in most other respects Three ranks in its normal position between Two and Four.
- **Flush Run** (or Running Flush). Three cards in suit and sequence such as 2–3–4 or Q–K–A. As between flush runs, the one with the highest-ranking top card wins. The Q–K–A hand, however, is not highest but is beaten by A–2–3, which can be beaten only by a prial.

- **Run.** Three cards in numerical sequence but not all of the same suit. The highest is A–2–3, followed by A–K–Q, K–Q–J, etc., down to 4–3–2.
- **Flush.** Any three cards of the same suit. As between competing flushes, the one with the highest top card wins, or second highest if tied, or third if tied again. Ace is highest, Two lowest, Three second lowest.
- **Pair.** Two cards of the same rank, the third one odd. A pair of Aces beats Kings, and so on, down to Threes and then Twos (lowest). If two players have a pair of the same rank, the one with the higher third card wins.
- **High card.** As between competing hands containing none of these combinations, the best is the one with the highest top card, or second if tied, and so on. Ace is high, Three and Two are low.

There are several varieties of Brag, and several related games based on Brag hands, but the most basic version is the Three-card game.

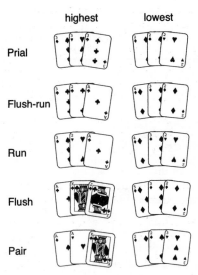

figure 32.1 Brag

Brag hands illustrated from highest to lowest (a prial of Threes to a pair of Twos)

Three-card Brag

Players. This form of the game can be played by, theoretically, any number of people from two to 17, but four to six is ideal.

Cards. Fifty-two, ranking from high to low AKQJ1098765432. By previous agreement one or more of them may be designated 'wild', which means you can use it to stand for any card in your hand. For details, see 'Variants' at the end of the main description. It is not customary to add a Joker for this purpose.

Structure. A game consists of any number of deals as long as all players deal the same number of times. Decide first dealer by any agreed means. The turn to deal and play passes always to the left.

Before play begins it is necessary to agree whether or not playing 'blind' is permitted (the following description assumes so), and whether or not to recognize any cards as wild (the following description assumes not).

Stakes. It is also necessary to agree on staking limits as follows:

- The ante, that is, the initial stake (if any) that everyone must put into the pot before play begins.
- The minimum and maximum initial bet. This sets a lower and upper limit on what the first player must bet to stay in.
- The limit (if any) on the amount by which the bet can be increased by each subsequent player.

These limits should be set low because the betting method of Brag tends to cause rapid increases. For the same reason, it is also necessary to agree what happens if a player runs out of money. Logically, they should drop out of play, but this is not much fun for the others, and Brag is by nature a more informal and sociable game than Poker. In real life, many players allow some form of lending and borrowing, but it is hard to draw up rules governing any such procedure. The simplest solution, to be getting on with, is to play the equivalent of 'table stakes' in Poker. That is, a player who runs out during the course of a hand can stake all they have left and remain in the game without paying. All subsequent stakes are paid to a second pot. When the second pot has been won, the hand that won it is compared with the hand of the player who went broke, and the original pot is won by the better of the two, or, if tied, by the hand that won the second pot. (For further discussion on this subject, see the Pagat website.)

Deal. Cards are shuffled at the start of play and immediately after any deal won with a prial, but not otherwise. Instead, the cards from the previous deal are just placed at the bottom of the pack and the new hands dealt from the top.

Deal three cards each, one at a time, face down, and place the remainder face up to the left to show the position of the deal.

Play. Players now look at their cards (unless playing blind, as explained below). Then, starting with the dealer's left-hand neighbour, each in turn must either stay in the game by pushing the amount of their bet towards the centre of the table, or renounce the pot by throwing their hand in. This is called folding, or stacking, and is done by placing one's cards face down on the top of the undealt pack.

Note. *It is a strict rule of etiquette that you may only fold when it is your turn to bet.*

The amount bet by the first player must be within the agreed limits for an initial bet – that is, not less than the minimum or more than the maximum. The amount bet by each subsequent player must be not less than the amount bet by the previous one, and may be more. If more, the additional amount must not exceed the previously agreed limit for a raise.

This continues until only two players are left in. They are then entitled to a further option, which is to 'see' the other player's hand by paying *double* the amount of that player's previous bet. If one of the last two sees the other, the player who was seen spreads their hand of cards face up on the table. The 'seer' can only beat this and win the pot by showing a better hand. If their hand is equal or lower, they needn't show their cards, and their opponent wins the pot.

If one of the two last players folds, or if all but one player fold in any round of betting, the one left in does not have to match their own previous stake but automatically wins the pot without having to show their hand.

In case you're already used to the betting system of Poker, you should take note of three important differences in the betting system of Brag:

• First, 'equalizing' the stakes does not cause a showdown. Thus, if everyone bets the same amount on the first round, the first player must bet at least that amount again in order to stay in the game, otherwise they must fold.

- The stakes at Brag increase more rapidly and less evenly than those at Poker, which can be disconcerting if you're not used to it.
- No showdown takes place until only two players are left in. Only then can one player see the other, and even then not by matching the other's previous stake, but only by putting in *twice* that amount.

Betting blind. Most schools allow players to bet blind, that is, without looking at their hand but leaving their cards face down on the table.

The advantage of playing blind is that every penny you stake counts as twopence – in other words, you only have to bet half the stake required at any given moment. Conversely, any non-blind or 'open' players must pay double the amount you bet in order to stay in the game. This continues until you cease to play blind by looking at your cards or taking your hand up. From that point on, you have to pay the full amount.

Note. *It is a strict rule of etiquette that you may only cease playing blind when it is your turn to bet and immediately before doing so.*

A further rule governing this method of play is that 'you can't see a blind man', unless you yourself are also playing blind. If you are, you can see your blind opponent in the usual way, by doubling their previous stake. But if one of you is playing blind and the other open, the situation is as follows.

The open player can only either fold or continue doubling the other player's stake, as long as the other remains blind. The blind player, however, can see the other at any time by equalizing the latter's stake (which counts as doubling it because of the relative stake values). In this event it is usual for each in turn, starting with the seen player, to expose one card at a time until one of them concedes defeat. As before, a pair of identical hands wins for the player who was seen.

It can happen that everybody else folds, leaving one blind man in theoretical possession of the pot with an unseen hand. They may then show the hand and win the pot, but are not obliged to do this. Instead, they may leave the pot to be carried forward to the next deal, keep their blind hand face down on the table, and be dealt another hand of cards, so that they are playing with two hands for the new pot.

In this case the new deal will leave two hands lying face down on the table before them, and they have the following options.

They may, if they wish, leave them both face down and play them blind in the usual way. If so, they must always match the previous stake in order to equalize, having now two hands to play at half a stake each.

Alternatively, they may immediately, or at any future turn to bet, take up one of the hands, look at it, and decide whether to play it open (in which case they must immediately fold the other hand without looking at it), or fold the hand they took and play the other one, either blind or open as preferred.

What they may not do, at any time, is to look at both hands and decide which one to play, or to play both hands open.

In the unlikely event that a person playing with two blind hands wins the pot again without having looked at either, they may not carry both of them forward to the next deal, but must fold one of them, without looking at it.

Example of betting procedure. Here is the score of a short game with five players, designed to illustrate how the betting system works.

	Arnie	Benny	Connor	Denny	Ernie
1	2	2	1 (blind)	4	2 (blind)
2	4	4	3 (blind)	6	3 (blind)
3	6	6	3 (blind)	6	3 (blind)
4	6	6	6 (open)	fold	4 (blind)
5	8	fold	fold	–	5 (blind)
6	10	–	–	–	10 (to see)

In round 1, Connor's single stake counts double because he is playing blind. Denny raises the stake to 4, which Ernie matches with 2 because he also is playing blind.

In round 2, Connor's bet of 3 amounts in effect to a raise from 4 to 6 because he is betting blind. In round 4, however, his courage fails him and he looks at his hand before betting the 6 required to stay in. Ernie, still playing blind, increases the stake by betting 4 instead of the 3 required of a blind man at this point.

In round 6, Arnie must either stake or fold: he is not allowed to 'see a blind man'. Ernie, however, decides to see Arnie. For this purpose he must double Arnie's last stake of 10, which in effect he does by paying 10, since a blind man's 10 is worth 20 of anyone else's.

In sum, Benny has lost 18, Connor 13, and Denny 16. If Arnie has the better final hand, Connor will have lost 27 and Arnie made a profit of 38 (74 less the 36 he staked). If Connor wins, Arnie will have lost 36 and Connor made a profit of 46 (83 less the 27 he staked).

Wild cards. A wild card is one that can be used to represent any desired natural card. For example, W–W–♥3 can be counted as ♥A–2–3 or a prial of Threes. Wild cards were originally called 'braggers' but nowadays are 'floaters', and appear to be more commonly employed in Four- and Five-card Brag than in Three-card. You can add Jokers as wild cards, but this is not usual. Instead, you may agree to designate one or more particular cards wild. The usual suspects are:

One card wild. This is often ♥K, the so-called 'suicide' King because in the commonest pack design he is shown apparently sticking his sword through his head. Traditionalists may prefer ♣J, the original 'bragger'.

Two cards wild. Often the 'one-eyed Jacks', namely ♠J and ♥J, being depicted in profile and therefore showing only one eye apiece. Alternatively, the two black Twos.

Four cards wild. Usually the Twos.

Natural cards beat wild cards. If the pot is contested between two identical hands of which one contains one or more wild cards, the one without wild cards wins, or the one with fewer wild cards beats the one with more.

Four- and Five-card Brag

Four or five cards are dealt to each player, who rejects any one or two (respectively) and plays the rest in the usual way. In this version there is nothing special about Threes, but in Five-card it is sometimes agreed that the highest possible hand is a prial of Fives.

Multi-card Brag

Brag-like games where more than five cards are dealt differ markedly from the games described above, in that instead of rejecting additional cards to reduce the hand to three, each player rearranges their cards into two or more hands and there is no vying (increase of stakes). All begin with everyone placing an agreed stake in the pot.

Six-card Brag

Each player receives six cards dealt face down one at a time. Anyone who can show four of a kind (four of the same rank) does so, and wins the pot outright with no further play. A higher-ranking four beats one of lower rank, though many play that four Sixes beat everything else.

If there were no fours of a kind, each player now divides their hand into two, in any desired way, and, of these two Brag hands, places the higher face down on the table to their left, and the lower to its right. For this purpose, unless otherwise agreed:

• a prial of Sixes outranks any other prial, from Aces down, and
• a hand containing no combination has no competitive value.

Starting with the dealer's left-hand neighbour, each in turn either exposes their left hand or folds.

Then, starting with the player showing the highest Brag hand, each in turn of those who have not folded either exposes their right hand or folds.

The pot is won outright, or split, or carried forwards, as follows:

A player wins the pot outright if each of their two hands is better than everybody else's equivalent hand, or if one of them is better and the other ties for best, or if each hand ties for best but with the equivalent hands of two different players.

Two (or more) players split the pot if their left hands are all equally high and so are their right hands.

In any other case everyone places an additional stake in the pot and it is carried forward to the next deal.

Variants (of Six-card Brag)

Either or both of the following optional extras are played in many circles.

1 A six-card running flush, such as ♥2–3–4–5–6–7, beats anything, including four of a kind, without further play.
2 In the event that every right hand (and, almost impossibly rarely, every left hand) contains no combination at all, the best hand is decided on a high-card basis. That is, the best is the one with the highest top card, or, if equal, the highest second card down, or, if still equal, the highest third card down.

Seven-card Brag

This is identical with Six-card, except that each player receives seven cards and, if no one has four of a kind, discards one before splitting the remaining six into a left and a right hand. In this case it is usual for Sevens to rank as the highest four of a kind or prial, and for a seven-card running flush to beat four of a kind.

Nine-card Brag

This is almost identical, except that each player receives nine cards and divides them into three Brag hands, placing the highest on the left, the lowest on the right, and the intermediate hand in between. The three hands are contested from highest to lowest, as before. If a player wins or at least ties all three hands, they win the pot. If two or more equalize on all three hands, they split the pot. In any other case the pot is carried forward to the next deal. Nines are the highest-ranking prial or four of a kind. Other sudden-death combinations may be recognized, such as a nine-card flush, two fours of a kind, four pairs, and so on.

Thirteen-card Brag ('Crash')

Four players receive 13 cards each and form them into four Brag hands, which they place face down in a row, rejecting the odd card. Each hand is then revealed in turn, in order from left to right or right to left but not at random, and the winner marks one point on a special scoring board. In some circles the last hand only scores if it is a pair or better. The game is won – over as many deals as it takes – by the first player to mark seven points, but if one player wins all four hands in a deal it is a 'crash' and they win outright. Anyone who has made no score at the end of a game may be required to pay extra to the winner, or to ante double stakes to the next pool. Scoring is usually often done on a purpose-made Crash board, consisting of a square of wood with two lines of 13 holes drilled from corner to corner like a St Andrew's cross. Each player pegs down one arm from a corner to the centre, and the winner is the first player to reach it.

See also

Entering the words 'Brag card game' in a search engine produces a large number of irrelevant entries and a small handful of vaguely relevant ones, of which most are worthless. This leaves:

http://www.pagat.com/vying/brag.html
http://www.pagat/partition/crash.html
John McLeod's Pagat website gives rules and variations of Three-, Four- and Five-card Brag derived from a multiplicity of authentic contributions. His Crash page describes further multi-card versions including the fascinating game of Crash, or Thirteen-card Brag.

33 poker

- for three or more players
- easy to learn
- a game of great skill

Poker is virtually the national card game of the United States, where it is played in thousands of homes and clubs in countless different forms and varieties and by millions of ordinary people. Throughout the rest of the world it has hitherto tended to move in the more restricted social circles of the professional classes, leaving everyone else to play their own national gambling game, such as Brag in Britain. In recent years, however, it has considerably increased in popularity throughout the western world, largely through the medium of the Internet and the expansion of on-line casinos and gaming rooms. It is, of course, universally known as a casino game, and World Poker Championships are held every year in Las Vegas.

The most advanced and globally successful member of an ancient family of games including Brag, Poker originated around New Orleans during the 1820s, and over the next 100 years evolved into the highly sophisticated game that it is today – one not to be taken or undertaken lightly. Contrary to the popular opinion of those who've never played it, it is as much a game of skill, not luck, as Bridge.

Definition of Poker

Poker differs from Bridge in two distinct respects. First, whereas Bridge involves the play of cards, cards in Poker are not themselves the instruments of play. In Poker, once you've been dealt your cards you do little or nothing with them other than (occasionally) look at them. What you actually play *with* is cash, or cash substitutes (chips), and the skills involved are, therefore, primarily those of money management and practical psychology, not 'card sense' in the traditional understanding of the term. And, second, Poker is not so much 'a game' as a whole family of games, boasting literally hundreds of variations, though all based on the same two defining principles, namely:

1 A Poker hand consists, *by definition*, of five cards. More may be dealt, but when it comes to a showdown it is the best five-card combination that wins.
2 There is a 'pot' of cash or chips which is gradually increased by a process of betting until somebody wins it, either by showing they were dealt a better hand of cards than anyone else (at 'the showdown'), or by frightening everyone else into giving up their hand ('folding') and so relinquishing all claim to the pot. This process is often designated by the technical term 'vying'.

Point 1 distinguishes Poker from other vying games based on hands of different constitutions, such as the three-card combinations of Brag, or the four-card hands of its Italian relative Primiera.

Point 2 distinguishes true Poker from other games that use Poker hands but do not involve vying, such as so-called Pai-Gow Poker, which is actually a banking game (like Baccarat).

Principal varieties of Poker

Of the many forms of Poker played today, only the three most widespread can and need be covered here. They are:

1 Draw Poker, the original and classic form of the game, still played widely throughout the world, especially in relatively domestic and private play.
2 Seven-card Stud, another classic variety still favoured by many serious and professional players.
3 Texas Hold'em, or just Hold'em, which became the most popular champions' game in the 1970s and has since seized the imagination of millions of on-line and casino players.

Before embarking on any one of these specific varieties, you need to understand the two factors that underpin all of them, namely the definition and constitution of Poker hands, and, second, the process of betting or 'vying'.

Standard Poker hands

In all forms of Poker, players bet as to which of them has the best hand. A Poker hand, by definition, is five cards. More may be dealt or held, but only five count in a showdown. These five may be totally unmatched, or may form one of the following universally recognized combinations.

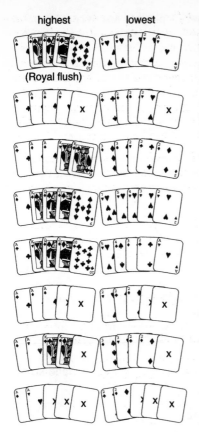

highest	lowest
(Royal flush)	

Straight flush Five cards in suit and sequence. Ace counts either low (A–2–3–4–5) or high. The highest (10–J–Q–K–A) is called a royal flush.

Four of a kind, or Fours Four of the same rank. The fifth card (x) can be anything.

Full house Three of a kind and a pair. Of two full houses, the one with the higher triplet wins (5–5–5–2–2 beats 4–4–4–K–K).

Flush Five cards of the same suit but not in sequence. Of competing flushes the one with the highest untied top card wins.

Straight Five cards in sequence but not flush. Of competing straights the one with the highest top card wins.

Three of a kind (triplet, trips, threes) Three cards of the same rank, plus two unpaired cards.

Two pairs Competing two pairs are decided on the higher pair, or the lower pair if equal, or the odd card if still equal.

One pair Two cards of the same rank and three unmatched cards. A higher pair beats a lower. A tie is decided by the highest of the three odd cards.

High card A hand containing no pair, flush or straight is called a high-card hand because when two or more of them compete the one with the highest card wins, or second highest if equal, and so on. Thus A–7–5–4–2 (Ace high) beats K–Q–J–10–8 (King high), which beats K–Q–J–10–7.

figure 33.1 standard Poker hands

At a showdown, which is when players discover who has the winning hand, a higher type of combination (shown higher up in the table) beats one of a lower type. As between two hands of the same type, the higher hand is one containing the highest-ranking top card, or second highest if equal, and so on. For this purpose, note that:

- Individual cards rank from high to low A K Q J 10 9 8 7 6 5 4 3 2, but an Ace may be counted low in a straight (thus 5–4–3–2–A is valid); and
- If two hands are equal as far as the combination is concerned – for example, two players each have a pair of Jacks, then they are decided on the rank of their accompanying non-matched cards, or 'idlers'. If still equal (both, for example, showing J–J–9–6–3), they are completely tied and split the pot. They cannot be decided on any other basis, because
- All suits are equal – no suit ranks higher than any other.

Evaluating Poker hands. To play Poker successfully you must become able to instantly assess each type of hand for its true worth. The following table indicates the relative value of Poker combinations by showing how rare or common they are. The first column of figures shows how many different hands there are of each type. The second expresses the same thing as a percentage of the total number of possible hands. The third shows the odds-to-one against being dealt such a hand straight from the pack (higher figures rounded to nearest 50):

hand	how many	frequency	odds
Straight flush	40	0.0015	65,000
Four of a kind	624	0.024	4,150
Full house	3,744	0.144	700
Flush	5,108	0.196	500
Straight	10,200	0.392	250
Three of a kind	54,912	2.13	46
Two pairs	123,552	4.75	20
One pair	1,098,240	42.25	1
High card	1,302,540	50.12	1
Total	2,598,960	(100%)	

This shows that about half the hands dealt will be nothing in particular, and the remainder mostly one pair. At an evening of ordinary Draw Poker, most of the pots will be won on two pairs or threes, while anything higher than a Full House would be something of an event. In case this sounds unexciting, it may be worth noting that different types of Poker game increase the frequency of winning on higher hands – for example, by dealing seven or more cards and allowing the player to choose the best five from them.

Poker is best played with proper Poker chips available from any good games shop. Chips come in various colours that may be used to represent any agreed scale of values. At least three colours are required, the lowest being white, the middle red, and the highest blue (whence the phrase 'blue chip' for an investment of high value). Typical scales of value are:

white	1	1	1	1
red	2	2	5	5
blue	5	10	20	25
yellow	25	25	50	100
black	100	100	200	250

For low-limit, conservative or beginners' games with five players you need about 100 in all, say 25 each of four denominations. For more players or wilder variations there should be something like 200 available.

Of course, the question on everybody's lips is what these pretty colours are really worth in terms of filthy lucre. One white unit may be set at one penny, one dollar, one pound, one handful of paper-clips, or any fraction or multiple thereof. It is obvious that the actual value will reflect the income bracket inhabited by the denizens of the table and the proportion of it which they are prepared to invest in the pleasure of playing. For convenience, one white should represent the agreed amount of the ante or minimum bet. If you can easily afford the price of this book, set it at 10p to start with. If buying the book is a small luxury make it 5p, and if you had to borrow it from the library then stick to the good old 'penny ante' game – and make sure you return the book in time to avoid having to pay a late fine on it.

In addition to settling the monetary value of the chips, certain other aspects of play need to be agreed beforehand, regardless of the variety of Poker being played.

Time limit. A time limit should be established and no deals made after it has expired. Many players quite reasonably agree to a time limit on pondering a hand, such that when that time is up the player must drop.

Expenses. It may be agreed that a given proportion or fixed amount be abstracted from each pot won for the purpose of defraying house expenses (cards, refreshments, worn carpet, etc). In some circles a kitty is established from which the losers are eventually compensated with a hand-out in proportion to their losses.

Pot limit. An agreed limit should be set on the maximum amount that can be bet or raised at any point in the game. The simplest arrangement, suitable for beginners, is fixed limit – say five chips for the sake of argument. A popular alternative is pot limit. This means that a player may bet or raise by anything up to the amount in the pot but not more. (It must be established by prior agreement whether this means the amount in the pot before or after the player has paid whatever it costs to stay in.) Similarly, a self-explanatory 'half-pot' limit is sometimes played, as even a pot-limit game can get excessively expensive when there are more than five at a table. Pot limit with a fixed maximum – say 50 whites – is a reasonable hybrid.

Table stakes. Playable with or without the additional discipline of a pot limit, this system entitles any player to bet up to the full amount of his stack and to 'tap out' when broke. No player may reduce the amount of his stack between deals, but may increase it by buying more.

Tapping out. This is a method of enabling a player who runs out of cash or chips to stay in the pot till the showdown, receiving more cards if the draw has yet to come, without paying. All bets made by other players in excess of the amount staked by the tapper-out are placed slightly to one side to constitute a side pot distinct from the main pot. If the tapper-out has the best hand at the showdown he wins only the main pot, the side pot going to the player with the next best hand. If not he is out of the game, unless permitted to buy himself back in.

No limit. A no-limit or sky's-the-limit game, as the name implies, is one in which no limitation is placed on raises, so long as the raisers can meet their debts when the day of reckoning comes.

Freezeout and Freewheel. These procedures may be regarded as opposite sides of the same coin. In Freezeout each player drops out when broke and the winner is the one left in at the end of the day – or week, or month as the case may be. In Freewheel a player when broke may stay in the game, participating to the extent of drawing cards, betting and calling, until he has won a pot, at which point he starts paying his way again. This is much the same as Poverty Poker, in which he may 'buy' from the bank a second or even a third stack of chips of the same size as the one he bought originally – all absolutely free of charge.

Raise limits. Limits may be placed on the number of raises that may be made, e.g. three per interval, or two or three per player in each interval. By the 'right to bet' system a player may not raise if the last player to speak before him dropped, but may do so otherwise. The limiting of raises is somewhat artificial but has the merit of preventing a situation known as the whipsaw or sandwich, in which three players remain in the pot and two of them keep raising to drive the third one out. In this case it may be agreed that the limit of three raises only becomes operative as soon as three remain in the pot.

Draw Poker

With slight regional variations, this is the original form of the game and the most widely played throughout the world. It differs in some respects from the form described in many English books, which I refer to as English Club Poker. It is also, but not quite accurately, sometimes known as Jackpots.

Preliminaries. From five to seven is a good number of players. With fewer, the game is dull because the average winning hand is very low; with more, there are not enough cards to go round in comfort. Each player should start with the equivalent of 200 chips in whites, reds and blues. Set a time limit on play and stop at the end of the deal in which the limit expires. Agree on the value of the chips, the amount of the ante (ideally, one white chip), the maximum permitted raise in the first betting round (e.g. five whites or equivalent) and the maximum permitted in the second round (e.g. ten whites or equivalent). Alternatively, agree to play 'pot limits' – i.e. the maximum permitted raise is the size of the pot at the time it is made.

Shuffling the cards. Theoretically, each new deal should be made from a thoroughly shuffled pack, and it is permissible to alternate between two packs so that one can be shuffled while the other is being dealt. In practice one pack is used continuously until a new one is called for – which anyone may do if they feel (rightly or wrongly) that the cards are 'running against them'. Also, in practice, there are people who prefer to play without shuffling the cards between deals, in order to produce 'more exciting hands'. There are such people who do this in all card games as a matter of course, but the practice has nothing to commend it in an honest game.

Anybody who wishes has a right to shuffle, but the dealer has the right to shuffle last. Before dealing, they should have the cards cut by the player on their right. The purpose of this is to prevent the bottom card of the pack from being seen by anyone, as may sometimes happen at the end of a shuffle. For similar but less tenable reasons, some players insist that the top card of the pack be 'burned' immediately before dealing – that is, transferred from the top to the bottom of the pack. (I suspect that 'burned' originated as a misreading of 'buried'.)

Ante. Before the deal, each player contributes to the pot by paying an ante of one white chip, placing it in the centre of the table.

Deal. Deal cards one at a time, face down, in rotation, starting at Dealer's left, until each player has received five cards.

Opening. Each player in turn, starting at Dealer's left, may fold, check, or bet.

- A player folds, if they don't think it worth competing for the pot, by laying their cards face down on the table and saying 'I'm out', or words to that effect.
- They check, if they wish to play for the pot but are either unwilling or unqualified to make the opening bet, by announcing 'I check' or knocking on the table.
- They open, if qualified to do so, by making an opening bet. For this purpose they are qualified only if their hand contains a pair of Jacks or better (unless previous agreement has been made to 'open on anything'). They do so by announcing 'Open for two', or however many chips it may be, and push that number forwards towards the middle of the table – though not actually in it with the antes, as it is necessary during the course of the game to be able to see exactly how much each player has so far bet, and so determine whether or not the bets have been equalized.

If no player has opened the betting before the turn comes round again to the first to speak, the cards are thrown in and the next deal ensues. The antes stay in the middle of the table as part of the next pot, to which a fresh ante is made by each player.

Continuation of first betting interval. Once somebody has opened, each player thereafter must do one of the following:

- Fold – that is, throw their hand in. This makes them an inactive player for the rest of the hand.

- Stay – by increasing the amount of their stake so that it equals that of the previous active player.
- Raise – by raising their stake to a level equal to that of the previous active player and adding an extra amount.

Example: *Player A says 'Open for two'. Player B says 'Fold' and throws in his cards. Player C says 'Stay for two', staking two chips to equal the stake of the opener. Player D says 'Stay for two and raise two', pushing four chips towards the pot. Player E says 'Stay for four', since D has increased the amount necessary to stay in the pot and E does not wish to raise further. Back round to player A again, and he must pay two if he wishes to stay, since he is two short of the amount so far staked by E and D.*

This continues until one of two things happens:

- Somebody raises and everybody else folds. The last raiser wins the pot without showing their hand and the deal is at an end.
- More usually, all bets are equalized between the two or more players who have stayed in the pot. Note that if one person raises and the others either fold or stay but do not re-raise, the betting interval is at an end: a player may not re-raise themself.

When all bets are equalized it is time for the draw.

The draw. The dealer now addresses each active player in turn, starting at his left, and asks whether they want to 'stand pat' (keep the cards they were dealt) or exchange any. If not standing pat, each player discards from one to three cards, face down, and receives the same number dealt face down one at a time from the top of the pack. When the dealer gets round to themself they must announce clearly how many they are discarding and drawing.

As it is silly to exchange more than three cards in the draw, some schools prohibit the exchange of more. Players should agree beforehand whether or not this rule applies. Serious players rarely draw more than two.

If the player who opened the betting did so on a high pair – Jacks or better – it is quite possible that they may want to discard one of them in the draw. This is known as 'splitting openers'. They don't have to announce that they are doing so, but they must keep track of their discards in case they win the pot, as they may then be required to show that they were qualified to make the opening bet.

Second betting interval. This time the first person to speak is not necessarily the player at Dealer's left but the one who opened the first betting interval. As before, they may fold, bet, or check. If they check, each player in turn after them has the same options. If everybody checks, the original opener may not check again but must either fold or open.

Once the betting interval has been opened, each active player in turn after the opener may fold, stay, or stay and raise. This continues in exactly the same way as the first betting interval. If all but one drop out, the one left in wins the pot without having to show their hand. Otherwise, betting continues until all bets have been equalized, at which point there is a showdown.

Showdown. All those still in the pot reveal their hands – they must do so, and must reveal them entirely – and the pot goes to the player with the best hand, or is divided equally if two have identical best hands. If the pot is won by the original opener and they cannot prove that they were qualified to open, it goes to the second best hand. If there is no second best (all but the opener having folded), the pot is carried forward to the next deal.

Irregularities. In the event of a misdeal, such as exposing a card, dealing in the wrong order or with an imperfect or unshuffled pack, the cards are gathered in and the same dealer deals again after shuffling and cutting. If she misdeals twice in succession she forfeits the deal, which passes to the left.

If a player bets out of order, they must do whatever they said they were going to do (fold, bet or raise) when their proper turn comes round. They can't say one thing at the wrong time and do something different at the right.

If too many players draw too many cards, there may not be enough left in the pack to go round. In this case the dealer deals cards from the pack as far as they will go short of the last card. This he keeps, and adds it to all the folded hands and discards of the other players, except the discards of the original opener in case he split openers and has to prove it later. The new pack must be shuffled and cut, after which the draw can be continued from it.

If a player runs out of chips during the course of a hand they may (by previous agreement) be permitted to 'tap out'. This means can stay in the pot free of charge, provided that they don't raise, and may even take part in the draw. All bets made after a player has tapped out are kept slightly apart from those made previously. If the tapper-out emerges the winner, they take only the main pot: all the bets made after they tapped out constitute a second prize which goes to the second best hand. If not, they are out of the game, unless permitted to buy themself back in.

The play

How you play depends largely on how everyone else is playing. A 'loose' game is one where players fool around, take reckless chances and reach bankruptcy at great speed. A 'tight' game is one where the participants are either mathematicians or money grubbers or both: the game is played in expressionless silence, the draws are all of one card if any, and the action is only enlivened by long periods of rumination before each player makes a move. Needless to say, a sensible game steers a middle course between two extremes. A game is a social activity and players should be sociable without being silly, otherwise it will not serve its primary purpose of generating enjoyment at the exercise of skill.

As a game progresses, it often gets looser. It also gets looser if the table is a mixture of loose and tight players. In order to counterbalance this, it may be best to err on the side of tightness without going so far as to become a po-faced skinflint.

Position counts. If you're first to speak in the first betting interval, you may have a hand qualified to open, but if it's the bare minimum, like a pair of Jacks, you have no way of knowing what the opposition is likely to hold. You could open and find yourself raised all around the table, or you might check and find the deal passed up by everybody. The dealer, on the other hand, is in the best position to make a positive decision, because they will have heard all their opponents' initial reactions to their hands before they come to speak. It is therefore sensible for a player in an early position to open with not less than a pair of Queens, Kings or even Aces, depending on how many there are at the table.

Throughout the game, it is useful to erase from your consciousness, from your vision if possible, those players who have folded, and see only yourself in relation to those left in the pot. Your actions may then be guided by whether the players on your immediate right and left are tight or loose players, whether they are winning or losing, and so on.

First betting interval. The first betting interval is rather more mathematical than the second. First, you must assess the strength of your hand by whether it is probably the best, or the worst, or about middling.

Since about half the hands dealt are nothing, and most of the others are a pair, you can immediately assess a low or non-pair hand as worthless. On average, about half the players round the table should get a pair, which is why the minimum worthwhile opening hand is a pair of Jacks. Remember that the more players there are, the more likely will at least one opponent be holding a strong hand, say two pairs or three of a kind.

Mathematics also enter into it because in the first interval you are only partly betting on what your hand is at the moment. More important to your assessment is what it may become after the draw. For this purpose the table on page 322 is helpful. The first column shows the type of hand you may be dealt and the amount of it you would keep when discarding. (A 'kicker' is an Ace accompanying the main combination, which you may keep hold of in hope of pairing it. With three of a kind, the kicker may be any rank.) The next shows how many cards you might exchange from it, followed by the type of hand you hope to get as a result. For each type of desired result, the final column shows the odds against actually getting it.

A word about odds and probabilities. It's not worth attempting to memorize them if you haven't got that sort of mind, but it is sufficient to know which combinations are worth going for and which are very long shots. If you do remember any of the figures, one way of using them is this: if the odds offered you by the pot are greater than those offered by the draw, make the draw; if not, don't.

For example, suppose there are 25 chips in the pot (including the ones you have so far staked) and it costs you five to stay in. Then the pot is offering odds of 25:5 or 5:1. It is therefore worth staying in on a high pair, since the odds of improving after discarding three are 3:1 against, which is shorter than the odds offered by the pot. But it's less worthwhile pursuing a two pairs hand, as the odds against improvement are 11:1.

Of course, the odds aren't everything – they are only a guide. Poker is primarily an intuitive game; but, just as there is no reason why intuition shouldn't enter your calculations, so there is no reason why calculations shouldn't contribute to your intuition.

Playing the dealt hand. If you are dealt a high five-card combination (straight, flush, full house or straight flush), you have no discarding problems and will stand pat. Mathematics hardly enter into it: your objective is the psychological one of betting hard enough to build up a good pot but not so hard as to frighten everybody out of it.

Four of a kind is similar, except that you have the option of standing pat or discarding the odd card just for fun. (But make sure you don't discard the wrong one or the joke will misfire.) There are those who think it immoral to discard one from four of a kind, but, fortunately, you are very unlikely to be placed in the happy position of so wrestling with your conscience.

Any of these combinations are likely to be winners in the first round. But it's not the first round that counts – it's the second. Bear in mind that players with worse hands may nevertheless convert them into better as the result of the draw. You don't want to bet so hard as to drive out such speculators, but you must remember that a pat hand, though probably the best going in, is not necessarily the best coming out.

Three of a kind is a good hand. It is usually the best going in and quite often the best even after the draw. It also gives you the greatest variety of options. You may discard two, giving yourself the best chances of making any improvement, or one, which gives fair chances and has the advantage of revealing no information about the shape of your hand, since one card is the commonest and least tell-tale draw in sensible Poker. Or, if not too many remain in the pot, you may even take a chance and stand pat on it.

Two pairs, by contrast, is the most awkward dealt hand to cope with, in many ways worse than one pair. The only sensible discard from two pairs is one card, and the odds against improving (a full house being the only possible improvement) are 11:1. The only advantage is that the one-card discard at least gives nothing away. The problem, of course, is that two pairs is usually the best hand going in, but rarely the best coming out. This applies especially if the pairs are low, since an opponent who went in with a high pair may well convert to a winning two pairs. Hence the best thing to do with two pairs is to bet hard in the first round if you bet at all, in order to drive out as much opposition as possible, and be prepared to relinquish it in the second period if it then seems unlikely to be the best round the table.

If you have a pair, discarding three is a dead give-away. However, you have the consolation of the best chances of making any improvement – 2½ to 1 according to the table, with a number of different hands as your ultimate prize. To give less away about your hand, you may keep the pair and a kicker and merely exchange two. The higher the kicker, the better. With a pair and an Ace, few players would discard the Ace. If in the sort of company that invariably draws no cards or one, you could be ridiculously cheeky and discard one, keeping two kickers. The odds of making any improvement at all are about 5:1, specifically 7:1 against getting two pairs and 221½ :1 against getting threes. But don't make a habit of it.

The only combinationless hands worth taking seriously are four-flushes and open ended four-straights, each of which is worthless in the first period and remains worthless in the second unless improved by the draw of one card, in which case they become very probable winners. Given four cards of a suit, the chances of drawing a fifth are about four to one against. If it fails you will either have to disown it in the second period or try to bluff it out, but at least it has the advantage of requiring the draw of only one card. Given four to a straight, it's only worth playing if they form an open-ended sequence fillable by either of two cards – such as 7–8–9–10, which can be filled by a Six or a Jack. The odds are only 5:1 in this case, but are less worth playing in the case of an inside straight (e.g. 6–7–rubbish–4–9) or a closed straight (i.e. A–2–3–4–rubbish or A–K–Q–J–rubbish). Here only one rank will do, and the odds are 11:1 against.

Related hands are the pair-bobtail (defined below) and four to a straight flush. The odds against improving a four-card straight flush are considerably shorter – 2:1 if it is open-ended, 3:1 if only one rank will do. In the former case, say ♠6–7–8–9, either of two cards will make a straight flush, any one of six others will make a straight, and any of seven others a flush.

hand dealt	cards drawn	hoped improvement	odds against
Ace high	4	1 pair Aces 2 pair inc. Aces	3 14
One pair	3	any 2 pair (any) triplet full house four of a kind	2½ 5 7 97 360
One pair + Ace kicker	2	any 2 pair (any) 2 pair inc. Aces triplet full house four of a kind	3 7½ 17 12 120 1080
Two pairs	1	full house	11
Threes	2	any full house four of a kind	8½ 15½ 22½
Threes + kicker	1	any full house four of a kind	11 14½ 46
Four-straight, double-ended	1	straight	5
Four-straight, one place open	1	straight	11
Fourflush	1	flush	4
Four-card SF, double-ended	1 1	straight or flush straight flush	2 22½
Four-card SF, one place open	1 1	straight or flush straight flush	3 46

A pair-bobtail is a four-card straight or flush and a fifth card of the same rank as one of the others. For example, J–J–10–9–8 is a pair and an open ended straight, while ♠J–♥J–7–4–2 is a pair combined with a four-flush. The question in these cases is whether to keep the pair and discard the other three, or to go for the higher combination by breaking the pair up. In the first case you finish up with a pair, which is not a strong hand, but better than nothing and quite capable of winning a pot. In the second, you may finish up with a probably unbeatable hand, but only if you make it – if not, the loss of the pair leaves you worse off than when you started. The odds favour keeping the pair in most cases, and forgoing the chance of the higher hand, especially if the pair is as high as Aces or Kings.

Second betting interval. This period is less mathematical and more psychological. You will have seen how many cards are being drawn by your opponents, they will have seen how many are being drawn by you, and everyone will be trying to relate this to their knowledge of how everybody else thinks and behaves over the Poker table.

The two most useful generalizations that can be made for this period and for all other forms of Poker generally are as follows.

First, if at any stage in the proceedings you really believe your hand is not the best round the table, drop it. You may be able to bluff your opponents into thinking your hand is better or worse than it really is, but you can't bluff the hand itself. The other side of the coin is that, having once decided that you are going to follow a hand through, do so with inner confidence. Never just string along in the hope that everyone else will drop out first and leave you to sweep the pot without showing your hand.

Second, the most dangerous property of a poor Poker player ('poor' in both senses of the word!) is predictability. Poker gives you plenty of opportunities for varying the way in which you draw cards and play the hands. If it becomes known that you always do the same thing – such as standing pat on two pairs or betting too hard on a low straight, or holding your cards tight and close to the chest when you are sure you have a winner – then more observant players will note and remember it. The true meaning of that much misunderstood word, 'bluff', lies in avoiding any sort of predictability in the way you play.

Seven-card Stud

Stud denotes a family of Poker games in which there is no draw. Instead, some of your cards are dealt and kept face up, so that everyone can see part of everyone else's hand. For this reason Stud is more suitable than Draw for larger groups of players, eight being a good table. There are endless variations on the basic theme, but we will start with the simplest.

Everyone antes the minimum amount before the deal, or else (and preferably) the dealer antes by putting up as many chips as there are players.

After the shuffle and cut, deal a round of two cards face down to each player – his 'hole' cards – followed by one card face up. Each player looks at his hole-cards, places them face down on the table before him, and covers them with his up-card.

The first betting interval follows, opened by the player showing the highest ranking up-card, or, in the case of a tie, by the tied player nearest to the dealer's left (dealer himself, if tied, counting as furthest from his own left). At this and each subsequent betting interval it is part of the dealer's duties to indicate which hand bets first. The first to speak must either bet or fold. At this stage no one is allowed to check or pass. Each subsequent player then folds, pays an equal amount to stay in, or raises by increasing that amount. After any raise there must be another complete round of announcements to enable each active player to fold, equalize or re-raise. This continues until all bets are equalized, or all but one player fold, in which case the one remaining wins the pot without exposing his hole card.

If two or more remain in the pot, deal each active player another upcard. Cards should be dealt with one hand from the top of the squared-up pack, which remains face down on the table. In some circles it is customary for the dealer to announce, as he deals each card, the best hand that could be held on the evidence of the player's up-cards at that moment, e.g. 'One pair', 'Ace high', 'Possible flush', etc.

The first to speak in this and subsequent betting intervals is the player showing the greatest number or highest value of paired cards if any, or the highest-ranking individual card if not, followed by the second highest in the event of a tie, and so on. First-to-speak may now check instead of folding or betting, if he wishes, and, if he checks, each subsequent player has the same three options until someone bets, after which the others must fold, call or raise. If everyone checks the betting interval ends and the next card is dealt. A second, third, and fourth up-card are dealt in this way, each followed by a betting interval.

At this point, everyone will be displaying before them six cards, the first two face down and the next four face up. Finally, one more card is dealt face *down* to each player, completing a hand of seven cards, only four of which are face up.

There is one more betting interval, and showdown is reached when the last person to raise has been called. At a showdown, each player selects any five of his seven cards to act as his final hand, and the best hand wins the pot. If everyone checks there is an automatic showdown. If one player raises and everyone else folds he wins the pot without revealing his hole card.

Strategy is the least of your worries at Seven-card Stud: the first thing you have to do is recognize potential hands when you see them. Not for nothing is Seven-card or Long Stud known as 'Down the River', as you may gather when you note that a player showing four rubbish cards may actually be sitting on four of a kind. A useful exercise is to deal out seven hands without looking at the hole cards and then make a note of what is the best hand that each player could possibly be nursing.

Hold 'em

Another family of Poker games is one involving communal cards, or 'flops'. As in Stud, everybody receives a number of 'hole' cards dealt face down, in this case two. A flop is a number of cards – in this case five – that are dealt face up to the centre of the table and count as 'communal' cards, which means that each player can use any of them – in this case three – to complete his final hand of five. So there is a sense in which Hold'em is a form of Stud, the only essential difference being that everybody shares the same visible (face-up) portion of their hand instead of claiming sole possession of it. A particular advantage of Hold'em is that it can accommodate a greater number of players than either Draw or Stud. Theoretically, you could have a table of 23 and still be left with one undealt card!

The exact procedure in Hold'em is as follows:

1 The first two players to the dealer's left place an agreed stake to start the pot. This is known as 'posting the blinds'. (A 'blind' is a blind bet – that is, one made without knowing what you're betting on.)

2 Deal two cards face down to each player. These are your 'hole' or 'pocket' cards. This deal is followed by the 'pre-flop', a round of betting initiated by the third player round from the dealer – that is, the one to the left of the player who last posted a blind. As in all forms of Poker, you can check, bet, raise, or fold.

3 When all bets have been equalized, deal three cards (the 'flop') face up to the centre of the table. A second round of betting follows, started by the first active player to the dealer's left. (An active player is one who has not folded and is therefore still in the pot.)

4 When all bets are equal, deal another card face up to the flop. This is known as the 'turn' card, and is followed by a third round of betting started by the first active player to the dealer's left.

5 Finally, when all bets are equal again, deal a fifth card face up to the flop. This is known as 'the river', and is followed by the final round of betting started by the first active player to the dealer's left.

6 When all bets are equalized, there is a showdown. The player to the left of the last caller reveals his hole cards and is followed by each other remaining player in clockwise rotation.

The pot is won by the player who can make the best five-card hand, counting for this purpose any five out of seven – that is, his own two and any three flop cards. In case of complete equality the pot is split. As in all forms of Poker, there is no showdown if all but one player throw their hands in, in which case the remaining player wins the pot without showing his hand. The average winning hand is in the straight-to-flush region, usually a full house if the flop include a pair.

It is not unusual for the dealer, immediately before dealing the flop, the turn, and the river, to 'burn' the top card of the pack by discarding it face down to one side.

The play

Let's start with a sample game to get an idea of what sort of hands to expect. We'll assume five players and give each of them a different structural basis. Ernie deals two cards each to Annie, Benny (who post the blinds of 2 chips each), Connie, Denny and himself as follows:

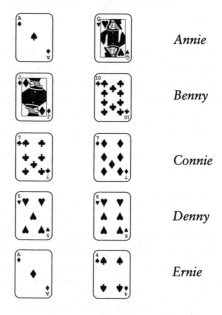

Annie

Benny

Connie

Denny

Ernie

figure 33.2

Annie and Benny have a fair start with high cards belonging to the same straight. Connie's pair of Sevens are worth opening, as pairs are good starts to possible trips or even full houses, and the fact that they are hidden gives her the potential for a strong element of surprise later in the play. She opens for 2.

Denny's Five, Six of hearts are two to a straight flush, but nothing to get excited about. He will soberly stay for 2 and dream of nothing higher than a possible straight.

Ernie folds immediately. You can squeeze a lot of profit out of players who open on Ace-and-nothing.

Annie and Benny decline to raise, so Ernie deals the following flop:

figure 33.3

Annie wisely folds. Benny now has an open-ended four to a straight and bets 2 chips. Connie hasn't caught a third Seven, but with 5–8–9 on the table a Six would fill an inside straight. This gives her six chances out of 47 (the number of cards she cannot see), or a 1 in 8 chance of winding up with better than two pair. To stay in would cost her 2 chips for a pot of 12 so far. Not good odds; but she pays and stays anyway. Denny's ♥5–6 needs a Seven or two hearts to convert into anything worth having, and he folds.

The 'turn' is ♠Q. This gives Annie a half-hidden high pair. She checks, to test the waters. Benny now has a straight, Queen high, and, since no one can possibly have trips, he can only be beaten by a King high straight or a club flush. Should he bet hard and either frighten everyone out or fall to a club flush, or merely keep the pot simmering? No wonder they call this card the turn – it really is a turning-point for so many hands. He decides to stay for 2. So does Connie, deciding that, having come this far, she might as well see it through. Annie folds.

The river card is ♣4, which is pretty academic, leaving Benny with the pot.

As a matter of interest, I dealt all the unused cards out in seven more flops of five to see what the best hand would have been if everyone had stayed in to the end. There were two flushes, one of them beating a lower flush and the other a straight; two straights, in each case beating nothing better than a pair; a triplet, in which Connie's Sevens beat Annie's pair of Queens; and two straights, each beating two players with a pair each. As a matter of further interest, none of the deals yielded a pair in the flop. An open pair, obviously, benefits everyone equally and tends to make for a higher average winning hand.

To generalize, at the pre-flop stage it is worth staying in with two high cards, a pair of Sevens or higher, two to a flush, or two consecutive ranks. Two unrelated cards should always be junked if one of them is low, even if the other is an Ace. (Ernie's opening Ace-Four, above, when subjected to the re-dealing test, converted twice into a four-card straight and once into a flush by the freakish deal of four more spades – which even then failed to win, as it was only Ten high to Annie's Queen high flush.)

At the flop, you can immediately see whether or not you have anything worth going for, and this is certainly the time to fold if you have nothing in realistic prospect. If you have an open-ended straight (such as 6–7–8–9, as opposed to 5–6–8–9) or a four-card flush at this point, it's worth pursuing; with only three in either case, it certainly isn't.

All these rules and calculations, however, are secondary to the fundamental winning rules applicable to all forms of Poker, namely: when you are convinced you have the best hand, maximize your gains by not betting so hard as to frighten everyone out of the pot; when not so convinced, be prepared to fold without worrying about what it might cost; study your opponents' methods and habits ('tells') to get some idea of what they are betting on from how they behave; and avoid giving yourself away by being so consistent that your own tells are self-defeating. That is the true meaning of bluff. If you think that Poker is just a game of bluff, and that bluffing consists in pretending you have a good hand when you really have a bad one, your losses will be well deserved.

See also

Poker vies with Bridge for being the most extensively covered card game on the Internet. For details of and links to other varieties of Poker see:

http://www.pagat.com/vying/poker.html

http://www.pagat.com/invented/poker_vars.html

ante   A fixed amount staked by the dealer, or by every player before cards are dealt.

auction   Preliminary part of a trick-taking game in which players bid for the right to specify conditions of play (such as the trump suit) in return for an undertaking to achieve a higher valued objective than anyone else.

bid   Offer to achieve a higher valued objective than anyone else in return for the right to specify certain conditions of play, such as the trump suit.

blind   See **widow**.

combination   A set of matching cards for which a score or payment may be due by the rules of the particular game.

contract   An irrevocable undertaking to achieve a certain objective after bidding higher than anyone else and specifying conditions of play.

court (card)   A King, Queen or Jack (originally coat card). Also *face card*.

declare   Various meanings according to context, but generally either (a) to announce the conditions of the game or the objective to be achieved, or (b) to show and score for a scoring combination of cards.

declarer   The soloist in solo games, otherwise that member of a partnership primarily responsible for declaring the contract.

defenders   In Bridge, the opponents of the declarer.

discard   (a) to reject an unwanted card from the hand (b) in trick-play, when unable to follow suit to the card led, to play a card from a suit other than trumps or the one led.

doubleton   Exactly two cards of a given suit remaining in (or dealt to) a player's hand.

draw   To take (or be dealt) cards from the stock and add them to one's hand, sometimes in exchange for unwanted cards.

eldest   The player sitting immediately to the dealer's left (or right, depending on the rotation of play), who normally has the privilege of bidding or playing first. In two-player games the non-dealer is elder.

exchange   To discard unwanted cards and replace them with fresh ones. In some games the discard is made before replacements are seen: in others, replacements are taken first and may form part of the discard.

flush Cards of the same suit.

follow (suit) To play to a trick a card of the same suit as the one led to it.

forehand Same as **eldest**.

game (a) complete period of play at the end of which all scores are settled – may be anything from one deal to a whole session (b) the target score which, when reached by at least one player, terminates the period of play and settlement – for example, a game described as '500 up' is one played up to a score of 500 (c) the stated objective and conditions of play for one particular deal – e.g. 'game in diamonds' means diamonds are trumps (d) in Bridge, the number of points still needed to win a game by a side that may already have a part-score (e) in contradiction of (a) above, several 'games' may constitute a larger self-contained period of play, see also **rubber**.

go out To play the last card from one's hand, in games such as Rummy where the aim is to be the first to go out.

guard(ed) In trick play, a card in the hand is guarded by at least as many lower cards (guards) as there are cards above it lacking from the hand. For example, if your highest spade is the Queen, you need two lower spades to guard it, so that when they have been thrown in turn to the Ace and King, your Queen will be the best in its suit (its 'master' card).

hand (a) the cards held in a player's hand (b) a player (as in 'eldest hand') (c) period of play between the point at which all cards have been dealt and the point at which all have been played.

head In tricks, to follow suit to the card led and beat all those that have so far been played. In some games it is obligatory to head the trick if possible.

honours Certain cards for which the rules of the game may prescribe a score of payment to their holder.

kitty (a) in gambling games, the pool or pot of cash or counters for which the game is played (b) a number of cards dealt face down to the table that can be taken up by the declarer or soloist in exchange for unwanted cards from their hand. Also called the **talon, blind,** or **widow**.

lead   To play the first card of deal or to a trick.

long suit   One in which you hold more cards than average. For example, if four players are dealt 13 each and you have four or more of a suit, your holding of that suit is 'long'.

make To fulfil a contract.

meld A winning or scoring set of cards that match one another by rank and or suit. To show or declare such a set.

misère An undertaking to lose every trick.

null Same as **misère**

numerals Cards other than court cards. Also called *spot cards*.

opponent Sometimes has also the specialized meaning of one who is playing against a solo player or declarer. Thus the opponents of the soloist are not necessarily opponents of one another.

ouvert (open) In trick-taking games, playing with one's hand of cards face up on the table.

overcall To make a higher bid than the preceding bidder.

overtrick A trick won in excess of the number required to win a game or fulfil a contract.

pass To make no bid when it is your turn to do so.

pip(-value)   Literally, a pip is a suit symbol printed on a card. (It is a contraction of *peep*). The pip value of a card is its value when captured, for example, in a trick. The term avoids confusion with 'points' in the scoring sense.

plain suit   One that is not trumps. Also *side suit* or *off suit*.

pot   The pool of stakes for which a (gambling) game is played.

rank   The denomination of a card as opposed to its suit, for example, Ace, King, Two, Three, and so on.

renege   Often used to mean 'revoke', but actually meaning to fail to follow suit in trick-taking games where special circumstances permit you to do so (as in Twenty-Five).

renounce   Loosely, to fail to follow suit; strictly, to play a card other than a trump when unable to follow suit.

revoke   To fail to follow suit, even though able and required to do so, for which a penalty may be exacted.

round   A round of play or bidding is complete when every player has had one opportunity to play or bid. Also, for example, 'third round of trumps' means 'third occasion on which a trump has been led to a trick'.

rubber   Equivalent to a match or tournament, the winner of a rubber being the first to win a certain number of games –typically three in Whist and Bridge.

ruff   A trump. To play a trump to a plain-suit lead.

run   A set of cards in numerical or ranking sequence, such as A–2–3 or 10–J–Q–K. In some games a sequence only counts if the constituent cards are also of the same suit.

sequence   Same as a **run**.

set   (a) a group of cards of the same rank in collecting games such as Rummy (b) defeated. A contract that has not *made* is said to be *set*, implying set back by so many points.

singleton   Exactly one card of a given suit remaining in (or dealt to) a player's hand.

slam   the winning of every single trick, called a 'grand slam' in games which also recognize a 'small slam' of every trick but one.

solo(-ist)   A solo game is one in which one player (not usually called the soloist, though it seems the best word) undertakes to win a certain number of tricks without a partner, playing alone against the combined efforts of everyone else.

stock   The undealt portion of the pack if not all cards are dealt.

talon   The undealt portion of a pack in games of French origin such as Piquet. See also **widow**.

tops   In Skat, a consecutive sequence of trumps from the top down, either held or not held by the soloist. (Translation of German *Spitze*. Called *matadors* in older books).

trick   In trick-taking games, a group of cards consisting of one contributed by each player in rotation.

trump   A card that exercises trick-taking power over another of a different suit, regardless of rank.

void   Having no cards of a given suit (e.g. 'I am void in spades' or 'I have a void in spades').

widow   A number of cards dealt face down to the table that can be taken up by the declarer or soloist in exchange for unwanted cards from their hand. Also called the **talon, blind,** or **kitty.**

wild card   One that may represent any card its holder wishes.